# Management for Professionals

The Springer series *Management for Professionals* comprises high-level business and management books for executives. The authors are experienced business professionals and renowned professors who combine scientific background, best practice, and entrepreneurial vision to provide powerful insights into how to achieve business excellence.

Lyle Yorks · Amy Lui Abel
Denise Rotatori

# Strategic Human Resource Development in Practice

Leveraging Talent for Sustained
Performance in the Digital Age of AI

 Springer

Lyle Yorks
Adult Learning and Leadership
Columbia University, Teachers College
New York, NY, USA

Amy Lui Abel
Executive Programs
The Conference Board
New York, NY, USA

Denise Rotatori
Global Technology
Bank of New York Mellon
New York, NY, USA

ISSN 2192-8096  ISSN 2192-810X  (electronic)
Management for Professionals
ISBN 978-3-030-95777-3  ISBN 978-3-030-95775-9  (eBook)
https://doi.org/10.1007/978-3-030-95775-9

This Springer imprint is published by the registered company Springer Nature Switzerland AG
The registered company address is: Gewerbestrasse 11, 6330 Cham, Switzerland

# Preface

As in many areas of professional practice, the level of uncertainty and ambiguity regarding the future of work is raising. At the individual, departmental, and organizational levels, workers, managers, and executives have to be continuously learning from current and emerging trends in order to strategically reposition themselves for performance and future possibilities. Doing so requires competencies in applying strategic learning practices and developing the personal capacity for navigating the complexities of a world in which people are interacting with "smart" digital technologies that are broadly grouped together under the umbrella term *Artificial Intelligence*. Strategic transitions requiring the transformation of organizations is more necessary than in the past as these digital technologies themselves are rapidly evolving and transforming the world more quickly than ever before. The popular acronym VUCA (Volatility, Uncertainty, Complexity, and Ambiguity) reflects the contemporary challenges confronting not only business, but all organizational sectors, including education.

It is for the purpose of providing tools and practices for strategically navigating this context of continuous change, and the learning and development implications for human resource development, that we have written this book providing methods and practices for engaging in strategic learning along with the theoretical frameworks on which they are based. It also provides a review of the evolution of the field human resource development as an academic discipline. The foundations of this book are the academic discipline of Human Resource Development and the practices of human capital/talent management that are being applied in various companies around the world during the time of an intensifying pace of change being driven by digital technologies. In today's world of rapid change marked by uncertainty and ambiguity, strategic agility is a necessity for individuals, departments, and functions within organizations and institutions. Individuals are now working within the context of a growing gig workforce with organizations making decisions about balancing full-time and contingent employees. Additionally, different sectors of the socio-economic environment are intersecting. For example, IBM has partnered with the American Council on Education; it has been determined that completing an apprenticeship program offered by IBM is equal to 45 college credits and can be transferred into a degree program. Another example is Google offering career certificates at high schools and colleges across the country. In this context of change, the concept and definition of strategic planning itself has to be reassessed.

The idea of "strategic planning" is rooted in the military with the process dating back to B.C.—many scholars trace the idea back to Sun Tzu's *The Art of War*. It became a central topic in the business literature in the late 1950s and 1960s as the pace of innovation began growing and the pace of change in the business environment began changing. Jump forward to the twenty-first century and as Willie Pietersen, a former CEO who is a Professor of Practice in Executive Education at Columbia University Business School, has argued, strategic planning needs to be preceded by strategic learning. Strategy formation is an individual, team, and organizational learning process. Planning follows strategic learning because in a time of new technologies the ability for strategically navigating through uncertainty is necessary at the individual, group/team, and organizational levels. The essence of strategy is allowing for the emergence of new insights which requires stepping outside one's traditional frameworks by seeking diverse perspectives on what is, and might be, trending, and then planning.

Drawn from research and work we have been doing with various companies who have been applying digital technologies to the talent management process and the academic field of human resource development, our focus is linking theory with practice and providing illustrations from case study settings. We are also integrating concepts from different areas of the literatures on strategy and human resource development. Each chapter provides a review of both the theoretical frameworks and practices relevant to the chapter topic. The need for strategic agility has implications for developing and managing the workforce; it is elevating the role of human resource management in general and particularly the learning and development function in organizations.

This book is an extension and update of Lyle's previous book on strategic human resource development published in 2005. It is intended as a text for HRD courses focusing on strategic human resource development practice, including strategy development as a learning process, connecting learning and adult development with organizational development and change, and talent development. Our focus is linking theory with practice and providing illustrations from case study settings. The book takes a scholar-practitioner perspective and can also be a resource for HRD practitioners and others who are assuming a talent management or learning and development role in their organization. Additionally, the learning practices described can be used for facilitating strategic learning and agility in organizations by HRD (L&D/talent management) professionals.

New York, USA                                                              Lyle Yorks
New York, USA                                                            Amy Lui Abel
New York, USA                                                         Denise Rotatori

# Acknowledgments

We acknowledge the support and valuable perspectives and information provided by our colleagues and members of The Conference Board as we researched and wrote this book. We also acknowledge the faculty and alumni of the Adult Learning and Leadership program in the Department of Organization & Leadership in Teachers College, Columbia University, and Executive Education at the Business School. They were too very supportive and made valuable contributions to our research.

# Contents

# Part I

# Chapters Providing the Foundations and Practices for Strategic HRD and Talent Management

# The Scope of Human Resource Development: Both an Academic Discipline and Professional Practice

The popularity of the acronym VUCA, (Volatility, Uncertainty, Complexity, and Ambiguity), reflects the contemporary challenges confronting organizations, functions, and groups within organizations, and individuals alike. "Lean Production," "Leadership and Organizational Agility," "The War for Talent," "Era of the Employee," and "Employee Engagement" are among many catch-all phrases commonly used by executives, consultants, and executive education faculty talking about the fluid context of today's task environment. Driving these fluid changes has been the continuing and intensifying pace of innovation in digital technologies and artificial intelligence (AI), with all parts of our world being hyper-connected while also presenting new political and security concerns in a simultaneously globalized yet segmented world. One consequence for organizations, their employees or members, and young people considering career options is the constantly changing needs for new skill sets and competencies, both real time and for the emerging future.

For organizations, forward-looking strategic talent management and adaptive organizational learning are essential for sustainable performance. A 2019 Deloitte Insights report, *Leading the Social Enterprise: Reinvent with a Human Focus*, documented that large companies were struggling to find the people with the skills and competencies their organization needed (Deloitte Insights, 2019). "Evolving work demands and skill requirements are creating an enormous demand for new skills and capabilities, while a tight labor market is making it challenging for organizations to hire people from outside" (p. 6). This trend has intensified since 2019 as technologies have continued to evolve at a more rapid pace.

For individuals, both those in and those entering the workforce for the first time, lifelong learning has become a necessity. Take, for example, the profession of engineering, long regarded as a prestigious and secure profession. In first decade of the twenty-first century, William Wulf, President of the National Academy of Engineering described the half-life of engineering knowledge as being from seven to two and half years and became an advocate for lifelong learning initiatives in the profession. In an article for the Christian Science Monitor in 2002 Terry Costlow wrote "In an era when high-tech gear becomes obsolete almost as fast as dairy

© The Author(s), under exclusive license to Springer Nature Switzerland AG 2022
L. Yorks et al., *Strategic Human Resource Development in Practice*, Management for Professionals, https://doi.org/10.1007/978-3-030-95775-9_1

products, many in the field feel they must advance at a steady pace or risk being cast aside." (Costlow, 2002). In the words of Jacobie Davis, a network support person at ATT, in 2016 "It's really hard to describe the vast difference between the things we're moving toward and the types of legacy technology I've been working on. It's like night and day" (Donovan & Benko, 2016, p. 71). While the pace of reskilling has been increasing for several years, as implied above in today's world, this need is an essential part of human–machine interaction. As machines learn so do humans need to learn from the augmented realities the machines increasingly provide. The future is already here. We have entered the age of 4.0; the so-called fourth industrial revolution.

Addressing these challenges involves learning and development processes that in many ways vary significantly from traditional practices of workforce and staff development. The roles of recruitment, performance management, and training, just to name three obvious ones, have come under reassessment resulting in a variety of changes in practice, and will continue to change as a result of the ongoing evolution of artificial intelligence. AI provides HR with an expanded spectrum of possible recruits from global databases, variables influencing performance levels previously not realized by managers are becoming visible creating enhanced or new Key Performance Indicators (KPIs) for roles, and traditional practices in the field of learning and development have been have become upended and transformed. Consequently, organizations have had to, and will continue to have to, reorganize and reposition the roles associated with human resources in different ways (Yorks et al., 2017). New senior and upper mid-level titles have emerged over the past couple of decades, such as Chief Learning Officer, Chief Talent Officer, Chief Knowledge Officer, People Officer, Engagement Officer, Director of Staff Development, and Director of Knowledge Management although the positioning of these roles varies from organization to organization. Simultaneously, HR executives and practitioners, like other employees, have had to develop a new mindset for strategically repositioning themselves in their organizations and acquire new skills and competencies (Yorks et al., 2017).

As the function of HR was being transformed from largely an administrative support function, and workforce development processes have been evolving from a focus on offering training programs to experience based learning, coaching, and self-directed learning, simultaneously a field of scholarship was evolving in higher education; *Human Resource Development*. As a field of scholarly research and professional practice HRD provides interdisciplinary scaffolding for addressing these continuing transformations. The term interdisciplinary is used in the previous sentence because while HRD is itself an academic discipline, it is grounded in diverse academic disciplines such as Adult Learning and Education, Organizational Psychology, Sociology, Political Science, and Economics, among others. As will be argued in this chapter, integration of such diverse perspectives also needs to be reflected in cross-functional perspectives and collaboration in practice. The purpose of this chapter is to define and layout this scaffolding, grounding it in the evolutionary trends that have, and continue to, define the field of HRD, and positioning it within the fast-changing ecosystem driven by increasingly cognitive technology.

Essentially, HRD provides a foundation for talent management and workforce development. This chapter provides an overview of how the scholarship and practices of human resource development have evolved framing a conceptual framework for the future of workforce development practices as we go through the pivotal fourth industrial revolution triggered by "intelligent" (self-learning) digital technologies. This evolution of the field of HRD reflects the changes that were, and are, taking place in world of talent management and workforce development. We begin with the basic question "what is Human Resource Development as an academic discipline?"

## 1.1 What Is Human Resource Development?

Human Resource Development (HRD) was established as an academic discipline with the creation of the Academy of Human Resource Development (AHRD) in 1993 at the American Society for Training and Development (ASTD) Professors' meeting, providing scholarship for advancing practices of learning and development. However, the term Human Resource Development is not widely used, or even understood, in many organizations. As reflected in the examples of titles mentioned above, HRD is not a formal professional title. We know of no organization, for example, with a chief HRD officer. However, the research and workshops conducted in the Academy of Human Resource Development are a source of research based applied knowledge valuable to the functions designated by these titles.

As the Academy of HRD has grown globally, bringing together scholars *and* practitioners from a diverse range of fields such as organizational psychology, sociology, economics, counseling, and adult education (to name a few), along with areas of related practices such as executive education, organizational development, and coaching, opinions and perspectives regarding the essence of HRD continues to provoke a rich discourse (Hamlin & Steward, 2011; Lee, 2001, 2014; Ruona, 2016; Wang & McLean, 2007). In order to frame the content that follows in this book we begin with a brief summary of the roots of the concept HRD and the perspective from which this book is coming from. These roots, we believe, remain as useful today as they were decades ago, in terms of conceptualizing HRD as an evolving practice that addresses the human capital challenges that confront organizations as technology transforms the workplace. The relevance of this will become evident as the material provided throughout this book unfolds.

### 1.1.1 The Roots of Contemporary HRD Scholarship and Practice

As documented by Alagaraja and Dooley (2003) in their comprehensive review of the literature on the origins and historical influences on HRD, the term human resource development has a diverse set of roots that have evolved over centuries preceding the formal academic language of "human resources" "human development" (or notions of "human capital" for that matter) reaching as far back as ancient primitive times (Nadler, 1970; Nadler & Nadler, 1990), Greek and Roman Civilizations (Swanson & Holton, 2001), early apprenticeship programs, early vocational education programs, and early factory schools (DeSimone & Harris, 1998). The challenge of preparing people for working productively and contributing to the needs of their communities is not new, only more challenging in today's world of rapidly changing technologies and increasing interconnectedness across organizational functions.

Within the Academy of HRD, Leonard Nadler is generally accredited with having created the term human resource development (Swanson & Holton, 2001). However, the term was previously part of a discourse taking place regarding the economic development of countries in the early 1960s. One example is the book *Education, Manpower, and Economic Growth: Strategies of Human Resource Development* by (Harbison and Myers (1964) that was a product of a joint project of the Industrial Relations Sections of Princeton University and the Massachusetts Institute of Technology. Part of an inter-university study of labor problems in economic development, the book was policy oriented with the objective of presenting "a generalized concept of human resource development which may be useful to economic planners and education and manpower planners, as well as to students of economic development and political and social modernization" (p. v). Their agreement is relevant for today's world given the implications for nations needing a learning culture valuing self-evaluation and improvement. Focusing on the national level of socio-economic development Harbison and Myers defined human resource development as:

> the process of increasing the knowledge, the skills, and the capacities of all the people in a society. In economic terms, it could be described as the accumulation of human capital and its effective investment in the development of an economy. In political terms, human resource development prepares people for adult participation in political processes, particularly as citizens in a democracy. From the social and cultural points of view the development of human resources helps people to lead fuller and richer lives, less bound by tradition. In short, the processes of human resource development unlock the door to modernization. (p. 2)

Harbison and Myers were conceptualizing human resource development for the purpose of developing measures of human development useful for fostering societal level economic development through classifying policy development by four levels of development; Underdeveloped Countries (level I), Partially Developed Countries (level II), Semi-advanced Countries (level III), and Advanced Countries (level IV).

At the same time, the century old processes of preparing and continually upgrading people's skills for roles in society, industry, government, non-profits, and professions had been continuing to develop. In 1943, a group of 15 training directors met in Baton Rouge, Louisiana for the first American Society of Training Directors meeting with the goal of creating an organization devoted to furthering the education and development of training professionals. By the 1960s, ASTD had been growing into a global organization for training and development practitioners. Leonard Nadler first introduced the term "human resource development" at the annual ASTD conference in 1969 (Yorks, 2005). The following year Nadler published the definition of HRD as "(1) a series of organized activities, (2), conducted within a specified time, and (3) designed to produce behavioral change" (1970, p. 3), later rephrasing it with his wife Zeace as "organized learning experiences provided for employees within a specified period of time to bring about the possibility of performance improvement and/or personal growth" (1992).

Nadler was using the designation HRD as an umbrella term for three different activity areas; (1) Employee Training, the focus of which was the job, (2) Employee Education, the focus of which was the individual preparing them for new positions and/ upward mobility in the organization, and (3) Employee Development, the focus of which was the organization preparing a flexible workforce for its future as it moves forward. He also argued that this same model defining the three activity areas "can be applied to organizations which are concerned with human resources who are not their employees" such as membership organizations (e.g. Association of Talent Development), labor unions, professional societies (e.g. American Medical Association), and community organizations. In short, to "society in general" as well as employees in any kind of organization (Nadler, 1970, pp. 37–39).

These three activity areas are even more relevant today than they were in 1970. With the advances in cognitive technologies continuously transforming the strategic opportunities and threats to organizations, having a flexible workforce is insufficient; organizations need highly agile workforces. Creating this agile workforce involves using AI to provide employees with the ability to evaluate opportunities for creating satisfactory and engaging career paths. As will be argued throughout this book, these three activities need to be strategically interconnected.

We turn now to the debates generated through the establishment of HRD as an academic discipline; debates that have relevance for the way learning and development practices are also being realigned in organizations.

### 1.1.2   Differing Perspectives and Key Commonalities in Understanding HRD

With the establishment of the Academy of Human Resource Development (HRD) has evolved into an academic discipline with graduate degree programs having been established in universities around the world. Generally, these programs are found in Colleges of Education or Business Schools with students focused on obtaining, or continuing, in learning and development roles in organizations. In addition to formal degree programs, courses in HRD/Learning & Development/Talent Management have been established in many other degree programs including adult education, organizational psychology, human resource management, and technology management. This has raised questions regarding the identity of HRD; is it a distinct field of research and professional practice and what, if any, is its relationship to emerging certifications such as executive coaching that essentially are full-time professional practices (Hamlin & Steward, 2011)? What would constitute an HRD professional certification? Additionally, the relationship of HRD to these various specialties such as coaching and organization development and whether HRD should be/is a separate professional practice or highly interconnected with permeable boundaries is part of an ongoing discussion (Ruona, 2016).

### 1.1.3  Moving Toward Coherence in Defining HRD

The first line in chapter one of Nadler's, 1970 book in which he defined HRD is "Defining a term is a hazardous occupation." He was certainly right. As an evolving field of research numerous alternative definitions has been introduced as new perspectives grow out of the academic discourse. Still certain core concepts were, and continue to be, present providing a unifying focus.

In seeking to develop a synthesis of the complex HRD domain encompassing both research and practice, Hamlin and Steward (2011) conducted a research study into how HRD has been defined. Following a robust research methodology and drawing data from published literature in academic journals and textbooks synthesizing the HRD, Organizational Development (OD), and Coaching literatures they identified 24 different, but often overlapping definitions. Based on their analysis of the "Intended Purposes" in the definitions, Hamlin and Stewart created four distinct "synthesized statements of purpose reflecting 'the intended purposes' of all the definitions…in each thematic category" (p. 210).

- "Improving individual or group effectiveness and performance";
- "Improving organizational effectiveness and performance";
- "Improving knowledge, skills and competencies"; and
- "Enhancing human potential and personal growth" (p. 210)

Twenty-two of the 24 definitions emphasized the development of knowledge, skills, and competencies, and 20 of the definitions imply or state a focus on work-related development and/or primarily in a work-based context. The four thematic categories remain as relevant today as in 2011.

Learning and development are central concepts in the field of HRD and the practice of talent management. Additionally, revisiting research studies Hamlin had previously done with Ellinger and Beattie (Hamlin et al., 2008) seeking commonalities in definitions of organization development and coaching, Hamlin and Stewart found high degrees of sameness or similarities between the intended purposes and processes of OD and HRD. And with regard to coaching, "there are high degrees of sameness and similarity between the 'intended purposes' of coaching the core purposes of HRD, even to the point of being perceived as near identical" (p. 212). There continues to be questions regarding how HRD relates to being a profession in the absence of formal qualifications defined by a professional regulatory body (p. 202).

However, learning and development are themselves constructs that are defined differently in different contexts. To quote anthropologist and cybernetics theorist Gregory Bateson, whose work intersected with many different academic fields and was seminal for adult learning theory, "The word *Learning* undoubtedly denotes

*Change* of some kind. To say what *kind* of change is a delicate matter" (Bateson, 1972, p. 283). We will discuss this later in Chap. 2. The concept of "development" also is also defined differently depending on a person's perspective. How learning and development are conceptualized and operationalized and have significant implications for talent management and human capital practices.

### 1.1.4 Recognizing the Need for Strategic HRD (SHRD)

Central to this ongoing discussion is the need for a strategic approach to human resource development in organization. Throughout its evolution as both an academic discipline and a professional practice, the need for a strategic approach to HRD linking learning and development interventions to the goals and performance of the organization has been an ongoing theme (Garavan & Carbery, 2012). In 1991 Thomas Garavan noted that the integration of training and development into wider business planning was a central feature of the literature on strategic human resource literature (Garavan, 1991). This included connecting to the organization's goals and objectives, collaboration with line management, and aligning with the organization's culture and values.

Achieving this required integrating HRD practices which at the time were primarily centered on training and development, with other human resource management functions. This would also require a transformation in the way HRD professionals saw themselves and presented themselves in the larger organization, including connecting their training and development programs and other initiatives to measurements of subsequent performance and organizational results (Gilley & Maycunich, 1998). This transformation to a strategic approach needed to focus beyond changes in the structures of various HRD functions to establishing coherence of SHRD efforts that connect with organizational performance (Walton, 1999). The literature on SHRD continued to expand, continuing with transitions and transformations in areas such as human resource management and organizational learning (Tseng & McLean, 2008). Garavan (2007) provided a comprehensive framework and literature review of the interplay between SHRD practices and the contexts within which the practices come into play: (1) the external global environment (defined as local, national, and multinational; (2) the internal context comprised of the organizations strategic focus, its organizational structure, its culture, and leadership; (3) the value placed on different jobs by the organization, (4) the expectations, employability, and careers of individuals in the organization. "SHRD is required to context with an appropriate mix of strategies in addition to an orientation that ensures horizontal alignment with the various elements of the context" (Garavan, 2007), p. 21). The focus on SHRD was making clear that training and development, organization development, and human resource administration were no longer separate support functions; rather they needed to become an integrated part of the organization's performance assessment.

We have provided a summary framing of SHRD. This literature is rich and continues to grow. With the pivot to the fourth industrial revolution, the need for SHRD in alignment both vertically and horizontally has intensified as the pace of change continues to increase. HRD has to play a central role in enabling the organization to be strategically agile.

## 1.2    Looking Beyond Coherence: The Traps of a Mindset of Unity in a World of Complexity

While the process of seeking a common definition has evolved toward coherence, some HRD scholars argue against a common definition. Monica Lee in her 2001 article A Refusal to Define HRD argues "the notion and practice of HRD is dynamic, ambiguous, and ill determined" (p. 327). Grounding her argument in philosophical, theoretical, and practice terms, Lee makes the case that both the context in which the topics and issues HRD addresses, and practices that are applied, have been continually evolving and emerging. Again, we note, these evolving practices reflect how the reality confronting organizations and individuals is increasingly evolving as technology intensifies the complexities inherent in the local and national socio ecosystems we inhabit. Keep this in mind as we continue our review of what constitutes HRD below.

Adding to the complexity of this continual evolution has been the globalization of national economies and the development of trans-national corporations (Hamlin & Steward, 2011) leading to the emergence of definitions of international human resource development (IHRD) (e.g., Debraw et al., 2000). Cho and McLean (2004) question whether a unifying definition of IHRD is even possible given the broad range of stages of development across countries and the variation of openness to accommodate cultural differences that exist in the global world. Given the range of difference between national socio-economic systems and their cultures, based on research by a collection of HRD scholars from 11 different countries, Cho and McLean conceptualize national human resource development (NHRD) as HRD "being used as national policy" (p. 382). The studies revealed that national level HRD goes beyond only being concerned with preparation for employment and related employment issues, but also with other considerations not typically connected to human capital and talent development.

Following a review of various documents and literature, including foundational theories in development economics and terms used in five NHRD models, Greg Wang (2008) concluded that although "with a right mind set and a right position in the overall development community, HRD scholars and practitioners can certainly play a significant role in accelerating the development process through policy analysis" (p. 313). However, Wang also noted that HRD professionals need to work collaboratively with the other development related professions for development at the national level, but the domain of HRD research and practice not be stretched to human development at the national policy level. Within the Academy of Human Resource Development, there continues to be a rich discourse regarding the essence of HRD work and its future direction (Ruona, 2016). This discourse is itself a valuable contribution to the evolution of learning and development within various contexts; one that has implications for challenges currently being confronted in organizations.

## 1.3    Returning to the Question "What is Human Resource Development?"

As the above summary describes, the answers to this question are diverse with the discourse continuing. Given the fluidity of the socio-economic task environment confronting organizations and nations, it is one that will continue to evolve as will the boundaries, interconnections, and role definitions of HR functions in organizations (Yorks et al., 2017). As Wang (2008) wrote almost two decades ago, "All my experience in HRD and life (not that I can easily separate them) points me to the belief in a world of becoming, one of process epistemology and negative capability" (p. 331). Going back further in time and revisiting Nadler's (1970) prescient work, regarding the function of HRD he wrote:

> HRD is here to stay! The name may change, and currently being heard is 'manpower policy,' 'manpower planning' and 'effective utilization of manpower.' In discussing manpower policy, the *Manpower Report of the President* said that such a 'policy' must have as its ultimate aim enabling every American to realize and utilize his full potential. This implies a concern for not only for occupational training but also for education at all levels (Washington, Government Printing Office, 1969, p. 4) (p. 9).

### Authors Side Note
While making important points, Nadler's quote's uses language reflecting the gender bias of the time that was systemic to the American, and all national cultures, demonstrating the need for critical reflection on embedded culture values as part of HRD/Talent Management processes including how these, and other, biases might be unintentionally coded into HR AI

As previously noted, the scope of Nadler's inclusion of *Employee Training, Employee Education, Employee Development, and Nonemployee Development* remains relevant today. In their initial discussion of HRD problems and issues involving developing "further value of high-level manpower for a more advanced economy," Harbison and Myers (1964, p. 17) noted the President of the Carnegie Corporation of New York, John W. Gardner, observations that the rate of innovative change being driven by technology required a high capacity for adjusting to changing social situations and innovation.

Really! the rate of innovation and change in 1964 was challenging people and organizations? With the rate of change more than "squared" today compared to 1964, Gardner's point is even more relevant now. Although with the rate of change more than "squared," it is not only the pace of change but also the intensifying complexity. To borrow a phrase from Reilly and Mcbreatry (2010), under conditions of complexity getting some place in terms of individual, organizational, or institutional spaces is "not a very neat circle or process" (p. 237). In today's world, more and more work needs to be done collaboratively across traditionally siloed functions. These collaborations require learning across functional lines of expertise and can be realized through the use of developmental action inquiry practices which are discussed in Chaps. 2 and 3.

Courtney et al. (1997) have identified four distinct levels of uncertainty:

1. *A clear enough future* where the residual uncertainty is irrelevant to making strategic decisions;
2. *Alternative futures* that can be described as having one of a few discrete scenarios. While the exact outcomes can't be identified, reasonable probabilities can be established;
3. *A range of futures* where a number of key variables describe the range of outcomes, the actual outcome can't be determined with any certainty;
4. *True ambiguity* where a number of dimensions of uncertainty interact creating an environment that is virtually impossible to predict.

While all four levels are always present, and of course a seemingly level one future can suddenly be disrupted, the overall business context of the early sixties through the eighties was essentially levels one and two. Now with the advent of rapidly spreading AI, the context for most companies, and many non-profits and government institutions, is shifting to level three and even level four.

The ability to navigate uncertainty is an important competency for executives and many professionals in a world where cognitive agility is essential for sustaining high individual and organization performance. In today's world of almost continuous complex change driven by technology, uncertainty is given. Developing this capacity in company leaders needs to be a priority for talent development professionals in organizations. Further, as will be discussed in other chapters, talent management and human capital strategies and programs in organizations must be targeted and designed taking into account the level of uncertainty of the specific context being addressed.

Further, the capability is necessary for HR functions, and HRD itself, as well. A 2017 study conducted by The Conference Board (Yorks et al., 2017) mapped out the process of an ongoing transformation process in six global corporations involving the realignment of the HR function in order to be more agile and included as a proactive contributor to the business. Consistent with Lee's view of HRD as needing to be a process of *ongoing becoming*, this transformation process is a continuously evolving process, not one with a fixed destination.

### 1.3.1   Our Definition of HRD

Building on the productive ongoing dialogues taking place within the Academy of Human Resource Development and the "boots on the ground" innovative changes taking place in practice, for purposes of this book, we define HRD as:

> *An integrative domain of professional practices with the purpose of improving effectiveness and performance at the individual, group/team, organization, and/or institutional and societal levels through continuous application of ongoing learning and development initiatives at the individual, teams, and organizational level through alignment of workforce planning and the organizational culture based on findings from rigorous research and successful practices and increasingly being informed, facilitated and transformed by Artificial Intelligent technologies.*

HRD is a legitimate institutionalized academic discipline with a growing number of graduate programs in accredited universities, four scholarly journals sponsored by the Academy of Human Resource Development, and other academic meetings such as the University Forum for Human Resource Development (Ruona, 2016). The knowledge and competencies advanced by the make-up of this discipline are itself multidisciplinary with members having training and continuing participation in related disciplinary societies such as the Academy of Management.

The contexts that HRD seeks to serve are increasingly temporal, shifting, and transforming, with those inhabiting them having to navigate emergent developmental challenges. As a somewhat multidisciplinary-interdisciplinary domain, HRD is significantly positioned for providing knowledge, methods, and competency-based practices for addressing these challenges especially in world that is moving toward transdisciplinary work.

### 1.3.2   Also, the Need for Continuing the Debates in the Academy

This doesn't mean that the ongoing dialogue and debates regarding defining HRD as a discipline and navigating the frontier beyond for HRD will end; should the Academy of HRD stand for professionalization or HRD or actively foster real transdisciplinarity (Ruona, 2016) is a fork in the road requiring one choice or the other. As Yogi Berra famously said, "When you come to the fork in the road, take it." The dialogue encapsulates many of the issues confronting the populations and settings the field seeks to serve. Navigating the need for transdisciplinary collaboration in the workplace along with professional grounding and certification in specific disciplines is the new reality in the workplace.

Both sides of the dialogue are important and in today's world of complexity will continue to co-exist. As Gold, Rodgers, and Smith (2003) argued back in 2003, HRD needs "to determine the core elements of its' disciplinary knowledge' This is not to argue for any kind of closure or unification of knowledge; …HRD should be characterized by diversity, creativity and debate about the meanings and practices that constitute its field" (p. 452). In 2010, complexity theorists Kurt Richardson and

Andrew Tait wrote in their chapter The Death of the Expert "So does an increasingly connected world signal the death of the expert? Certainly not … However, exploring complex problem spaces requires a different kind of expertise than that has traditionally been given priority" (Richardson and Tait, 2010, p. 37).

More specifically, organizational life is becoming increasingly complex and, as a consequence, rapidly changing. The domain of HRD research and practice is comprised of a broad network of professionally trained scholars and practitioners many of whom are also connected to other networks and sub-networks. As such HRD as an academic discipline and a practice domain is well positioned to inform the development needs of the individuals, organizations, and societies that are increasingly both diverse and interconnected. "Complex network organizations are continually emerging…*innovative organizations…are always in the process of becoming rather than ever reaching equilibrium*" (Rycroft & Kash, 1999, pp. 66–67, italics in original quote). As discussed in Chap. 3, this process of becoming is evident in current trends of transformation in HR and developing human resources and organizational processes in business and other organizations. By the second decade of 2021, this process of becoming has intensified, requiring members of the workforce to engage in ongoing becoming, both individually and collectively. By extension the practices of talent management and organization systems and culture, the process of becoming are intensifying as well. We conclude this chapter with a brief summary of how this process has been unfolding and provide a model for conceptualizing the practices of HRD in the digital age.

## 1.4  Human Resource Management, Learning and Development, and Organization Development—And Leveraging AI Technology

Since the mid-1990s, contemporary human resource functions have been increasingly confronted with the need for reconceptualizing and reorganizing their services in order to reduce cost and provide more value to the business. Since the late 1990s when David Ulrich popularized the role of the Human Resource Business Partner (HRBP), the term has been adopted in many businesses in very varied, and often not very meaningful, ways. At times, the person with the title HRBP would continue to handle many administrative tasks while reporting into a senior HR executive who dealt with people related business issues with the senior team. As the HRBP role continued to evolve other changes in how HR was organized began to materialize. Administrative responsibilities such as compensation, compliance issues, and some traditional areas of employee relations and labor relations were centralized into shared services and centers of expertise. Being driven by digital technology and AI, the pressures for change intensified in second decade of the twenty-first century as increasingly administrative tasks were digitalized requiring less HR oversight.

At the same time the so-called War for Talent has created a place for HRD related practices at both the strategic and operational levels of organizations. As the administrative components of the traditional HR role continue to become digitalized, the human resource management planning process, learning and development, and organizational development are becoming more and more coordinated, and in some instances integrated, through the role of talent management.

A guiding principle of the workforce planning aspect of human resource management can be expressed as *positioning the right people for the highest possible achievable performance to meet the organization's strategic goals.* Putting this principle into practice involves continually raising and answering questions such as: What kind of people do we need in terms of abilities and motivation? How many people do we need? Where/how do we find them? How do we position them in the organization? How do we motivate and retain them? How do we administer them?

A guiding principle of learning and development functions in organizations can be expressed *Preparing and continually developing people and learning systems for the highest possible achievable performance to meet the organization's strategic goals.'* Executing this principle in practice involves continually addressing questions such as: What kind of learning is needed? How do we allocate learning opportunities? How do we keep track of our people's competencies and capabilities? How do we recognize the tacit knowledge of our employees? How do we document learning from our employees' experience for the organization? How do we manage knowledge and the social and intellectual capital of the organization?

A guiding principle of organizational development can be expressed as *getting our processes and systems aligned for organization effectiveness, growth and development while fostering values and behaviors that will sustain this alignment.*

AI is increasingly useful for significantly enhancing the implementation of these three guiding principles. As will be discussed in later chapters, it is already transforming processes for identifying and recruiting talent, onboarding them, and providing new avenues for continuous learning and development for career development. Sustainable organization performance requires the coordination/integration of all three domains for effective talent management. The foundations of decades of HRD scholarship and practice summarized above provides the scaffolding for the ongoing transitions and transformations confronting today's organizations and institutions. Additionally, advances in AI have made collaboration between the Chief Information Officer and Chief Human Resources Officer critical as AI is a pivotal factor in how these domains are coordinated (Abel & Yorks, 2018). No longer separate support functions, the technology and human resource functions are critical for the strategic success of companies as reflected in three questions that continuously need to be addressed:

- What opportunities exist, or are potentially emerging for us, that provide new services and products through the technological innovations of AI?
- What are the implications of these innovations for our future talent needs?
- How will we effectively address these future talent needs through recruitment, continual development of employees, and focused retentions of key employees?

The implications of these questions are that human resource executives and managers need to be conversant with the emerging AI technologies, and technology executives and managers need to be aware of the implications of how technologies are impacting the wider workforce. These collaborative discussions are central to the strategic positioning of the organization. One reality that is already here is that HRD is increasingly about human–machine interaction producing new insights and learning across organizations through machine enabled intelligence. For example, Kaiser Permanente, an organization with over 175,000 employees across the United States adopted a social learning tool to increase the sharing of best practices and information across the regions. Called The learning Forum, the tool was developed to provide weekly 15 to 30 minute interactive learning sessions. Topics include technical skills, personal health and well-being, and innovation among others. The live sessions are recorded and made accessible in a searchable repository. Combining KP Standard tools, WebEX, and voice through landlines and their enterprise social networking tool Ideabook, users can "participate in live, interactive learning sessions, explore a virtual exhibit hall containing an organized collection of learning opportunities, rate the learning sessions and share their own thoughts through follow-up discussion groups." The social learning platform grew in 2 years from 500 users to more than 30,000.

The use of machine enabled technologies will be discussed in more detail in Chap. 4.

## 1.5    Summary

As every reader already has experienced, the workplace is being continuously rocked by changes that often involve uncertainty and, at times, considerable ambiguity. The so-called fourth industrial revolution that is driving these changes is intensifying the pace of change. The challenges that mark these changes typically involve acquisition of new employees along with the repositioning of current staffing, require continual development of new skills and competences, and changes in organizational structures, systems, and processes. The scholarly field of HRD, although originally rooted in training and development, provides insights for transdisciplinary connections across all of three of these sectors of organizational practices rooted, respectively, in human resource management, learning and development, and organization development which have traditionally been largely separated. Brought together they provide the foundations for viable strategic talent management (see Fig. 1.1).

The coordination of HRM, L&D, and OD leveraged through AI depicted in Fig. 1.1 is increasingly an important part of the talent management process for maintaining organizational agility and driving strategic changes necessary for sustainable maximum performance (Ruona & Gibson, 2004). How the role of talent management is structured varies across organizations and it doesn't imply a hierarchical structure with other functions reporting to talent management (Yorks & Able, 2013). It's the degree of alignment among the initiatives that is the key to the success of talent management for organizational performance. Talent management professionals within HR can be playing the roles of broker, consultants, and facilitators.

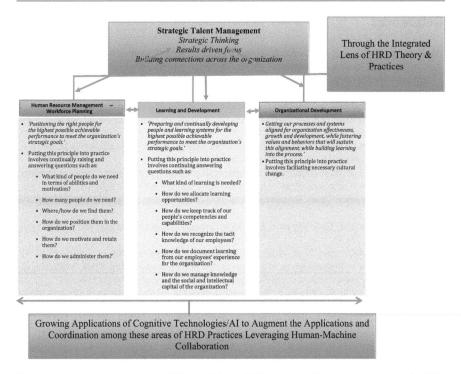

**Fig. 1.1** The systemic interplay of HRM, L&D, and OD for strategic talent management in HRD practice increasingly facilitated by technological innovation involving human–machine interaction

Strategically positioning talent management for playing these roles requires the strategic repositioning of HR itself. Accomplishing this involves engaging in strategic learning across HR, the talent management function, the technology function, and the larger organization.

Implementing digitally intelligent systems for learning and development also changes the culture of the organization as learners engage with the systems. Changes in systems facilitate cultural change; monitoring the emerge cultural changes and supporting them with other HR and L&D initiatives are an important part of HRD (talent management) practice. IBM has been enabling a culture of learning through mobile and social engagement. On demand, learning is provided through social and mobile platforms. A culture of learning and collaboration at IBM is enabled and infused into the daily life of employees through a social enterprise platform called "Connections." IBMers use connections to exchange ideas, share knowledge, and immediately learn from experts across the company.

Details of the content of the collaborative initiatives across functions will vary but strategic alignment is essential. As will be discussed in Chap. 3, this involves developing a strategic learning mindset and practices. First, we turn to the diverse, and potentially complementary theories of learning that are central to, and foundational for, HRD.

## References

Abel, A., & Yorks, L. (2018). Artificial intelligence: The key unifier between the CIO and CHRO. *CIO Review,* December, 8–9. Reviewed from https://hr.cioreview.com/cxoinsight/artificial-intelligence-the-key-unifier-between-the-cio-and-chro-nid-27155-cid-48.html

Alagaraja, M., & Dooley, L. M. (2003). Origins and historical influences on human resource development: A global perspective. *Human Resource Development Review, 2*(1), 82–96.

Bateson, G. (1972). *Steps to an ecology of mind: A revolutionary approach to man's understanding of himself.* Chandler Publishing.

Cho, E., & McLean. (2004). What we discovered about NHRD and what it means for HRD. *Advances in Developing Human Resources, 6*(3), 382–393.

Costlow, T. (2002). A short circuit for U.S. engineering careers. Faced with foreign competition and an ever faster pace, many engineers are dropping out of a once safe field. *Christian Science Monitor, December 26th.* Retrieved from https://www.csmonitor.com/2002/1226/p02s01-usec.html

Courtney, H., Kirkland, J., & Viguerie, P. (1997). Strategy under uncertainty. *Harvard Business Review, 75*(6), 67–79.

Debraw, Y. A., McGovern, I., & Budhwar, P. (2000). Complementarity or competition: The development of human resources in a south Asian growth triangle: Indonesia, Malaysia, and Singapore. *International Journal of Human Resource Management, 11*(2), 314–335.

Deloitte Insights. (2019). Leading the social enterprise: Reinvent with a human focus. *2019 Deloitte Global Human Capital Trends.* Retrieved from https://www2.deloitte.com/content/dam/Deloitte/ro/Documents/HC_Trends_2019_C_TT-FFF-06291_ro_2019_General_Document_en.pdf?nc=1&utm_campaign=HC_Trends_2019_C_TT-FFF-06291_ro_2019_General_Email_en&utm_medium=email&utm_source=Eloqua&_ga=2.85901849.1844194341.1624655207-2105781350.1624655207

DeSimone, R., & Harris, D. (1998). *Human resource development* (2nd ed.). The Dryden Press.

Donovan, J., & Benko, C. (2016). AT&T's talent overhaul. *Harvard Business Review, 94*(10), 68–73.

Garavan, T. N. (1991). Strategic human resource development. *Journal of European Industrial Training., 15*(1), 17–30.

Garavan, T. N. (2007). A strategic perspective on human resource development. *Advances in Developing Human Resources, 9*(1), 11–30.

Garavan, T. N., & Carbery, R. (2012). Strategic human resource development. In J. P. Wilson (Ed.), *International human resource development: Learning, education, and training for individuals and organizations* (3rd ed.). Kogan Page Limited.

Gilley, J. W., & Maycunich, A. (1998). *Strategically integrated HRD: Partnering to maximize organizational performance.* Addison-Wesley.

Gold, J., Rogers, H. M., & Smith, V. (2003). What is the future for the human resource development professional? A U.K. perspective. *Human Resource Development International, 6*(4), 437–455.

Hamlin, R. G., Ellinger, A. D., & Beattie, R. S. (2008). The emergent 'coaching industry': A wake-up call for HRD professionals. *Human Resource Development International, 11*(3), 287–305.

Hamlin, B., & Steward, J. (2011). What is HRD? A definitional review and synthesis of HRD domain. *Journal of European Industrial Training, 35*(3), 199–220.

Harbison, F., & Myers, C. A. (1964). *Education, manpower, and economic growth: Strategies of human resource development.* McGraw-Hill.

Lee, M. M. (2001). A refusal to define HRD. *Human Resource Development International, 4*(3), 327–341.

Lee, M. M. (2014). Dilemmas in defining HRD. In N. E. Chalofsky, T. S. Rocco, & M. L. Morris (Eds.), *Handbook of human resource development* (pp. 97–111). Wiley.

Nadler, L. (1970). *Developing human resources.* Gulf Publishing.

Nadler, L., & Nadler, Z. (Eds.). (1990). *The handbook of human resource development.* Wiley.

Reilly, R. C., & Mcbreatry, M. (2010). Getting there is not a very neat circle or process: An illustrative view of complexity within a knowledge management learning community. In A. Tait & K. A. Richardson (Eds.), *Complexity and knowledge management of social networks* (pp. 237–265). Information Age Publishing, Inc..

Richardson, K. A., & Tait, A. (2010). Death of the expert ? In A. Tait & K. A. Richardson (Eds.), *Complexity and knowledge management of social networks* (pp. 23–40). Information Age Publishing, Inc..

Ruona, W. E. A. (2016). Evolving human resource development. *Advances in Developing Human Resources, 18*(4), 551–565.

Ruona, W. E. A., & Gibson, S. K. (2004). The making of 21st century HR: An analysis of the convergence of HRM, HRD, & OD. *Human Resource Management, 43*(1), 49–66.

Rycroft, R. W., & Kash, D. E. (1999). *The complexity challenge: Technological innovation in the 21st century*. Pinter Publishing.

Swanson, R. A., & Holton, E. F. (2001). *Foundations of human resource development*. Berrett-Koehler Publishing, Inc..

Tseng, C.-C., & McLean, G. N. (2008). Strategic HRD practices as key factors in organizational learning. *Journal of European Industrial Training., 32*(6), 418–432.

Walton, J. (1999). *Strategic human resource development*. Pearson.

Wang, X., & McLean, G. M. (2007). The dilemma of defining international human resource development. *Human Resource Development Review, 6*(1), 96–108.

Wang, G. G. (2008). National HRD: A new paradigm or reinvention of the wheel? *Journal of European Industrial Training, 32*(4), 303–316.

Yorks, L. (2005). *Strategic human resource development*. Thompson.

Yorks, L., & Able, A. (2013). *Strategic talent management: Where we need to go. Executive report*. Conference Board, September.

Yorks, L., Abel, A. L., Devine, M., Bang, A., & Nair, S. (2017). *What's next for 21st century HR? Continuous strategic transformation*. The Conference Board, December.

# Foundations of Learning Theory for HRD Practice

**2**

Learning has become a central topic in twenty-first century discussions of individual, team, and organizational performance, as well as personal career growth and sustainability. The need for effective applications of learning focused interventions in organizations and the broader society is the focal link between HRD workforce development practices and organization strategy, operational processes, functional units, teams, and individuals. While learning has been of increasing importance throughout the past century, in a socio-economic context where innovation in digital technologies is a constant process, it is now essential for providing value to customers and addressing talent management issues such as employee engagement and retention.

For example, one of the talent management challenges for a global consulting firm headquartered in Washington D.C. that provides strategic and technological focused services to business and government organizations is retaining the young professional staff providing these services. After a couple assignments, they begin looking for other employment opportunities in order to gain broader experience. To address this retention problem, the firm implemented what they call the three-year cycle plan. When one of these professional staff members has been on an engagement with a client for 2 years, during the third year, the firm provides the staff member with an overview of emerging new client projects. The talent management staff initiates a conversation regarding which new project the staff member would like to join to continue his or her professional development. Of course, in joining the new engagement, the staff member will also be bringing his or her prior experience to the new engagement. Professional development occurs across the team working on the engagement. This is an example of addressing the HR challenge of staff retention by aligning the process of assigning professional staff to projects with the career related purposes of professional staff members and enhancing their engagement on projects. These kind of retention initiatives are being augmented by artificial intelligent technologies that track emerging job opportunities across the organization, match the skills needed by the jobs, and provide suggestions to employees regarding potential career path opportunities.

In today's world with increasing emphasis on lean horizontal engagement across organizational functions, teams, and centers of expertise, learning must flow both ways, back and forth between individuals and organizational groupings and levels. This chapter reviews the learning and development theories that provide a base for ongoing research and practice in HRD and by extension, individual and organizational learning and development in practice.

That said, we need to note that the scope of learning theory is very wide with a considerable number of different theoretical perspectives, many of which supplement or augment each other in practice. Covering the entire terrain of learning theories is beyond the scope of this chapter, which is intended to provide a foundational background for strategic learning and HRD practice in a world of intensifying change driven by technology. Specifically, we primarily focus on (1) *Transformative Learning*, (2) *Experiential Learning*, (3) *Adult Development*, (4) *Somatic Learning*, (5) *Team*, and (6) *Organizational Learning*. Together these theories provide a heuristic framework for application in HRD, along with how digitalization, particularly AI, is augmenting learning practices. Periodically *Formal, Informal, Incidental Learning* and *Self-directed Learning* are also discussed within the context of the six theories we focus on and throughout the book. If you have a formal training in these theories, you can go on Chap. 3.

We start with a very basic question. What do we mean by learning?

## 2.1    What Is Learning? An Overview of the Theoretical Terrain

What is learning? A very basic question, but also somewhat complicated. As previously quoted in Chap. 1, Gregory Bateson wrote about levels of learning, but declined to define it, writing, "The word *learning* undoubtedly denotes *change* of some kind. To say what *kind* of change is a delicate matter" (Bateson, 1972, p. 283). Although declining to define learning, Bateson captured the defining characteristic of learning: it involves personal change stimulated though some encounter. The domains in which the change could take place are many including skills (motor or intellectual), acquiring knowledge, cognitive development, mindful awareness, or attitudes. These domains have been broadly captured in the management learning literature as abstract knowledge, involving *know-what* and *know-why*, and knowing in practice, involving *know-how* and *care why* (Quinn, 1992).

## 2.2    Knowing What—Knowing How—Two Distinct Spheres of Learning, Yet Interconnected

The distinction between *knowing what* and *knowing how* parallels the differentiation made a century earlier by the pragmatist and psychologist William James (1925) between *knowledge about* and *knowledge of acquaintance*. In short, this is the difference between abstract knowledge and the ability for applying one's knowledge in practice. Creating bridges between these two spheres is in many ways at the heart of HRD practices for learning and development.

Two Distinct Spheres. The first, *know-what and knowing why*, involves "talking about" a practice and is descriptive, explanatory, and systematic. The second, *know-how and care why*, involves "talking from within a practice" and is performative and ad hoc (Fox, 1997, p. 30). Peter Vaill (1996) addressed learning in a similar vein writing about the learning challenges for surviving in a future "world of permanent white water" as a result of continuously emerging technologies, defining learning as "Changes a person makes in himself or herself that increase the know-why and/or know-what and/or the know-how the person possesses with respect to a given subject." (p. 21).

The distinction between knowing what (knowledge about) and knowing how (knowledge of acquaintance) is an important framing in thinking about the purposes and the delivery methods of learning interventions for talent development in the twenty-first century. Is the learning need being addressed one of knowing content and information or the ability to perform? What information is needed in going forward; are there levels of content that need to build on each other. Also, how might the content be understood from different perspectives given that the meaning of information is socially constructed and people often leave a workshop or meeting with different interpretations of the meaning of key words or ideas. One of the authors still remembers an experience with the operating committee of a small company supplier to several fortune 500 manufacturing companies. In addressing a problem around scheduling projects, the president of the company held a meeting and made a statement about priorities that was followed by very little discussion. Asked if the statement for guiding priorities was clear, all the members of the committee agreed. In working with members of the committee during day, it became clear there were at least three different definitions of "priority." One interpretation was continuing to schedule work as it has been scheduled unless there is a crisis. The second was continuing to "pursue all three sets of production needs but proportion resources according to the priorities." Third interpretation was sequential, doing priority one first, priority second next, then the third priority. None of these executives was trying to spin the information or play political games; each had interpreted the information through his own frame of reference.

If the need is *knowing how,* then first-hand encounters in practice are necessary. While knowing how can be expressed in one's personal mental models, the learning is embedded in the person's capacity for enacting the knowing learned through experience. Polanyi (1964) called this personal knowledge. While a range of skills and competencies can be developed through practice sessions, role plays, and simulations, it is important to recognize the contextual differences between such formal training experiences and the pressures and complexities of applying them in actual practice. As these contextual elements increase or become more intensive, learning through supervised field experience is necessary.

While target practice on a shooting range is necessary for initial skill development and is useful preparation for soldiers, the target doesn't shoot back. Nor is there any need for understanding the target's intention. If one's job potentially involves the necessity of exchanging gunfire in combat, full knowledge of acquaintance cannot be acquired through training although repeated trainings are necessary for as much preparation as is possible. These trainings involve simulations and war games to provide for vicarious experience extending basic skill training on the firing line. Of course, neither encompasses the fear and emotion experienced in actual combat. The same is true for police officers making a traffic stop or intervening in a crime scene in which socialized subconscious biases, along with emotions energized by the event, come into play.

Another example of knowledge of acquaintance and knowing how, in the developed economies of the world, the use of digital technologies is part of Generation Z's embedded knowledge. They have grown up living in the digital world. Using technology has been part of their formal, informal, and incidental learning (See Box 2.1 for definitions).

Box 2.1 Defining Formal, Informal, and Incidental Learning **Formal Learning:** The goals or objectives of the learning are set by the institution or managers and take place in a structured setting, such as a classroom, workshop, or an organized series of events. **Informal Learning:** The goals or objectives for the learning are set by the learner who may pursue them by enrolling in structured learning initiatives or pursuing the learning independently through seeking advice from others, personal research, or practice. **Incidental Learning:** Is unplanned and takes place in the context of the learners' experiences when engaged in another activity that could be an intended structured experience or just doing work or interacting with others. It may be conscious or tacit. Marsick & Watkins, 2001

## 2.2.1  Yes Distinct, but Interconnected Spheres

Although the analytical distinction between knowing what (knowledge about) and know-how (based on knowledge of acquaintance) is a powerful distinction, often the relationship between them is as important to understand as the difference. Knowledge about provides the framework through which one enters into a particular setting in practice. Then, as one engages in practice, this framework is modified as a result of their knowledge of acquaintance. In an academic setting, this is reflected in new experimental designs or through action research. In practice settings, it can involve after action reviews in which models for future plans are changed or become more contingent in their designs. This interconnectedness is embedded in theories of experiential learning (e.g., Kolb, 1984, 2014) to be discussed in more detail below with particular attention to AI. First, we review learning frameworks that extend this distinction.

## 2.2.2   Four Types of Learning—Edward Cell's Learning Framework

Edward Cell (1984) identifies four types of learning that are useful for organizing and deepening our thinking about learning beyond the basic distinction between "knowing what" and "knowing how": (1) response learning; (2) situation learning; (3) transsituational learning; and (4) transcendent learning:

1. Response learning. Cell defines *"response learning"* as a change in the way a person is prepared to respond or act in a particular situation. At its base, response learning is what B.F Skinner called "operant conditioning" and includes rote learning. Behavioral modeling training to prepare supervisors for responding with a prepared set of answers when disciplining an employee for lateness and attendance problems or customer service staff for handling certain customer issues are examples of this kind of learning. Response learning can also involve being able to apply a sequence of skills in somewhat complex situations such as using certain negotiating tactics when engaged in a contentious negotiation. Many of the roles built around the need for response learning are being replaced by AI such as online customer service representatives although customer service staff needs to be available for responding to situations that the AI. can't address. Professional staff and managers need to participate in trainings for certain situations, such as responding to a subordinate who is exhibiting symptoms of stress. These situations require response learning. Of course, a critical question is whether the staff and managers are really motivated to learn or are just "checking off" the box of a requirement of organizational policy.

2. Situation learning. Cell describes *"situation learning"* as a change in one's ability for doing response learning involving a change in how a person organizes his or her understanding of a situation. Cell's point is that response learning is dependent on situation learning, since our response is shaped by how we interpret the situation. For example, what a supervisor perceives as being punishment, if the workforce doesn't respect management, it might be seen as positive reinforcement enhancing an employee's status in an ongoing labor organizing campaign. Situation learning involves a change in one's meaning-perspective or point of view (Mezirow, 2000a, 2000b), recognizing and interpreting situations differently and making judgments about how to react. Programs addressing issues such as affirmative action, discrimination, and sexual harassment ideally result in increased awareness leading to changes in participant meaning perspectives. This is likely on the part of participants who respect others but were not aware of how their actions impact others (situation learning leading to response learning). However, in terms of the motivation to learn, other participants with strong bias are less likely to modify their points of view although they may change their actions to avoid disciplinary punishments.

3. Transsituational learning. Transsituational learning is the third type of learning described by Cell—learning *how to change* one's interpretations of a situation; what many HRD professionals call learning-to-learn. Transsituational learning

involves reflecting on one's learning process and questioning the assumptions one is making about a situation. The learner has to reflect on the processes that characterize his or her learning, applying reflexive inquiry practices to critically self-reflect on *how* they have engaged in testing their assumptions and attributions about situations. As will be discussed in the Chap. 6, the digital, or fourth revolution with AI has opened, and will open even more, transsituational possibilities, many of which will have HRD implications.

4. Transcendent learning. The fourth kind of learning in Cell's typology is *transcendent learning;* modifying or creating new concepts. Cell argues that this kind of learning conceptualizes new possibilities and practices for interpreting situations and events. Examples from the relatively recent past include how terms such as "servant leadership," "empowerment," "talent management," "machine learning," and "artificial intelligence" have changed how leadership and management are discussed, opening new opportunities for research and practice. Each has been an avenue for social transactions and as they have been operationalized, they have become tools for facilitating changes in how people construct meaning of their socio-economic context. Managers and other leaders have long understood the importance of language, and especially new concepts, for stimulating actionable change. Extending the possibilities of transsituational learning, transcendent learning opens the doors for new strategic directions for an organization.

The distinctions between situation, transsituational, and transcendent learning describe progressively deeper forms of transformational learning, an area of adult learning scholarship and practice that has been evolving since the 1970s.

## 2.3    Transformative Learning

In 1975, adult educator Jack Mezirow wrote a research report based on 36 case studies of women's reentry programs in community colleges. The focus of this report was how the women who were returning to school in time of a growing women's movement were experiencing transformation of their meaning perspectives as the central process occurring in their personal development from participating in college reentry programs. Mezirow defined meaning perspectives as the "psychological structures within which we locate and define ourselves and our relationships" (Mezirow, 1975, p. 7). Originating in the mid-sixties and continuing to spread in the seventies, Mezirow saw these programs as facilitating transformative change in the meaning perspectives of the participants as they were embarking on a process of repositioning themselves, and the role of women in general, in society and the workplace. Drawing primarily on the work of Jurgen Habermas (1984), an internationally recognized critical theorist associated with the Frankfurt School in Germany, he went on to connect the findings from the study to a more general critical theory of adult learning (Mezirow, 1978, 1981, 1991; Mezirow & Associates, 1990, Mezirow & Taylor, 2009), work that initiated a new branch of adult learning theory creating a rich dialog within the field (e.g., Dirkx, 1997; Yorks & Kasl, 2002; Taylor & Cranton, 2012, 2013; Illeris, 2014; Cranton, 2016). Transformative learning is a process that involves what Cell subsequently described as situational and transsituational learning.

Central to transformative learning theory is the concept of "frames of reference," the meaning perspectives held by people comprised of the assumptions and beliefs through which they filter their perceptions and impressions of their encounters with their world. Frames of reference shape what one sees, hears, and how one reacts to these encounters, framing the way they make sense of their experiences. Essentially, frames of reference are the lens that a person has constructed of their beliefs; beliefs that he or she may be aware of or have subconsciously internalized through having assimilated them in the process of enculturation and socialization. They are the personally held "mental frame" or "lens" through which Edward Cell's concept of "situation learning" occurs.

Frames of reference are comprised of *habits of mind* and *points of view*. Habits of mind consists of the aforementioned broad assumptions that serve to orient how one interprets the meaning of one's experiences and his or her reaction. A point view is the set of specific expectations, beliefs, feelings, and judgments a person applies when thinking about, or interacting with, a particular individual, event, or situation. While shaped by, and generally aligned with, one's habit of mind applied to a particular person or setting one's frame of reference might vary. For example, although a person might hold a negative bias of a racial or ethnic group (his or her habit of mind), he or she might view a certain individual in a more favorable perspective (their point of view).

Research has shown that the process often evolves in recursive ways (Taylor, 2000). While providing the details of transformative learning theory beyond the scope of this book, a couple of key points are very relevant. The *first* is that the "trigger" point for transformative learning is confronting a *disorienting dilemma*. These disorienting trigger points occur when a person is confronted by either external or personal upheavals such as disruptive natural disasters, changes in the socio-eco system, being confronted by disturbing contradictions between one's belief systems and experience, or a series of cumulative experiences and self-changes (Mezirow, 1991). The *second point* is the importance of engaging in open dialogue and critical self-reflection around the disorienting experience, including surfacing and critically reflecting on the assumptions that underlie one's frame of reference that is being disrupted—consistent with Cell's description of situation learning. The *third* is awareness of and reflecting on the affective aspects of emotion and feelings as one engages in the inquiry process—the process of engaging in Cell's notion of transsituational learning. Transformative learning not only entails a cognitive change, but also how a person affectively experiences the world (Yorks & Kasl, 2006; Kasl & Yorks, 2016). The *fourth* is acting based on one's new perspective, integrating it into one's life. Transformative learning embodies a form of Cell's transcendent learning and conducting it typically requires Cell's situational and transsituational learning.

Facilitating transformational learning is increasingly integral to HRD practice. As organizations confront the need for strategic change, realigning their culture, enhancing organizational performance through diverse cross-departmental change, and leadership and development, transformative learning on the part of individuals is required. Strategic agility requires transforming the frames of reference that have been shaped by the past successes of the organization. Ideally, HRD professionals provide disorienting dilemmas in the service of fostering the process before the external market realities trigger disorienting dilemmas that are initially dismissed by key decision makers in the organization. However, the latter is typically the case, as illustrated by Blackberry and Microsoft's fall from domination in their market space.

## 2.4    Connecting the Terrain with Experiential Learning

In describing the theoretical terrain of learning above the focus is on the kind of learning a program, workshop, or other interventions such as coaching, is intended to produce; change involving acquiring a body of knowledge, new skills or competencies, or a changed mind set. The intention is to enable or enhance either current or future performance. This framing treats learning as a *noun*—an outcome. The framing is useful in terms of thinking about what kind of learning is needed for addressing/enabling effective action and performance. Delivering the needed learning requires understanding learning as a process—seeing learning as a verb. Designing and facilitating effective learning interventions require being able to connect desired learning outcomes with effective learning processes. The concepts of single, double, and triple loop learning processes connect with Cell's four kinds of learning.

### 2.4.1    Single Loop Learning

Sequential response learning involves single loop learning when very different kinds of outcomes from the action taken are not what is needed (Argyris & Schön, 1974). Kolb essentially represented it in his experiential learning cycle of experiencing an outcome, reflecting on what happened, conceptualizing an alternative set of actions, which are applied (Kolb, 1984). Single loop learning involves changing one's actions within an existing framework of thinking or mental model. These alternative actions might be drawn from a repertoire of previously learned actions or created in the moment. In short, it takes place within the context of the existing strategic focus, assumptions, or rules (Fig. 2.1).

**Fig. 2.1** Single loop learning (Argyris & Schön, 1974) represented by Kolb's (1984) experiential learning cycle

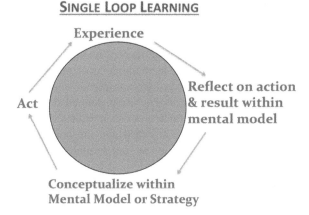

**Fig. 2.2** Kolb's learning cycle adapted to represent double loop learning

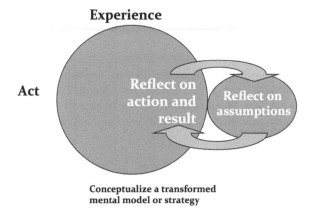

## 2.4.2 Double Loop Learning

Situation learning involves double loop learning; rethinking and changing one's assumptions, leading to a shift in one's framework or mental model allowing one to perceive a situation from a new perspective. It involves a change in strategy or changing the rules embedded in the system. Double loop learning can also open the door to a transcendental situational insight. The differentiation from single loop learning is the reflection on the learning cycle; stepping back and reflecting on the assumptions that are underlying one's strategy (See Fig. 2.2). Accomplishing this involves surfacing one's assumptions though dialogue and getting alternative perspectives. Doing so often triggers disorienting dilemmas.

### 2.4.3   Triple Loop Learning

Although triple loop learning is clearly an extension of Argyris' and Schon's double loop learning, the origins of the concept are not clear. Triple loop learning is reflexive in nature, seeking to learn about *how* a person learns, strategizes, and envisions possibilities. As such it is a process aligned with putting into practice Edward Cell's concept of *transsituational learning*, defined above as *learning how to change one's interpretations* of a situation. As such triple loop learning potentially contributes to one's developmental state, enriching the outcomes of double loop learning and enhancing the possibilities of transformative learning insights. In various forms, triple loop learning is characterized as critical self-reflection on how a difficult or challenging conversation was conducted and personally experienced, *how* one is in relationship with the ambiguity of the situation and learning from one's reaction to the ambiguous encounters with the challenge being confronted. Returning to its potential for potentially contributing to one's developmental state, triple loop learning is about intentionally enhancing one's capacity for learning from strategic learning practices. From an HRD perspective, building single loop, double loop, and triple loop into strategic learning conversations develops both the competencies and capacity for generating new strategic insights. Figure 2.3 summarizes the connections.

The concepts of double and triple loop learning highlight the importance reflection playing in the learning process, expanding the way in which reflection is conceptualized in Kolb's model. As illustrated above, double loop learning requires what Jack Mezirow describes as "premise reflection" bringing one's presuppositions and existing attributions into conscious awareness; triple loop learning requires

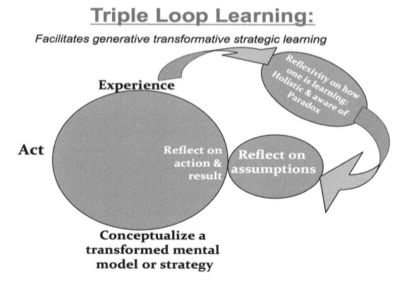

**Fig. 2.3** Kolb's model adapted to represent triple loop learning

critical self-reflection in how one engages in the process of double loop learning which speaks to enhanced self-awareness that can foster one's developmental capacity for avoiding self-imposed blocks to new insights and perspectives. One way of conceptualizing triple loop learning is *learning how to learn* while *learning how to act for producing necessary results*. When applied with rigor, these processes produce learning in action that is productive.

It is critical that the learner tests the validity, or soundness, of the conclusions drawn from the reflective process. Depending on the circumstances that have been reflected on this can be done through dialogue with others with whom the learner can share his or her thinking and/or testing his or her new perspective through taking new actions. The ladder of inference can be a useful framework for continuing to assess what subsequently occurs. Of course, these "tests," like the experiential learning cycle itself, are an ongoing process of constructivism.

### 2.4.4  Assessing Kolb's Framework and Experiential Learning

Kolb's framework has been a foundation for understanding how learning from experience is understood and still widely used in today's world. It has also come under criticism in the academic community for being too simplistic and underrepresenting the complexities of the experiential learning process. In their critique of Kolb, and other experiential learning theorists, Bergsteiner and Avery (2014) argue that his model involves the "violation of categorization principles, confusing four important classes of variables, each with its own subset of variables": six modes of *learning* "(concrete, active, primary, abstract, passive, secondary), *learning senses,* or combination of senses that these activities predominately engage (kinesthetic, visual, aural), *learning stages* (information gathering and sense making, conceptualizing, planning and doing)" and *learning-activity types* "(engage in, write about, observe, hear/see, read, hear)" (p. 258). They also note that reflection takes place at all stages of the learning process, not just as a stage in a cycle. Their model captures the complexity of the learning process and the learning practices in play in a way useful for future research and reflection as a way of being in the learning process as one is learning through doing.

Learning through experience is a function of one's openness for critically looking at one's own performance and the complexities of one's social context and constructing new meaning perspectives on the social setting. Doing this is in part a function of one's competence in applying learning practices and also one's developmental capacity, bringing us to a model that will be discussed in Chap. 3: *Insight* is a function of *competency* X *capacity*. As implied by the model, the experiential learning dimension of the learning terrain is connected to competency; conceptual *knowledge about* and the ability for *knowing how* to apply skills and methodologies in specific situations. Developmental capacity is another part of the learning terrain. We turn now to this other dimension of learning theory, adult development.

## 2.5    Adult Development Theory

For several decades, numerous stage development theories have been provided (e.g., Gilligan, 1982; Kohlberg, 1969; Perry, 1970; Fowler, 1981). In 1983, Bartunek, Gorgon, and Weathersby laid out the implications of adult development for management development programs for preparing managers to lead effectively in complicated and complex situations. Citing Karl Weick's (1979) advice to managers to "complicate yourself" (p. 261), they note Weick's argument that "most people perceive and interpret events from narrow frames of reference" (Bartunek et al., 1983, p. 273). Having such a restricted framework frequently leads to unproductive actions on the part of managers. In order to be effective when addressing complicated or complex situations "managers should develop the ability to generated several interpretations and understandings of organizational events so the 'variety' in their understanding is equivalent to the variety in the situation" enabling them "to register accurately the complex nature of many of the events they face, as well as to choose actions most suited for dealing with particular problem situations … Theories of cognitive complexity suggest that people who are more cognitively complex are more capable than others of applying such multiple perspectives" (pp. 273–274).

That said, while the 1980s were experienced as complicated because of the emerging changes in technology, they were relatively stable compared to today's context. Bartunek, et al.'s argument makes clear the relationship between competency and capacity and the relevance of adult development theory for human resource development in the age of increasing uncertainty and ambiguity. However, we will argue below that a more holistic understanding of adult development, connecting the cognitive and affective aspects of development is necessary for maximizing the implications of adult development theory.

Two adult development theories particularly relevant to leadership and talent development are Robert Kegan's Constructive Developmental Theory (1980; 1982; 1994; Kegan & Lahey, 2001) and William Torbert's Action Logics (1991; Torbert & Associates, 2004, Rooke & Torbert, 2005). Both extend Jean Piaget's theory of cognitive development across the lifespan describing additional developmental stages in adulthood. Kegan's theory explicitly builds a model of possible development that enables more complex meaning making processes from a psychological perspective. Torbert's theory parallels Kegan with an emphasis on the evolution of leadership actions. A third theory with particular relevance to HRD and strategic talent development is John Heron's (1992) developmental framework that provides a holistic view of the developmental process, with implications for fostering the developmental process in an age of intensifying complexity and diversity.

### 2.5.1    Kegan's Constructive Developmental Theory

Kegan's theory of adult development consists of five stages, the first two of which are characteristic of early childhood through adolescence and the next three reflecting possible development through adulthood.

- *The Impulsive Mind:* Impulses frame one's meaning-making. Movement and sensation drive immediate single point reaction.
- *The Instrumental Mind:* One's needs, self-interests, preferences, and desires frame meaning-making and simple tit for tat reciprocity.
- *The Socialized Mind:* Interpersonal relationships frame one's meaning-making. Conformity to rules through a concrete point of view in order to "fit in" and "gain acceptance" from those who one wants to be accepted by, have mutual reciprocity with, and social role consciousness shapes behavior.
- *The Self-Authoring Mind:* Self-authorship of identity, ideology, individualization, actions to meet goals frame one's meaning-making. Multiple-role consciousness, perceiving relations between abstract systems, and self-formation of relationship-regulating forms shapes behavior.
- *The Self-Transforming Mind:* Dialectics between ideologies, groups, and systems frames one's meaning-making. Trans-ideological or post ideological, testing of formulation, paradoxes, and contradictions in the relationship between institutional forms and interpenetration of self and others shapes behavior.

The transformation from one stage to another in adulthood is gradual, if it occurs at all, involving growing awareness of beliefs that been subjectivity embedded in the person and not called into question and beginning to question and reflecting on them. What has been subjectively framing one's meaning-making becomes the object of one's personal reflection. For example, a person with the socialized mind comes to understand themselves as their actions and behaviors being shaped by the views of important others from whom they want to receive acceptance and approval. What has been subject in one's pre-consciousness become object that can be reflected on with gradual emergence of a new subject embeddedness of themselves being autonomous and self-creating. Metaphorically, the process can unfold as going from a socialized mind to two thirds and one third self-authoring, to fifty-fifty, to one third socialized mind and two thirds self-authoring, to essentially self-authoring.

## 2.5.2   William Torbert's Action Logics

William Torbert frames the developmental stages as *Action Logics,* explicitly connecting adult development theory with leadership (Rooke & Torbert, 2005). He also adds the expert action logic (stage) between the equivalent of Kegan's Socialized mindset and self-authoring mindset that particularly applies to individuals in a professional or certified occupation. Further, Torbert's model defines additional action logics (stages) evolving through the post-conventional self-transforming mindset in Kegan's model. Torbert's seven stages of action logics are as follows:

- *The Opportunist Action Logic:* Needs rule impulses. Focus is self-oriented and manipulative to win any way possible.

- *Diplomat Action Logic:* Social norms rule needs. Wants to belong and rarely rocks the boat.
- *Expert Action Logic:* Craft logic, expertise, and rational efficiency rule social norms.
- *Achiever Action Logic:* Strategic goals rule craft logic. Achieves goals through teamwork, effective juggling of duties and external demands.
- *Individualist Action Logic:* Creates unique structures for resolving breaks between strategy and performance interweaving personal and organizational action logics.
- *Strategist Action Logic:* Self-amending effectiveness rules reflexive awareness. Through mutual inquiry and vigilance of both the short and long term generates organizational and personal transformation.
- *Alchemist Action Logic:* Mutual processes of interplay of principles/action generate material spiritual and social transformation.
- (Adapted from: Torbert & Associates, 2004; Rooke & Torbert, 2005).

One's developmental stage becomes evident in how a person interacts when pursuing significant tasks in groups or leading others. Using data collected through a sentence-completion survey developed by psychologist Susanne Cook-Greuter and administered to thousands of managers and professionals in large American and European companies over a period of decades, Torbert and colleagues analyzed the connection between action logics and organizational and individual performance (Rooke & Torbert, 2005). The data collected by Torbert suggested that only *five percent* of individuals serving in leadership roles in businesses at the time were at the opportunist stage of action logic. Experts and achievers were the most prevalent action logics, with *twelve percent* assessed at the diplomat action logic, *thirty-eight percent* as having an expert action logic, and *thirty percent* were achievers. In contrast, individualists made up *ten percent*, strategists *four percent*, and alchemists *one percent* of the managers and professionals assessed, outcomes that remain fairly consistent from contemporary organizational interventions and workshops.

Their studies found that performance, at both the corporate and individual levels, varied by action logics. More specifically, leaders assessed at the opportunistic, diplomat, and expert level "were associated with below average corporate performance" and "were less effective at implementing organizational strategies than … achievers." Only individualists, strategists, and alchemists demonstrated "consistent capacity to innovate and to successfully transform their organizations" (Rooke & Torbert, 2005, p. 68).

Opportunistic action logics translate into a leadership focus on winning through taking advantage of world of situations and others for personal gain. Others are treated as objects with whom they are in competition for valued outcomes. Being carried over from childhood experiences, they justify their actions as necessary in a world of tit for tat outcomes and their success in achieving leadership roles through ignoring having to work with collaboratively with others. Driven by an egocentric mindset they disregard feedback, blame others for failure, and retaliate harshly.

Returning to the issue of transforming from one stage/action logic to the next, like Kegan, Torbert acknowledges that is a gradual process, if it happens at all.

> The leader's voyage of development is not an easy one … Some people change little in their lifetimes; some change substantially. Those who are willing to work at developing themselves, and becoming more self-aware can almost certainly evolve over time.

Below we will discuss developmental practices for facilitating the possibility of such transitions. First, however, we turn to a third framework that also parallels Kegan's and Torbert's models, with additional implications for understanding the challenges and dynamics of the developmental transition process.

### 2.5.3   John Heron's Developmental States

A third developmental theory we find particularly relevant for understanding the process of leadership and human development is John Heron's (1992) developmental states. Whereas, Kegan's framework explores the evolution of cognitive complexity of adult development stages and Torbert's focuses on how developmental stages are manifested in different ways of leading, Heron's model looks at development from a holistic learning perspective providing a complex description of the human development process. He describes eight states of personhood, using the term "states" instead of "stages" to avoid implying

> … a temporal progression with one stage leading to the next … while some broad generalizations can be made about stages of development, which hold universally, people have a way of making some very idiosyncratic journeys toward self-realization … What you can say is that the bottom four occur, developmentally, before the top four. They comprise the loam, the ground, the humus out of which the top four grow. (Heron, pp. 52–53).

His point is that while one state may be predominant, people move between states as part of the developmental process. In describing the developmental process, Heron uses the term *psyche* to refer to:

> … the human mind and its inherent life as a whole, including its unexpressed and unexplored potential, as well as what is manifest in conscious development … 'The psyche' is simply a convenient generic term to when talking about some of the basic structures and dynamics of the human mind. (p. 14).

The psyche has four modes, *(1) Affective, (2) Imaginal, (3) Conceptual,* and *(4) Practical*, that comprise an "up-hierarchy" that underlies four *ways of knowing:* (1) *Experiential knowing*—largely preconscious, tacit, and embodied, internalized through experience; (2) *Presentational knowing*—expressive engagement with one's world through metaphors, analogies, storytelling, movement, drawing or artistic creation; (3) *Propositional knowing*— stated in logical formulations through language and/or mathematical formulations to assert facts and theoretical generalizations about relationships that coherent, rationally grounded in evidence, and without any internal contradictions; (4) *Practical knowing*—translating the prior three ways of knowing into effective action through knowing how to do something. In the words of Heron, "Practical knowledge is the final outcrop of this up-hierarchy of knowledge, from experiential to presentational, to propositional" (1992, p. 172).

Each of the four modes has two polar functions: individualizing and participatory. In the affective mode of experiential knowing, the psyche's individualizing function manifests as "emotion" and the participatory as "feeling." Acknowledging "special usage" for the word "feeling," Heron defines feeling as the participatory expression of human affect, calling it, "the capacity of the psyche to participate in wider unities of being …. This is the domain of empathy, indwelling, participation, presence, resonance, and such like" (p. 16). This development enables transformation toward a habit of being with capacity for presence of self *and* other.

Heron's eight states are as follows:

- *The Primal Person:* Fusion of the primordial psyche with its fetal world;
- *The Spontaneous Person:* The uninhibited psyche expresses inmate impulses;
- *The Compulsive Person:* Wounded psyche has defensive splits and repressions from interactions with others;
- *The Conventional Person:* Socialized psyche has defensive splits and repressions from interactions with others;
- *The Creative Person:* Psyche is autonomous in external behavior and actions;
- *Self-Creating Person:* Psyche is autonomous in healing and self-actualizing;
- *Self-Transforming Person:* Psyche realizes its psychic and spiritual potential;
- *Charismatic Person:* Continuously transfiguring.

In the early states of development, emotion dominates as the person experiences periodic traumas and oppressions creating compulsive states that become "interwoven with the conventional person" (p. 55) who grows to adopting the cultural norms of the group. In later states, the participatory function of feeling becomes stronger and acts as a filter for emotions. Heron describes the first four states as being *prepersonal* with the person largely internalizing the values, norms, and beliefs of their cultural-social system. *Personhood* begins with the transition from the socialized conventional person to the state of a creative person who is in his or her own relationship with the broader system. The transition into the creative person begins the process of transcending and unraveling conventional and compulsive behavior through reflexive thinking. As this process continues one can move between creative, self-creating, and self-transfiguring states in different contexts as the developmental process continues with the potential for realizing, although rarely attained, the state of the charismatic person.

## 2.5.4  The arc of Adult Development

Although the specifics in the frameworks vary somewhat, the arc of the development process in each is parallel. This arc is the developmental shift from a focus on

**Table 2.1**  Comparison of developmental frameworks by Heron, Torbert, and Kegan

| Heron's Developmental States | Torbert's Action Logics | Kegan's Constructive Developmental Cognitive Stages |
|---|---|---|
| **Charismatic Person:** continuously Transfiguring | | |
| **Self-Transfiguring Person:** Psyche realizes its psychic & spiritual Potential | **Alchemist:** Mutual process (interplay of principle/action) rules principle | |
| **Self-Creating Person:** Psyche is autonomous in healing and self-actualizing | **Transforming:** Self amending effectiveness rules reflexive awareness | |
| - - - - - - - - - - - - - - - - - | **Redefining:** creates structures & processes to & for bridging gaps between strategy, performance, & among people's action logics | **Self-Transforming Mind:** Dialectic between ideologies, Groups, and systems frames one's meaning making |
| **Creative Person:** Psyche is autonomous in external behavior and actions | **Achiever:** System/group effectiveness rules norms/craft logic | **Self-Authoring Mind:** Self-authorship of identity, ideology, actions to meet goals frame one' meaning making |
| - - - - - - - - - - - - - - - - - - - - - - - *[Transition from pre-person to personhood]* | **Expert:**  Craft logic, expertise and rational efficiency rules norms | - - - - - - - - - - - - - - - - - - - - - |
| **Conventional Person:** Socialized psyche adopts culturally defined social roles | **Diplomat:** Social norms rule needs | **Socialized Self:** Interpersonal relationships frame one's meaning making |
| **Compulsive Person:** Wounded psyche has defensive splits and repressions from interactions with others | **Opportunist:** Needs rule impulses | **Instrumental Mind:** One's needs, interests, desires frame meaning making |
| **Spontaneous Person:** Uninhibited psyche expresses innate impulses | **Impulsive:**  impulses rule behavior | **Impulsive Mind:** Impulses frame meaning making |

one's self to awareness of the interconnectedness of one's self with the larger environmental context. This developmental growth is critical for enabling people, and especially professionals and leaders, to function in the environment of continuous change and hyper-connectivity of the twenty-first century. Table 2.1 summarizes the commonalities and differences between the three frameworks reflecting the different interests of the theorists.

Facilitating development requires ongoing extensive practices. While awareness of its importance can be introduced in a training session or two- or three-day workshop, this is essentially knowledge about. With the exception of sessions in which participants have voluntary joined the session with personal motivation for self-development, defensive routines can be initially triggered. Making accurate appraisal of one's cognitive stage or action logic requires careful assessment and a supportive holding environment for participants to continue to assess how their position in the arc of development shifts, either progressively or falls back, in response to particular events. In short, critical self-reflection is part of the process. Self-reflection and awareness of how we engage with others facilitate development. (Kegan & Lahey, 2001).

Torbert's process of *developmental action inquiry* provides a lens for self-reflection with awareness of three interconnected spaces of inquiry: first person awareness, second person speaking, and third person inquiry. First person awareness involves four territories of experience:

1. First territory of Intentional Attention, meaning presenting awareness of one's vision, intuition, aims, and goals;
2. Second territory of one's Action Logics, shaping one's strategies, schemas, ploys, and typical modes of reflecting on experience;
3. Third territory of one's Own Sensed Performance, in terms of skills, pattern of activity, deeds as sensed in the process of enactment;
4. Fourth territory of Outside Events, observing results, consequences, and environmental effects.

Mindful awareness of the four territories is a foundational practice for being conscious of how one is a self-comprised systemic entity that is also acting within and being influenced by a larger system of entities. This consciousness provides insights of one's action logic in play at the moment. Critical reflexivity in the moment has the potential for supporting further development. Returning to Heron's model, in instances when strong emotions have been triggered the potential for fostering feeling can be enabled through first person awareness.

Second person speaking involves awareness of how one is communicating with the other, especially in complex and/or emotionally tense conversations. Torbert (2004). defines four parts of speech; (1) *Framing* one's intention or purpose, (2) *Advocating* one's proposal, strategy, or plan, (3) *Illustrating* with a story of how what is being advocated might by applied, and (4) *Inquiring* into others thoughts and reactions with the intention of learning from them. This manner of speaking is essential for engaging in developmental action inquiry. Understanding the four parts of speech is easy; incorporating them into one's daily conversations as a manner of speaking is not. In real work conversations, whether is group work in workshops or in meetings and task forces, the old habits of jumping into advocacy and debate take over. Like Kegan and Lahey, Torbert calls attention to how one speaks shapes both how we lead and work and subsequently the outcomes we produce, which connects with third person inquiry; how we are in relationship with the socio-economic echo system and are organizing our resources and taking action in the world.

The essence of third person inquiry is our personal interactions with others in our immediate networks and those with whom we might never come in contact with, or with each other, but will be influenced by our actions. Again, emerging digital technologies is continuously interconnecting and changing these networks. Third person inquiry must be done with conscious awareness of the four territories of first person experiencing. While conceptually described as specific spaces of inquiry, the three are continuously interacting with each other, subconsciously and ideally at times intentionally.

Intentional practice of being aware of how one's thoughts and emotions are dominating one's actions and shifting to consciously changing how one is speaking and intentionally holding one's self in the three spaces of inquiry can facilitate one's development through the arc of development. This is a change in how one is in relationship in the larger socio-eco system by not letting emotions block one's indwelling in the world and resonating with how it is (Heron, 1992, p. 23). Mindful engagement with somatic learning, discussed below, also facilitates this process of development.

It is important to note that the process of development isn't strictly linear. While a person's mindset maybe largely centered in one developmental stage/state, "fall back" to a prior state can occur when dealing with particular people or situations (Livesay, 2015). Also, on occasion someone may exhibit characteristics reflective of a more "advanced" stage as a result of a particular set of circumstances, for example, working on resolving an issue of high importance to them within a setting in which very open dialogue and listening are being facilitated.

## 2.6    Somatic Learning: Mind-Body Awareness for Self-Development

Somatic learning involves a process of working with the interdependent systems of the body consisting of thoughts, emotions, and neuromuscular physiology (Damasio, 1994; Lakoff & Johnson, 1999). Mind and body are worked with as a functional living wholistic system consisting of what one feels, thinks, and expresses (Strozzi-Heckler, 2007). Returning to the concept of learning as a verb, knowledge subjectively arises first and foremost from the body's interaction with the environment resulting in sensations, emotions, and feelings leading to cognitive, conscious interpretative thoughts. This is consistent with Heron's up-hierarchy of ways of knowing and Polyani's concept of tacit knowledge with "bodily knowing as central to all acts of knowing" captured in his famous saying "I know more than I can say" (p. 75).

Somatic learning connects with mindfulness, emphasizing not only the need for mindful awareness of one's thoughts, but also one's sensations in the body that activate largely though subconscious neural patterns. This is done through body-based practices that develop the learner's capability for intervening with their own neurology (Brendel & Bennett, 2016). This is accomplished through having learners engage in activities that bring this awareness into consciousness. Using somatic learning is a growing practice, being delivered in both workshop formats and coaching. Practices include centering for developing a felt sense of being aligned and balanced, peer exercises such as the grab where participants walk side by side and one suddenly grabs the other's wrist, and blending which also involves moving toward each other to walk side by side with arms touching (blending) together. Through these kinds of exercises participants become aware of how one responds to being with others in conversations or other relationships. While initially skeptical, as participants become more aware of their strong sensations and connecting these with his or her strong default values and their tendencies that connect with workplace behaviors, significant changes occur.

Brendel and Bennett provide a three-phase process integrating mindfulness and somatics:

- Phase one—Expanding awareness to receive mind-body insights to connect sensations in the body with thoughts and actions through mindfulness and somatic practices;
- Phase two—Engaging in critical reflection and dialogue around mind-body insights generated by participation in the practices to transform behaviors;
- Phase three—Transforming practice into more attuned and accepting ways of being through continuous body-based practices that "reshape" the mind bringing it into alignment with one's intentions.

Not surprisingly becoming competent in delivering these learning practices requires experiential learning on the part of the facilitator.

Somatic learning is becoming increasing a part of leadership development initiatives in prominent businesses. It is also relevant in terms of preparing staff for working in diverse teams and their personal development in terms of how they perform in uncomfortable situations. In terms of constructive developmental theory, mindful somatic learning brings subjective reactions into objective awareness, providing for developmental growth through subsequent reflection on the emotional impulses, the behaviors they have triggered, and the state of one's mindset. Somatic learning provides a pathway for fostering a participatory mode of psyche in terms of Heron's developmental framework.

## 2.7    From Individual to Team and Organizational Learning

The models presented above describe the multi-dimensional aspects of learning as an individual phenomenon. When individuals have similar learning experiences, there is a shared set of mental models or frames of references that bind them together as a community. Paradoxically, this can potentially create walls between them and members of other communities who have a different set of shared experiences, especially when developmentally they have conventional socialized mindsets or action-logics. This is often a key underpinning of the "tribal" conflicts that can exist between communities. In organizations, work is often done in groups or teams and much of this work requires addressing issues requiring innovative solutions produced by group members from diverse functions with very different skill and mindsets. Group members need to learn together when addressing these kinds of situations. Teams are more effective than individuals in solving unstructured or ambiguous problems assuming the group members are engaged in effective team learning processes. In the digital driven world of the twenty-first century teams working across functions will become even more common as roles evolve as a result of artificial intelligence and lean management is increasingly implemented in various sectors. Team learning theory is bridge connecting learning & development and organizational development practices. While our initial focus here is on team learning, effective team learning is also connected to processes of organizational learning, the two are interconnected.

## 2.7.1    Frameworks of Team Learning

In the 1990s, scholars began researching teams from the perspective of being collective learning units (Edmondson, 1999; Edmondson et al., 2001; Hackman, 1990; Kasl et al., 1997; DeChant, Marsick & Kasl, 1993; Yorks et al., 2003). Elizabeth Kasl, Victoria Marsick, and Kathleen DeChant's research produced a team learning model describing four learning modes describing the extent a team is collectively learning as a group:

- Fragmented learning: Individuals learn, but their learning is not necessarily shared with others on the team and not with the entire team;
- Pooled learning: Sub-groupings within the team learn as members share information among themselves, but the entire team doesn't learn;
- Synergistic learning: The team as a whole learns as members create knowledge mutually, integrating divergent in new ways as the new knowledge is integrated into individual meaning perspectives;
- Continuous learning: Synergistic learning becomes habitual within the team.

These modes are not linearly progressive stages of development, but phases through which the team may move back and forth. Going from fragmented to phases of more collective learning, either within pooled groups or synergistic teams, involves a learning process of:

- framing the initial perceptions;
- reframing initial perceptions through reflecting on data and the group's experience to date;
- experimenting through group action to test the framing and/discover impact;
- crossing boundaries through interactions with individual's or units sharing ideas and information including seeking insights from "devils advocates"; and,
- integrating perspectives by the group synthesizing their divergent views and resolving conflicts through "dialectical thinking" not compromise or majority rule. (Kasl et al. 1997).

Typically facilitating the process of team learning begins with individual learning and as the team becomes more cohesive transitions toward a more synergistic phase of learning. Three general sets of learning conditions are necessary for this progression to take place:

- Appreciation of teamwork: The openness of team members for hearing and taking others' ideas into consideration, acting in ways that help the team build on the synergy of its members;

- Individual expression: The extent to which the team members have the opportunity to participate in the team's goals, influence the team's operation, and are comfortable in expressing their objections;
- Operating principles: The extent to which the team has organized itself for effective operations and established a set of commonly held beliefs, values, purpose, and structure that balances working on tasks with building relationships among the team members (Kasl et al., 1997).

Getting a newly formed team off to a good start is an important first step in creating a learning team. As organizational psychologist Richard Hackman noted in 1989 assuming that team members have the skills they need to work effectively in the team is one of the "trip wires" that can block the formation of learning teams "… whatever occurs when a team is created—when members first meet and begin to come to terms with one another and the work they will do—has enduring effects" (Hackman, 1990, p. 503). Getting a team off to a good start, minimizing the potential of the storming phase through integrating norming practices into the forming stage through having team members brainstorm what norms will guide their work can have an enduring effect. Although norms will vary across situations, how leadership, decision-making, and conflict resolution will be handled are important.

The initial lists of norms provide a framework for what Mezirow called process reflection, activating what Kasl, Dechant, and Marsick frame as operating principles and appreciation of teamwork. This framework can be structured with each statement followed by a 5-or-7 point-scale. Periodically, the team can collectively reflect on their norms and have a dialogue around how well the team is adhering to its norms. First team members individually scale each question. Without discussion, the team then creates a frequency distribution for each of the norms. The team members can then have a dialogue around any norm where there are significant differences in opinion about how the group is functioning or any norm with a relatively low mean, inquiring into specific examples and what could be done differently. If done with reasonable frequency, this process can be done efficiently and before team learning, dynamics become problematic in terms of group dynamics. The process reinforces learning practices that facilitate reframing and sensemaking from experimenting with ideas.

This kind of learning process is important when teams are launched, when completing cycles of complex and challenging tasks, and when teams are intended to be organization learning mechanisms crossing boundaries. The above processes are especially important for teams dealing with uncertain or even ambiguous tasks such as strategy development in today's socio-economic environment. The dynamics of the team learning process will vary within different types of teams, such as those with stable membership and those with changing or fluid memberships and how stable the tasks are (Clutterbuck, 2002). Clutterbuck has provided a framework defining five types of teams with regard to the stability of tasks performed and the stability of team membership:

1. *Stable teams* with steady membership and performing unchanging tasks. Team members rarely engage in learning;
2. *Cabin crew teams* whose membership is regularly changing but the task performed by the teams are unchanging. Team members rarely engage in learning;
3. *Hit teams* with stable membership who are together only for brief periods of time while performing new or changing tasks. Any learning being scattered as the team disbands;
4. *Evolutionary teams* performing changing or new tasks with members changing. As original members of the team coalesce through sharing of their knowledge and applications and continue to learn, new members who lack this experience may find it difficult to integrate into the team.
5. *Virtual teams* that come together informally and are comprised of both consistent and new members to address both stable and new tasks. Knowledge is the currency that brings the team together and members that don't have this currency are excluded limiting the learning opportunities for less experienced or lower level staff.

In today's world of necessary agility, preparing managers and executives for coaching teams to use learning processes that break through the boundaries of different types of teams is an important item on the HRD agenda. So is facilitating the launching of teams dealing with critical strategic issues facing the organization and requiring organization change. This can require team learning on the part of the HRD team as HR is strategically realigning itself. This will be discussed in Chap. 3.

The impact of learning machine technologies is shifting the prevalence of certain types of teams; specifically as traditionally stable tasks become increasingly automated by AI the length of time before members of stable or cabin crew teams become confronted with either their team having changing roles and the need for learning new skills (becoming evolutionary teams) or joining new teams (that are perhaps hit teams) or leaving the organization is shortening. Anticipating these changes and planning for them are central HRD role.

## 2.7.2   Organizational Learning

Team learning is a form of organizational learning which in turn requires individual learning, especially when teams engage in boundary crossing sharing and incorporating information and learning from other teams. Leveraging this shared information is a critical part of the organizational learning process. Boundary crossing, along with integration of perspectives across teams as well as within them, is crucial for the horizontal integration of work activities in today's world of lean management and production. In his book, *The Fifth Discipline*, Peter Senge made this connection, writing "teams, not individuals are the fundamental learning units in modern organizations. This [is] where the 'rubber meets the road'; unless teams can learn the organization cannot learn" (1990, p. 10). This doesn't negate the role of individual learning in the organizational learning process as Senge clearly emphasizes in his discussion of personal mastery later in the book; "Organizations learn only through organizations that learn. Individual learning does not guarantee organizational learning. But without it, no organizational learning occurs" (p. 139).

While Senge's book made organizational learning part of mainstream conversations about management and leadership practices in both academic research and practice, the topic had been a part of the discourse and debate in organizational theory for some time (Argyris & Schön, 1978; Fiol & Lyles, 1985; Heberg, 1981; Shrivastava, 1983). At the heart of the debate was whether organizations can truly learn or if only individuals learn on the organization's behalf.

Despite this debate bridges were forming that linked the two sides shifting the conversation toward conceptualizing organizational learning. The early theories of James March and Herbert Simon characterized rules and procedures in organizations similar to habits in individuals; standardized ways of handling routine events or decisions. Their theories were not entirely inconsistent with emerging theories of organizational learning by Bo Heberg (1981), Marlene Fiol and Marjorie Lyles (1985), and Paul Shrivastava (1983), arguing that learning takes place at multiple organizational levels and can be conceptualized as embedded in the procedures, systems, and practices of an organization and dependent on individual's learning. Just as individual habits are the product of learning, so are organizational procedures. Heberg (1981) connected individual learning with organizational learning because only individuals have brains and senses necessary for organizational learning to occur. However, with the emergence of fourth industrial revolution, the human brain is being augmented by machine learning. Organizational systems increasingly have their own "brains."

The concept of organizational learning continued to have growing popularity in both theory and management practice, the latter being driven by the increasing pace of change in technology and its impact on the socio-economic context of the organization. It was increasing accepted that the rate of individual and organizational learning would become the basis of sustainable competitive advantage (Adler & Cole, 1993). Particularly in knowledge-intensive industries (Stata, 1989), there was a growing consensus in the literature that while the distinction between individual learning and organizational learning was useful for thinking about issues of adaptive organizational change, there continued to be significant differences in how this distinction was addressed in both the research and practitioner literatures.

Popper and Lipshitz (1998) addressed this issue by providing an empirically based framework that would address the issue of anthropomorphism and operationalized the concept of organizational learning for purposes of both research and practice. Based on empirical research, their framework distinguishes between "learning in organization" (LIO) and "learning by organization" (LBO). Learning-in-organization occurs when members learn on behalf of the organization; learning-by-organization when the individual learning has organizational outputs that are taken and utilized widely throughout the organization. These outputs could include informal norms and/or changes in formal procedures and practices. The connection between LIOs and LBO takes place through organizational learning mechanisms

(OLMs). OLMs are "institutional structured and procedural arrangements that allow organizations to systematically collect, analyze, store, disseminate, and use information relevant to the performance of the organization and its members" enabling organizational learning (p. 170). OLMs are systems operated by "organizational members" making "it possible for organizations to learn to attribute to organizations a capacity to learn" (p. 170) and avoiding the theoretical problem of anthropomorphism proposed by March and Olsen.

Popper & Lipshitz's model (1998, 2000) makes clear the connection between individual, team, and organizational learning. It also illustrates the necessary integration of HRM, L&D, and OD in HRD practices to create organizational learning mechanisms. Organizational learning requires an organizational cultural of learning, in which mistakes are opportunities for learning, transparency is a norm, as is responsible behavior. Of course, organizations are "federations" comprised of various groupings that in turn encompass larger groups. Some of these groupings are more or less tightly coupled and more or less autonomous depending on the extent, the organization's structure is centralized or decentralized. Learning intervention practices need to be designed and implemented based on the particular characteristics of the setting as will be discussed in Chaps. 3, 4, and 7. This is particularly true in the age of AI.

Organization learning continues to be an area of interest, with research demonstrating that it is an essential factor impacting organizational performance in today's world of constant technological change. And as will be discussed in later chapters, performance models are another component of HRD theory and practice.

## 2.8  Self-Directed Learning

We conclude this chapter with self-directed learning because in the age of digital systems, self-directed learning is an increasingly necessary personal characteristic. As will be discussed in later chapters, learning resources for the workforce are being provided in the flow of work. It is the learner who needs to access the resources when he or she needs them. As Alvin Toffler, author of *Future Shock* (1970), quoting psychologist Herbert Gerjuoy, famously wrote, "Tomorrow's illiterate will not be the man who can't read; he will be the man who has not learned how to learn" often restated as "The illiterate of the 21st century will not be those who cannot read and write, but those who cannot learn, unlearn, and relearn."

The establishment of self-directed learning as a significant theoretical concept in the field of adult education is generally attributed to the writings of Cyril Houle (1961) and two of his doctoral students, Allen Tough (1971) and Malcolm Knowles (1970, 1975). In particular, Knowles' (1970) differentiation between pedagogy and andragogy as a guide for understanding and facilitating how adult learn became the initial foundation for self-directed learning. Knowles defined self-directed learning as:

Self-directed learning is a process in which individuals take the initiative, with or without the help of others, in diagnosing their learning needs, formulating learning goals, identifying human and material resources for learning, choosing and implementing appropriate learning strategies, and evaluating learning outcomes (1975, p. 18).

A rich stream of literature on self-directed learning emerged over the course of the next several decades, Brookfield (1985, 1986), Grow (1991), Candy (1991), Caffarella (1993), Garrison (1997), providing a range of perspectives on the concept. The literature on self-directed learning has continued to expand over the past decades, including how teachers in schools and colleges can develop self-directed learning as a critical competency for the twenty-first century. With content now available online with open access being able to critically access information in terms of its usefulness, validity is an important part of self-directed learning.

Apart from accessing tangible materials in the form of articles, videos, virtual reality presentations, and receiving coaching or attending workshops, self-directed learners also engage supervisors and other individuals in their network of contacts in informal conversations as a way of learning. In today's fluid and highly skills based and gig workplace, fostering a culture supportive of self-directed learning throughout the workforce is critical. Doing this involves managers and HRD professionals having dialogues with members of the workforce defining their career *goals*, *analyzing* what learning and development needs they must address for realizing these goals, *planning* how they can address these needs, building *awareness of the resources* available for doing so, taking *actions* utilizing these resources, and *reflecting* on their progress. In short, being supportive of the motivation and engagement necessary for fostering their development, not directing it.

## 2.9    Summary

In this chapter, we have presented major theoretical frameworks that provide grounding for HRD practices. While each framework provides a particular lens for understanding learning, they also interconnect with some sharing concepts that parallel one another and others complementing different frameworks. As previously mentioned, Cell's *situation, transitional, and transcendental learning* are essentially progressively deeper forms of *transformative learning. Situational* learning, especially around situations in which a person has been culturally socialized, been deeply embedded in and emotionally attached to, involve at minimum a transformed *point of view* and possibly a transformed *habit of mind,* depending on the depth of learning. Both require a level of *double loop* learning as one reassess the appropriateness of actions taken/to be taken and assumptions framing this reassessment as one learns from her or his *experiences. Transitional* learning involves transforming one's *habit-of- mind* requiring the reflexive application of *triple loop* learning on one's own meaning making processes. More open habits of mind enhance the possibilities of innovative outcomes through *transcendental* learning when engaging in creative conversations in diverse groups.

The potential and richness of all these connections are bounded and enabled by the *developmental* state of the learner(s) involved. As Kegan has written, the developmental states or stages constitute the "forms of our meaning making" shaping the relationship one has with what they are learning about. Developing a more complex form of meaning-making is itself transformative. "What is 'object' in our knowing describes the thoughts and feelings we say we have; what is 'subject' describes the thinking and feeling that has us. We 'have' object; we 'are' subject" (2000, p. 53). Change in the learner's *developmental state/stage* is a significant dimension of *transformative* learning that also enables or limits transformation of one's, *point of view* or *habit of mind*; or to use Kegan's chapter title "What 'form' Transforms?" Developmental transformations are a function of awareness of how we talk (Kegan & Lahey, 2001; engaging in action inquiry (Rooke & Torbert, 2005) and *somatic* learning (Brendel & Bennett, 2016) and can holistically facilitate developmental transformations. These dynamics are all in play in *team learning*.

## References

Adler, P.S. & Cole, R.E. (1993). A tale of two auto plants. *Sloan Management Review, 34*, 85–94.

Alvin, T. (1970). *Future Shock*. New York: Random House.

Argyris, C., & Schön, D. A. (1974). *Theory in practice increasing professional effectiveness.* Jossey-Bass.

Argyris, C., & Schön, D. A. (1978). *Organizational learning*. Addison-Wesley.

Bartunek, J. M., Gordon, J. R., & Weathersby, R. P. (1983). Developing a "complicated" understanding of administrators. *Academy of Management Review, 8*(2), 273–284.

Bateson, G. (1972). *Steps to an ecology of mind: A revolutionary approach to man's understanding of himself*. Chandler Publishing.

Bergsteiner, H., & Avery, G. A. (2014). The twin-cycle experiential learning model: Reconceptualising Kolb's theory. *Studies in Continuing Education, 36*(3), 257–274.

Brendel, W., & Bennett, C. (2016). Learning to embody leadership through mindfulness and somatics practice. *Advances in Developing Human Resources, 18*(3), 409–425.

Brookfield, S. (1985). Self-directed learning: A conceptual and methodological exploration. *Studies in the Education of Adults, 17*(1), 19–32.

Brookfield, S. (1986). *Understanding and Facilitating Adult Learning*. San Francisco: Jossey-Bass.

Caffarella, R. S. (1993). Self-Directed Learning. *New Directions for Adult & Continuing Education, 57*, 25–35.

Candy, P.C. (1991). *Self-direction for Lifelong Learning: A Comprehensive Guide to Theory and Practice*. San Francisco, Jossey-Bass.

Cell, E. (1984). *Learning to learn from experience*. State University of New York Press.

Clutterbuck, D. (2002). "Passport": How teams learn. *Training and Development,* March, 67–69.

Cranton, P. (2016). The art of questioning. *Journal of Transformative Education, 14*(2), 83–85.

Damasio, A. R. (1994). *Descartes' error: Emotion, reason, and the human brain*. Grosset/Putnam.

DeChant, K., Marsick, V. J., & Kasl, E. (1993). Towards a model of team learning. *Studies in Continuing Education, 15*(1), 1–14.

Dirkx, J. M. (1997). Nurturing soul in adult learning. *New Directions for Adult & Continuing Education., 1997*(74), 79–88.

Edmondson, A. C. (1999). Psychological safety and learning behavior in work teams. *Administrative Science Quarterly, 44*(2), 350–382.

Edmondson, A. C., Bohmer, R. M., & Pisano, G. P. (2001). Disrupted routines: Team learning and new technology implementation. *Administrative Science Quarterly, 46*(4), 685–716.

Fiol, C. M., & Lyles, M. A. (1985). Organizational learning. *Academy of Management Review, 10*(4), 803–813.

Fowler, J. W. (1981). *The psychology of human development and the quest for meaning.* Harper Collins.

Fox, S. (1997). From management education and development to the study of management learning. In J. Burgoyne & M. Reynolds (Eds.), *Management learning: Integrating perspectives in theory and practice* (pp. 21–37). Sage.

Garrison, D.R. (1997). Self-directed learning: Toward a comprehensive model. *Adult Education Quarterly, 48*(1), 18–33.

Gilligan, C. (1982). *In a different voice: Psychological theory and women's development.* Harvard Press.

Grow, G.O. (1991). Teaching learning to be self-directed. *Adult Education Quarterly, 41*(3), 125–149.

Habermas, J. (1984). *The Theory of Communicative Action. Reason and The Rationalization of Society.* Volume One. Boston: Beacon Press. (Translated by Thomas McCarthy—originally published 1981, Frankfurt am Main).

Hackman, J. R. (1990). Conclusion: Creating more effective work groups. In J. R. Hackman (Ed.), *Groups that work (and those that don't): Creating conditions for effective team work* (pp. 479–504). Jossey-Bass.

Heberg, B. (1981). How organizations learn and unlearn. In P. Nystram & W. Starbuck (Eds.), *Handbook of organizational design: Adapting organisations to their environment* (pp. 1–27). Oxford University Press.

Heron, J. (1992). *Feeling and personhood: Psychology in another key.* Sage.

Houle, C. O. (1961). *The inquiring mind.* University of Wisconsin Press.

Illeris, K. (2014). Transformative learning and identity. *Journal of Transformative Education, 12*(2), 148–163.

James, W. (1925). *Pragmatism.* Longmans and Green.

Kasl, E., Marsick, V. J., & Dechant, K. (1997). Teams as learners: A research based model of team learning. *Journal of Applied Behavioral Science, 33*(2), 227–246.

Kasl, E., & Yorks, L. (2016). Do I know you? Do you really know me? And, how important is it that we do? Relationship and empathy in differing learning contexts. *Adult Education Quarterly, 66*(1), 3–20.

Kegan, R. (1980). Making meaning: The constructive-development approach to persons and practice. *Journal of Counseling & Development, 58*(5), 373–380.

Kegan, R. (1982). *The evolving self.* Harvard University Press.

Kegan, R. (1994). *In over our heads: The mental demands of modern life.* Harvard University Press.

Kegan, R., & Lahey, L. L. (2001). *How we talk can change the way we work: Seven languages for transformation.* Jossey-Bass.

Knowles, M. S. (1970). *The modern practice of adult education: Andragogy versus pedagogy.* Association Press.

Knowles, M. S. (1975). *Self-directed learning: A guide for learners and teachers.* Association Press.

Kohlberg, L. (1969). Stage and sequence: The cognitive development approach to socialization. In D. A. Goslin (Ed.), *Handbook of socialization theory* (pp. 347–480). Rand McNally.

Kolb, D. A. (1984). *Experiential learning: Experience as the source of learning.* Prentice Hall.

Kolb, D. A. (2014). *Experiential learning: Experience as the source of learning and development* (2nd ed.). Pearson Education, Inc..

Lakoff, G., & Johnson, M. (1999). *Philosophy in the flesh: The embodied mind and its challenge to western thought.* Basic Books.

Livesay, V. T. (2015). One step back, two steps forward: Fallback in human and leadership development. *Journal of Leadership, Accountability and Ethics, 12*(4), 173–189.

Marsick, V. J., & Watkins, K. E. (2001). Informal and incidental learning. *New Directions for Adult and Continuing Education, 2001*(89), 25–34.

Mezirow, J. (1975). *Education for perspective transformation: Women's re-entry programs in community colleges.* Centre for Adult Education, Teachers College, Columbia University.

Mezirow, J. (1978). Perspective transformation. *Adult Education Quarterly, 28*(2), 100–110.

Mezirow, J. (1981). A critical theory of adult learning and education. *Adult Education Quarterly, 32*(1), 3–24.

Mezirow, J. (1991). *Transformative dimensions of adult learning.* Jossey-Bass.

Mezirow, J. (2000a). Learning to think like an adult. In J. Mezirow and Associates (Ed.), *Learning as transformation: Critical perspectives on a theory in progress* (p. 8). Jossey-Bass.

Mezirow, J. (2000b). *Learning as transformation: Critical perspectives on a theory in progress.* Jossey-Bass.

Mezirow, J. & Associates. (1990). *Fostering critical reflection in adulthood: A guide to transformative and emancipatory education.* Jossey-Bass.

Mezirow, J., & Taylor, E. W. (Eds.). (2009). *Transformative learning in practice: Insights from community, workplace, and higher education.* Jossey-Bass.

Perry, W. G. (1970). *Forms of intellectual and ethical development in the college years: A scheme.* Holt, Rinehart, and Winston.

Polanyi, M. (1964). *Personal knowledge.* Harper and Row.

Popper, M., & Lipshitz, R. (1998). Organizational learning mechanisms: A culture and structural approach to organizational learning. *Journal of Applied Behavioral Science, 34*(2), 161–178.

Popper, M., & Lipshitz, R. (2000). Organizational learning: Mechanism, culture and feasibility. *Management Learning, 31*(2), 181–196.

Quinn, J. B. (1992). *Intelligent enterprise.* Free Press.

Rooke, D., & Torbert, W. R. (2005). Seven transformations of leadership. *Harvard Business Review, 83*(4), 66–76.

Senge, P. M. (1990). *The fifth discipline: The art & practice of the learning organization.* Doubleday/Currency.

Shrivastava, P. (1983). A typology of organizational learning systems. *Journal of Management Studies, 20*(1), 7–28.

Strozzi-Heckler, R. (2007). *The leadership DOJO: Build your foundation as an exemplary leader.* Frog Books.

Taylor, E. W. (2000). Analyzing research on transformative learning theory. In J. Mezirow (Ed.), *Learning as transformation: Critical perspectives on a theory in progress* (pp. 285–328). Jossey-Bass.

Taylor, E. W., & Cranton, P. (Eds.). (2012). *The handbook of transformative learning: Theory, research and practice.* Jossey-Bass.

Taylor, E. W., & Cranton, P. (Eds.). (2013). A theory in progress? Issues in transformative learning theory. *Eur J Res Educ Learn Adults, 4*(1), 35–47.

Torbert, B. (2004). *Action inquiry : The secret of timely and transforming leadership.* Berrett-Koehler.

Torbert, W. R. (1991). *The power of balance: Transforming self, society, and scientific society.* Sage Publications.

Tough, A. (1971). *The adults' learning projects: A fresh approach to theory and practice in adult learning.* Ontario Institute for Studies in Education.

Vaill, P. B. (1996). *Learning as a way of being: Strategies for survival in a world of permanent white water* (p. 21). Jossey-Bass.

Weick, K. E. (1979). *The social psychology of organizing.* Random House.

Yorks, L., & Kasl, E. (2002). Toward a theory and practice for whole-person learning: Reconceptualizing experience and the role of affect. *Adult Education Quarterly, 52*(3), 176–192.

Yorks, L., & Kasl, E. (2006). I know more than I can say: A taxonomy for using expressive ways of knowing to foster transformative learning. *Journal of Transformative Education, 4*(1), 1–22.

Yorks, L., Marsick, V. J., Kasl, E., & DeChant, K. (2003). Contextualizing team learning: Implications for research and practice. *Advances in Developing Human Resources, 51*, 103–117.

# Strategically Positioning HRD Practice in Organizations

The rapidly changing socio-economic context confronting organizations being driven by technology has generated a rich debate regarding the role of HR for the twenty-first century. Articles such as "Why We Hate HR" (Hammonds, 2005, *Fast Company, August*) and "It's time to blow up HR and build something new. Here's How"(Cappelli, 2015 *Harvard Business Review*) represent a pivotal turning point in what was an increasing frustration with the traditional administrative mindset of many HR functions. Although the titles of these, and many other articles and presentations during the first decade in the twenty-first century carry negative connotations, the general theme is that human capital talent continues to be critical for organizational success and sustainability. The HR function is now an important strategic contributor to the business. That being the case, as of 2018, research finds that while the transformation of HR from an administrative support function to a strategic partner in the business is under way in many companies, it is still a work in process.

Strategically positioning HR and talent management within the ecosystem of the organization requires engaging in effective strategic advocacy, a process that involves achieving alignment of HR's strategic objective and the strategic objectives of the organization with the needs of the most important customers and stakeholders. We now describe a political economy framework that is helpful for assessing the ecosystem and identifying key linkages for making the strategic connections in the HR transformation process. We then present a more specific model based on a series of case studies of how this transformation is unfolding that can be used as an assessment tool for where an organization is in the process.

## 3.1 A Political Economy Model for Understanding Strategic Connections

A political economy approach to organizational repositioning and change is a way of framing how leaders in the organization need to leverage the opportunities and constraints imposed by the fluid interdependencies among the economic and political elements comprising the system. The concept of political economy has been used in organizational analysis for several decades including analysis of the YMCA (Zald, 1970) comparative analysis across organizations of the diffusion of job redesign efforts (Yorks & Whitsett, 1989), marketing analysis (Arndt, 1983; Stern & Reve, 1980), strategic applications of information technology in organizations (Langer, 2013), and HRD strategic leadership practices (Yorks, 2004). An organization's political economy is comprised of both an external and internal dimension. The external economy consisting of relationships around acquiring capital assets, availability of talent, competitors, product markets, and emerging technologies requires both adaptive and generative strategies and tactics. While implementing these strategies can involve taking direct action on economic variables such as pricing, compensation levels, location of assets, or staffing practices, often they involve negotiating with other actors and entities in the external environment. These negotiations can be bounded and influenced by various factors shaped by the political context such as government regulations and policies that in turn are the outcomes of political action by groups such as lobbyists, industry associations, and activists' groups. Building cooperative relationships in the larger ecosystem of the organization is often a major determinate of successful strategic action.

The internal dimension of the political economy is equally complex; anticipated and realized return-on-investment from products and programs, wage and salary structures, incentive systems, cost factors, and budget allocations to name a few. How these decisions are made is a function of how power and influence are exercised within the structures and mechanisms that reinforce these actions (Zald, 1970). Organizations are simultaneously political and economic systems with power relations embedded in the cultural fabric of the organization. These power relations comprise coalitions that both facilitate and constrain the ability of the organization to be adaptive and generative to changing environmental contexts.

Bridging the interconnection both within and between the external and internal polities and economies of the organization through strategic advocacy is central to strategy development and execution. Creating and implementing strategy require exercising executive agency mediating the alignment between the external and internal political economies (see Fig. 3.1).

The framework presented in Fig. 3.1 maps at a high-level element and interconnections of the political economic ecosystem of organizations. Additional elements can be added with regard to specific settings, and details will vary from organization to organization. In practice, of course, the ecosystem is a dynamic open complex system with elements interacting and changing in non-linear and often in unexpected ways. Adding to the complexity is the multiple levels to the political

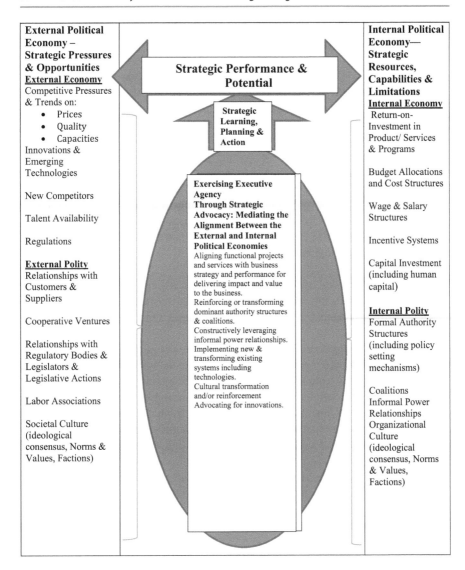

**Fig. 3.1** A conceptual framework of political economy for analysis of strategic advocacy options and comparative organization analysis (Adapted from Yorks (2004) and Yorks and Whitsett (1989))

economy ecosystem; the organization level, function level (i.e., HR), subcomponents of the function (i.e., talent management), or subgroups that must be aligned.

We turn now to how the human resource function is repositioning itself, and by extension HRD practices, in a diverse set of companies; a process that translates political economy theory into a practical tool for diagnosing and leading strategically focused organizational change.

## 3.2  How HR Is Repositioning Itself: The Changing Political Economy of HR

As previously discussed in Chap. 1, HRD practices encompass activities traditionally housed in the HRM, L&D, and OD functions. As HR strategically repositions itself in response to the changing business landscape, these activities are being reallocated across the organization. In the process, new HRD related needs are being created within the HR function itself as well as in the broader organization. This repositioning process requires new competencies on the part of HR executives including using sophisticated analytics, business acumen, and a forward-looking mindset. Although enabled by technology, a study by The Conference Board in 2017 (Yorks, Abel, & Devine) found that this "transformation involves more than adding new technology for extracting data from systems" (p. 4). The HR function in many companies is now in engaged in a process of strategic transformation consisting of four phases of progressive change:

- *Phase One: Initiating and Activating*—Enacting a diagnostic mindset initiating conversations with key stakeholders across the business, beginning to drive change efforts and making initial shifts from transactional administrative work to strategic.
- *Phase Two: Scaling*-Enacting a mindset that is experimental with various strategies for redesigning/reenergizing the HR service delivery model, implementing any necessary new technologies and monitoring ongoing progress and impact.
- *Phase Three: Sustaining*-Enacting an adaptive mindset in providing solutions that drive business results, connect across the business to identify and deploy value-creating opportunities, develop the capabilities for encouraging data-driven decisions, and continuously learn and integrate changes with the HR function.
- *Phase Four: Continuously Transforming*-Enacting a future-oriented strategic mindset, continuing to innovate HR systems and practices in response to emerging trends in the business and technology, facilitating dynamic conversations with key internal and external stakeholders and continuously transforming the HR function.

Six core elements of the transformation process were identified as encompassing the progression through the four phases. Each of these core elements transitions through what can be conceptualized as four phases of the transformation process although not always in alignment with each other:

- *Aligning HR with the business strategy*—Realigning HR in order to be structured to deliver services and strategic insights to the business;
- *Delivering impact and value to the business*—Providing outcomes that demonstrate the value of HR to the business and key stakeholders;
- *Applying HR technology*—Using technology to enhance and deliver HR services;
- *Using human capital analytics*—Linking systems or partnering with different resources for gathering data and developing insights to drive decision-making;

- *Enhancing employee experience*—Particularizes HR's attention and actions for creating employee-engaging programs and initiatives;
- *Building HR's strategic capacity*—Developing the mindsets and competencies necessary for mobilizing and executing efforts in each phase of the transformation and navigating the business terrain of the twenty-first century.

Organizations move flexibly through the four phases with the start and end points of the six elements often differing, "contingent upon an organization's readiness to transform and the amount of time and resources it spends juggling competing tasks and priorities" (Yorks, Abel, & Devine, 2017, p. 10). Table 3.1 presents the key actions that comprise the practices for transiting the elements through the phases of transformation.

The core elements described above encapsulate exercising strategic executive agency involves mediating the interwoven alignment of the internal and external political economies through an evolving process of repositioning the HR function. HRD practices, Human Resource Management-Workforce Planning, Learning & Development, and Organizational Development described in Chap. 1 (Fig. 1.1 in Chap. 1) are embedded in this transformational process as both HR and the broader organization strategically reposition themselves in the changing competitive environment. Applying HRD practices is necessary for facilitating the HR transformation and its continuing impact on the business. Underlying this process is the ability of senior HR executives leading the process to be positive playmakers initiating and sustaining the change process with both political and business acumen.

## 3.3    Strategic Political Acumen

Political acumen refers to understanding and dealing with the relationships mediated by power, authority, diverse interests, and personal needs that shape how decisions are made in the organization's ecosystem and strategically taking actions that lead to good outcomes. For example, returning to the core element of aligning HR with business strategy in Table 3.1 above, political acumen is a key competency for gaining buy-in from senior leaders, creating teams for governing the process of transformation and alignment with priorities of the business (phase one) and co-leading with other functions oversight of changes made as part of transformation, [e.g., HR & Legal, HR & IT] (phase three).

The word "politics" typically carries a negative connotation being associated with engaging in actions that are manipulative, power seeking, and self-serving. However, all human systems have a political dimension; being able to constructively navigate the political terrain is a necessary competency for strategically positioning one's self, one's team or department, and the organization. While some actors in the system are manipulative, others recognize the nature of human systems and seek ways of resolving and aligning people's interests and connecting them with the goals of the organization.

**Table 3.1** Phases and elements of HR transformation (Adapted from Yorks, Abel, & Devine, 2017)

| Core elements | Phases | | | |
| --- | --- | --- | --- | --- |
| | Initiating and activating transformation | Scaling transformation | Sustaining transformation | Continuously transforming |
| Aligning HR with the business strategy | Assess how well the organization & HR are structured for delivering strategic value; Develop a vision for what HR wants to become to align with business strategy; Gain buy-in for the vision from senior leaders; Create teams to govern the process of transformation and alignment with priorities of the business | Identify what value HR will deliver to the business and how the value will be delivered; Develop a detailed execution strategy for how HR infrastructure, systems, and processes will align with business needs and strategy; Create a design for how resources will be allocated between shared services, outsourcing centers of excellence leaders; Develop integrated dashboards for HR administration and monitoring of the HR transformation process. | Build a process for getting continuous feedback from business on HR performance; Have ongoing discussions with business leaders about the potential challenges to the business; Exchange talent across HR and non-HR functions using HR as a talent "hot spot"; Co-lead with other functions oversight of changes made as part of transformation (e.g., HR & Legal, HR, & IT) | Develop new strategies to identify emerging business needs and realign HR to address those needs; Buy and build staffing resources from within the organization and beyond in alignment with business priorities; Engage with external stakeholders to promote brand and strategies that drive high performance and long-term value. |

(continued)

**Table 3.1**  (continued)

| Core elements | Phases | | | |
| --- | --- | --- | --- | --- |
| | Initiating and activating transformation | Scaling transformation | Sustaining transformation | Continuously transforming |
| Delivering impact and value to the business | Identify efforts that are cost efficient and provide monetary ROI; Develop understanding of value and impact HR can bring to the business; Assess current and future workforce needs and align with the business goals; Create a new value proposition and clearly articulate the impact HR wants to make in the organization; Identify measures to evaluate if HR is responding to the pressures of the business; Identify companies recognized for creative and people-friendly policies and practices. | Increase strategic conversations and collaboration with senior leaders; Monitor performance and impact of HR strategies on a regular basis; Develop robust workforce planning tools and systems to proactively identify workforce needs and trends; Conduct pilots to assess the impact and value of transformative HR initiatives; Develop milestones to track HR's transformation— Where HR is in the transformation process and what new strategies should be devised to move to the next level. | Identify opportunities for creating value within the business; Assess impact of HR programs and initiatives on business impact; Support routine and systematic efforts across the organization that demonstrate HR's value on an ongoing basis; Expand transformation efforts to other regions and functions in the enterprise. | Co-create value between businesses, across the enterprise and with external community; Track macrotrends in the external and internal environment and their impacts on talent and the business; Influence how the organization is perceived externally (i.e., by publishing and branding its people strategies that have created long-term value for the organization; Achieve public awards that demonstrate HR value (e.g., "best place to work"). |

(continued)

**Table 3.1**   (continued)

| Core elements | Phases | | | |
| | Initiating and activating transformation | Scaling transformation | Sustaining transformation | Continuously transforming |
| --- | --- | --- | --- | --- |
| Applying HR technology | Develop understanding of leading HR technology tools and associated vendors; Identify gaps in how technology is used across the enterprise; Assess organization's readiness to adopt new technologies with: <br> • Senior leadership buy-in <br> • End user readiness <br> • HR/IT capacity and skills to transform <br> • Governance to oversee compliance to security and privacy policies <br> • Technology and infrastructure casts and capabilities <br> • Other… <br> Determine what HR processes will be automated; Create change management strategies for rolling out and scaling use of HR technologies. | Roll out technology solutions with self-service capabilities that allow customization, if needed; Automate HR processes that map to employee paths of development (i.e., employee databases, time and attendance, performance management processes, onboarding/ off-boarding, etc.); Initiate processes of moving from local data formats to one global format or a globally integrated system if needed; Develop easily comprehensible operating manuals for fast and easy adoption of technology across the organization; Track user experiences (i.e., Improvements and challenges using the new technologies. | Articulate and demonstrate the impact of a comprehensive technology system to maximize speed and value; Look for new ways to connect technology and use the holistic/ combined data it generates; Measure progress and speed of delivering HR services (speed to execute); Identify redundant jobs/ roles because of automation and redeploy people/ positions; Make business-led-decisions about further investments in HR technology. | Develop custom-made tools and apps that fit the specific HR needs of your organization; Continuously look for ways to innovate with technology; Develop and deploy smarter systems, enabling users to be more productive and motivated. |

(continued)

**Table 3.1** (continued)

| Core elements | Phases | | | |
| --- | --- | --- | --- | --- |
| | Initiating and activating transformation | Scaling transformation | Sustaining transformation | Continuously transforming |
| Using human capital analytics | Assess how data will be gathered from multiple technologies and data sources; Develop plans to move beyond reactive analyses of data (done at a simple descriptive level); Communicate need to tap into data and analytics to provide strategic insights to business; Create a new value proposition and clearly articulate the impact HR wants to make in the organization; List skills and capabilities critical for analyzing data and making data-driven decisions; Draw resources and data analysts (form within and outside HR) to help with mining HR-related data unit HR has develop the capability to do this. | Pull talent and business data from HR technologies or implemented systems; Begin using data warehousing tools to draw inferences and insights; Design employee training programs based on HC analytics; Meanwhile, focus on developing HR capabilities to analyze and use data to drive business and talent decisions; Continue to rely on external resources and analysts (outside HR, if needed) to help organize and interpret employee-related data. | Integrate data and automate reporting processes; Ask pertinent questions of the data. Create a single, unified story about employees and the business; Leverage advanced business intelligence tools and resources to draw insight; Implement training programs and strategies to build and retain employee capabilities; Develop confidence to analyze data and devise data-driven strategies. | Continue to innovate and spread knowledge about the effective use of HC analytics; Create a culture of using data for problem-solving and decision-making; Gather data about the organization, across organizations and from the environment to draw useful linkages and impactful connections; Use predictive analytics to predict future risks and benefits (i.e., future turnover of critical talent and identifying talent pipelines of high potentials) |

(continued)

**Table 3.1** (continued)

| Core elements | Phases | | | |
|---|---|---|---|---|
| | Initiating and activating transformation | Scaling transformation | Sustaining transformation | Continuously transforming |
| Enhancing employee experience | Collect data about employee experience once a year; Shift from offering standard one-size-fits-all products/program to offering flexible solutions; Develop and protect the "human" dimension of work. Begin focusing on healthy workplaces, health and wellness, meaningful work; Distribute responsibility and ownership of driving employee experience with others in the organization. | Begin to collect data systematically on employee experience across the organization more than one a year; Diversify product and service offerings for employees; Expand opportunities for real-time feedback-via apps, video tools-aimed to create an empowered and mobilized staff; Develop and implement tailored served delivery models and programs; Draw on granulated, real-time data to manage and enhance employee experience proactively; Communicate need to share ownership of employee experience collectively; Communicate need to share ownership of employee experience across the organization. | Offer employees services with self-service capabilities and automated HR transactions; Gather information continuously and aggregate multiple data points (e.g., engagement surveys and tools) to form a holistic view of an employee's experience; Collaborate with other functions to co-lead organization-wide efforts to enhance employee experience collectively; Assign dedicated resources/and senior leaders to lead employee experience efforts (e.g., chief of employee experience). | Look for newer approaches and offerings to address the needs of employees with speed and agility; Be publicly recognized for effective approaches to enhancing employee experience; Create places and conditions where employees can learn and grow. |

(continued)

**Table 3.1** (continued)

| Core elements | Phases | | | |
|---|---|---|---|---|
| | Initiating and activating transformation | Scaling transformation | Sustaining transformation | Continuously transforming |
| Building HR's strategic capacity | Business awareness to create business value; Advocacy and facilitation skills to gain buy-in; Strategic change management skills to drive change and transformation; Technology awareness to support HR delivery with the right platforms and tools; Innovative design skills to map processes to business strategy and employee experience. | Communication and influencing skills to inspire change; Change management skills to execute change strategy; Develop others to mobilize others to change; Collaborative skills to build relationships across HR teams and functions; Readiness to redesign HR processes to support new HR strategy. | Resilience and strategic persistence to manage continuous change; High-level business acumen and financial stewardship to direct HC strategies; Strategic consultancy to build credible relationships with business leaders; Outcome-focused with ability to articulate the impact of business decisions on talent; Strategic coach to build tomorrow's leaders and executives. | Strategic thinking to look forward and outward for business solutions; Self-directed and agile to learn continuously and respond to new business demands; Disruptive to challenge the status quo and push boundaries of HR role and function; Connector to link people and ideas inside and outside the business; Highly curious and inquisitive to always consider what's best and what's next for HR. |

Only framing politics in a negative way sets up a false dichotomy. Joel Deluca (1999) distinguishes between Machiavellian, Responsible, and Leader political styles. The Machiavellian has a negative view of politics and essentially looks out for him or herself. Responsibilities hold a more neutral view seeing politics as "comes with the territory" and engage in political action out of "obligation" (p.11). Leaders, while "aware of the negative side of politics" see politics as part of leading people and using political acumen to be an impactful play maker seeking to create "innovative ways to combine and satisfy apparently opposed interests" (pp. 19–20).

Focusing on the Machiavellian and Leader ends of the continuum of initiating politically attentive action what differentiates them is their intentions: *self-interest* or the *interests of self and others*. As Deluca states Machiavellians manipulate using power as lone wolves for their own ends and Leaders are "play makers" who influence others using power and authority strategically and ethically for getting things done with others. Deluca's definition of ethical influence is that "others know what you are trying to influence them toward and why" (p. 32). The conversations around the issue at hand are framed openly, explaining the need for and intended actions going forward. This is consistent with engaging in strategic advocacy through developmental action inquiry previously presented in Chap. 2 and discussed further below in this chapter.

However, given the complexity of the real world it is important to acknowledge the dilemmas one faces when needing to discuss controversial and/or emotionally sensitive issues confronting an organization, such as possible restructuring, mergers, or implementing artificial intelligence technologies and reducing job levels. Strategically implementing change involves working through the moral dilemma of situations in which ends can be justified as ethical, but initial actions can't be transparent to everyone. This requires strategic agility of striving to balance the interaction within and between the subsystems of the organization comprised of various levels of responsibility and authority across interconnected yet separate functional units. As mentioned above, this agility is reflected in Table 3.1 for aligning HR with the business strategy and also the core element of building HR's business capacity through strategic advocacy and facilitation to gain buy-in, collaboratively building relationships across HR teams and functions, and being a connector linking people and ideas both inside and outside the business. While some organizations are fortunate to have executives who have these capabilities, HRD practices and tools are core for developing the necessary competencies for making this transition happen both inside HR and other functions across the business.

### 3.3.1  Mapping the Political Territory

One tool that can be very helpful for strategically positioning HRD in the organization is mapping the political territory. When strategizing around repositioning HR, HRD, or positioning new developmental learning programs, visualizing the sociopolitical context is often helpful especially when the changes might be met with resistance from some significant decision makers in the organization. Joel Deluca developed a mapping framework that is very useful for visualizing the territory and strategically thinking about how to best proceed to have proposed changes or proposed programs get a constructive hearing. Five basic questions underlie the map:

1. Who are the key players, who can influence the decision regarding the proposed changes, programs, or issues on the table;
2. What's their relative influence/ power in the organization regarding the proposals in question—ranked on a scale of 1 (low) to 10 (high);
3. To what extent are they applying their influence either in support of or against the proposal in question—depicted on a scale ranging from −10 (against) to +10 (for) the proposed change with 0 being not actively applying or "a fence sitter."
4. How easily can their applied influence be changed—illustrated as a square for low (can't or not easily changed, a circle for medium possibility, and an inverted triangle for very possible or easy).

5. What *significant* relationships exist among the key players, negative or positive—a solid line for positive and a dotted line for negative.

Figure 3.2 is Deluca's political data sheet for the answers to these five questions. These data can then be transferred into a map of the political territory (see Fig. 3.3).

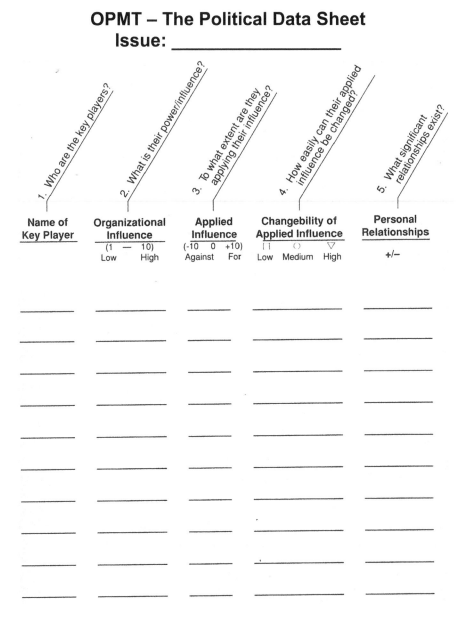

**Fig. 3.2** The political data sheet. Source: Joel DeLuca, *Political Savvy: Systematic Approaches to Leadership Behind the Scenes. Evergreen Business Group, Berwyn, PA*

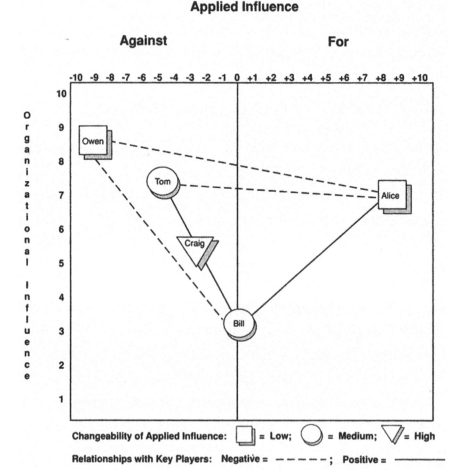

**Fig. 3.3** A map of the political territory: Source: Joel DeLuca. *Political Savvy: Systematic Approaches to Leadership Behind the Scenes. Evergreen Business Group, Berwyn, PA*

As illustrated by Fig. 3.3, the map provides a visual overview of the interrelationships among the key players as a proposed project or issue goes forward, along with their relative level of influence on the issue (the vertical dimension of the map), the direction and degree each is applying their influence (the horizontal dimension), and how changeable is each player's position (the geometric symbol beneath each player's name). While people think about the various individuals who are involved in getting a significant proposal approved, having the interrelationship and positions of the players displayed as a system provides a comprehensive perspective useful for thinking strategically about how to go forward. It can also reveal the need for building and strengthening new relationships. See the case "A Financial Services Firm Mapping the Political Territory When Adopting Cloud-Based Technologies" in the second section of the book for an example.

### 3.3.2  Analyzing the Map

Mapping the political territory is a learning process. In preparing a map, it's important to be aware of what assumptions are underlying how people are being characterized on the map. Here Donald Schon and Chris Argyris' metaphor of the Ladder of Inference is useful. Looking at the map "what data/experiences" I am drawing on with regard to how supportive or not a person will be toward the proposal and how fixed is his or her position? Are there alternative explanations for these experiences? How can I test them, perhaps through informal conversations using action inquiry (described in Chap. 2) or paying careful attention in taking initial steps forward. Testing one's assumptions is an important element of strategically advocating for a proposal.

Another lens for strategically analyzing the map is Peter Block's (1991) trust-agreement matrix. The two variables, trust and agreement, provide a useful differentiation between *allies, opponents*, *adversaries, bedfellows,* and *fence sitters*:

- Allies are individuals you both agree with and you can trust to be open and straight forward with you regarding their thoughts, opinions, and actions.
- Opponents are individuals whom you often disagree with, but you can trust them. They won't go behind your back.
- Adversaries are those who not only do you disagree with; you don't trust them.
- Bedfellows are adversaries who on a particular issue you can work with even though your overall level of trusting them is low.
- Fence sitters are undecided on the initiative or practices being advocated, but you don't trust them. They could potentially be bedfellows or adversaries regarding the issue at hand.

In looking at the map it is useful to identify who are your allies, opponents, adversaries, fence sitters and potential bedfellows, and the relationships that exist among them, as you strategize the how to get the proposal or issues you are presenting to be effectively listened to and heard.

It is also important to remember that the map is static reflecting a particular point in time. A quote often used by the military is very applicable here; "the map is not the territory." The territory may change in a moment. There is also what Deluca refers to as the X factor. The map "can appear to contain all the relevant information, but in real life, there is always an X factor...relationships unknown to those creating the map." (p. 75). And, of course, the purpose of strategically advocating is to change the territory.

The map can also provide insights into the agility of the organization. For example, the patterns of lines reveal how open and fluid or contentious communications around issues can be in the organization. Also, what "closed" networks might exist. To quote DeLuca, the map shows how fixed or dynamic the political situation is at a given moment. "Many squares indicate entrenched positions...A high percentage of triangles signals a very unstable situation where a comprehensive strategy can have enormous impact." (p. 73).

### 3.3.3    From Mapping to Strategic Leadership Action

As stated above, the map is not the territory, and the territory can change in a moment. HRD leaders and professionals must pay attention to how the territory is changing. More importantly they must be taking action utilizing the map to exercise influence in the service of the strategic, tactical, and operative initiatives of the organization; not as support function, but as an initiator of change. When proposing innovative initiatives that are often likely to encounter initial resistance from some influential people on the map there are five approaches for exercising influence with political acumen:

- Linking Agendas—In reviewing the map, identify the opportunities that exist for connecting the HRD initiative to the agendas of the functions of others on the map that aligns with the organization's strategy. What multiple agendas exist and where are the win-win possibilities are key questions when engaged in strategic advocacy.
- Utilizing Currencies—Currencies are resources that are useful to others in the organization and therefore have exchange value in terms of, and can be used in, building and sustaining alliances (Cohen & Bradford, 1989). Some currencies are tangible, such as information, time, or task support, while others are more intangible such as providing personal support, acceptance, recognition, or visibility to others. Strategizing from the map involves linking agendas and identifying what currencies these executives will find useful.
- Following the Credibility Path—The connecting lines in map can suggest who has credibility with the key decision maker(s). The credibility path rests on the principle what influencing someone on a decision about a HRD proposal often turns on who is the messenger delivering the proposal. Convincing others of the value of a proposed initiative or intervention frequently depends on who communicates the idea. Effective influencers often let whoever has the most credibility take the idea forward.
- Challenging Assumptions—When assessing the opposition depicted on the map, particularly those who are only moderately opposed, a key question is, "What assumptions are they holding that are the basis for their opposition and how might we have them reflect on them?" (while of course also reflecting on our own assumptions.) Accomplishing this requires having open conversations, in the office or sometimes over lunch or dinner (what a former Chief HR Executive of a global retail company who was a client of Lyle's used to refer to as "having sh—t house conversations").
- Facilitating Learning—Influencing others on change initiatives is often an educative process and having learning focused conversations is part of the strategic advocacy process. Skillfully applying developmental action inquiry practices discussed in Chap. 2 (paying attention to the four territories of experience and how one is engaging in the conversation through framing, advocating, illustrating, & inquiring into other's thoughts).

Little of importance, good or bad, happens without the exercise of political influence; the reality is that exercising influence is a key leadership responsibility. In doing so it is important to exercise influence in an ethical manner. Deluca (1999) defines ethical political action as behavior that one is comfortable defending whenever the agenda becomes public, meaning that the goals of those engaging in it are beneficial to others and to the organization; they are not simply self-serving. In the final analysis, the personal reputation of HRD leaders is their most important asset. What happens behind the scenes is as important as more visible actions of leaders.

## 3.4 Summary

Effectively positioning HRD practices and initiatives in an organization requires paying attention to the political economy ecosystem of the organization and suborganization divisions and functions that must align with it. Exercising influence is a key responsibility of all leaders across the organization including those in HRD related roles. When initiating new initiatives and changes in HRD practices within the organization, it is important to understand the political territory and how the connections within the territory can be ethically leveraged for implementing the initiatives.

In this age of 4IR engaging in strategic change to continuously reposition HRD practices is essential. And these are transformations, not gradual transitions. Doing so effectively requires engaging in effective application of political savvy competencies. HRD initiatives need to be aligned with the business strategy and use human capital analytics to provide continuous learning and reskilling opportunities in ways that enhance the employee experience. We turn now to Chap. 4 for a discussion of AI and its current and potential impact on HRD practices.

## References

Arndt, J. (1983). The political economy paradigm: Foundation for theory building in marketing. *Journal of Marketing, 47*(4), 44–54.

Block, P. (1991). *The empowered manager: Positive political skills at work*. Jossey-Bass.

Cappelli, P. (2015). It's time to blow up HR and build something new. Here's how. *Harvard Business Review, 93*(7/8), 56–61.

Cohen, A. R., & Bradford, D. L. (1989). Influence without authority: The use of alliances, reciprocity, and exchange to accomplish work. *Organizational Dynamics, 17*(3), 5–17.

Deluca, J. (1999). *Political savvy: Systematic approaches to leadership behind the scenes* (2nd ed.). Evergreen Business Group.

Hammonds, K. H. (2005). Why we hate H.R. *Fast Company, 97*, 40–47.

Langer, A. M. (2013). *Strategic IT: Best practices for managers and executives*. Wiley.

Stern, L. W., & Reve, T. (1980). Distribution channels as political economies: A framework for analysis. *Journal of Marketing, 44*(3), 52–64.

Yorks, L. (2004). Toward a political economy model for comparative analysis of the role of strategic human resource development leadership. *Human Resource Development Review, 3*(3), 189–208.

Yorks, L., Abel, A., & Devine, M. (2017). *What's next for 21st century HR? Continuous strategic transformation*. The Conference Board, December.

Yorks, L., & Whitsett, D. A. (1989). *Scenarios of change: Advocacy and the diffusion of job redesign in organizations*. Praeger.

Zald, M. N. (1970). *Organizational change: The political economy of the YMCA*. University of Chicago Press.

# Digitalization, Artificial Intelligence, and Strategic HRD

The fourth industrial revolution is changing both the strategic ecosystem of organizations and the way in which talent management processes are executed. New talent management challenges are emerging including talent acquisition, reskilling, and cultural agility. It is important that executives and managers over seeing HRD practices have an understanding of what AI is, how it has and will continue to evolve, and current and potential applications in talent management. We begin with a brief discussion of how AI has evolved over the past three decades followed by a definition of what AI is and isn't. A framework providing a foundation for assessing the potential applications in one's function is described. We then turn to how the age of digitalization is changing the ecosystem of HR in general and HRD in particular, as a business partner in the C-suite, and the future of talent management.

## 4.1    Pivotal Moments in the Evolution of AI

The term *"Artificial Intelligence"* is attributed to John McCarthy as defining the topic of a research project workshop held at Dartmouth College during the summer of 1956. Titled the Dartmouth Summer Research Project on Artificial Intelligence it was held for 8 weeks between July 18th and August 17th, and attended by 20 computer scientists and mathematicians, some for the full time and others for part of the time, plus periodic visitors, is generally considered to be the founding of AI as a formal field of study. It brought together a diverse stream of research that had been growing over the past decades on machine intelligence being stimulated by the emergence of the computer technology.

L. Yorks et al., *Strategic Human Resource Development in Practice*, Management for Professionals, https://doi.org/10.1007/978-3-030-95775-9_4

### 4.1.1   The Historical Evolution of the Thinking Machines: A Brief Overview

Historically, the philosophical roots foundational for the development of logical thinking machinery date back to antiquity times in ancient Greece, India and other parts of the world 100 BC and earlier as philosophers endeavored to illustrate the process of human thinking with the mechanical manipulation of symbols. Through the centuries, logics seeking to mirror human intelligence were evolving. In the early twentieth century, these roots were becoming much more explicitly expressed in both academic and fictional forms (consider the humanoid robot in the 1927 movie *Metropolis* that impersonated Maria and the Tin Man depicted in the 1939 film *The Wizard of OZ*). By the time of the Dartmouth project, the question of whether machines could be taught to think was being explored by various academics who had the possibility of thinking machines culturally assimilated in their minds (Anyoha, 2017). In 1950, Alan Turing, a young British polymath, wrote an influential paper, *Computing Machinery and Intelligence,* detailing a logical mathematical framework for building intelligent machines and testing their intelligence. Putting his framework into practice however was challenging because (1) computers were only beginning to be capable of storing commands; they could only execute them and (2) computing was extremely expensive so only prestige universities or large corporations could extend the research. (Anyoha, 2017). However, the question "can machines learn?" continued to be pursued. With funding from RAND Corporation, over the Christmas holidays in 1955, Allen Newell, Herbert Simon, and Cliff Shaw created the Logic Theorist program that mimicked human problem-solving skills and presented it at the Dartmouth conference.

From the mid-50s to the mid-70s, work related to machine learning flourished as computer gradually became more capable of storing information and also were more affordable. Jack Kelly and Robert Noyce created the microchip in 1959 and by the mid-1960s, computers were shrinking in size. In the mid-1970s, some people were using computers to communicate with each other. Along with these developments in computer technology programs like Newell and Simon's *General Problem Solver* and Joseph Weizenbaum's language interpretation program *Eliza* demonstrated the potential of machine learning. Also the continuing enthusiasm generated by the Dartmouth program. However, during, the late 70s progress lagged a bit, in part because of drops in funding sources and the need for even more capacity for information storage in computers. However, interest in machine learning regenerated throughout the 1980s. Throughout the 1990s ongoing innovations in computer technology by companies like IBM, interwoven with the evolution of Big Data, were leading to the fourth industrial revolution.

### 4.1.2   A Brief Overview of the Historical Foundations of Big Data

The evolution of practices of data analysis took place in parallel with the evolution of technology with the two becoming increasingly intertwined. Like logical thinking machinery, the roots of data analysis data back to antiquity, such as the early development of accounting for tracking herding and crop growth following each season's harvest in Mesopotamia. Accounting practices continued to develop over the centuries with the Roman Emperor Augustus using accounting methods to track spending on grants of land to individuals, building temples, and to the military among other expenders for planning purposes. Jumping ahead several centuries, in the thirteenth century Europe transitioned from a bartering to a monetary economy with merchants using bookkeeping to track transactions and using double entries for making decisions about growing their businesses. In 1494, Luca Pacioli wrote Summa de Arithmetica, Geometria, Proportioni et Proportionalita, considered by historians to be the earliest written book on double entry bookkeeping. Accounting principles continued to grow and data analysis was being used for addressing other social issues. In 1663 John Grauunt collected and analyzed data on the rate of mortality in London to raise awareness of the bubonic plague's effects on society. While statistical analysis continued to advance the use of data for addressing significant institutional and societal challenges continued to be limited by the time required to gather and analyze relevant data.

In the late nineteenth and early twentieth centuries, technological innovations provided new tools for expanding the speed and scope of data analysis. For example, in 1881, Herman Hollerith invented the Hollerith Tabulating Machine, based on the punch cards that controlled patterns woven by mechanical looms. Hollerith worked for the U.S. Census Bureau that was struggling with processing the data from the 1880 census. The Census Bureau projected it would take 8 years to process the data. Worse, it was anticipated it would take 10 years or more to process the data from the 1890 census. Hollerith's machine reduced the 10 years to 3 months. The connection between data and machines was strengthened throughout the twentieth century. In 1943, the British created Colossus, a data-processing machine for deciphering Nazi codes in World War II that searched for patterns in messages by processing 5000 characters per second. The U.S. National Security Agency (NSA) was established in 1952 decrypting messages during the cold war. In 1989, Tim Berners-Lee created the world-wide web providing the foundation for sharing information. Throughout the 1990s, the creation of data grew as multitudes of devises capable of using the internet were created. These connections were increasingly facilitated by the continuing development of super computers capable of process billions of calculations per second. Big data was created. These are just a selected set of examples of the innovations taking place during the twentieth century moving increasingly toward access and analysis of big data by technology. The foundation for the 4IR was established.

## 4.2   Understanding AI in 4IR

As described above, while the artificial intelligence was formally established as an academic discipline in 1956, its evolution started when humans started having the capacity to store data. However, the true AI revolution started in the 1940s and

1950s when capacity began to grow for providing storage of huge volumes and vast varieties of structured and unstructured of data such as images, videos to be stored on smaller devices with tremendous capacity leading to the fourth industrial revolution.

To understand AI and its impact on HRD, we utilize the framework developed by Anand Rao that differentiates three gradations of artificial intelligence, *Assisted Intelligence*, *Augmented Intelligence*, and *Autonomous Intelligence* (Rao & Verweij, 2017):

- *Assisted Intelligence* is AI systems assisting humans in making decisions or taking action by collecting and processing information and providing it to humans. These systems are hardwired, but do not learn from their interactions. An example from HR are platforms used in the talent acquisition function that review resumes based on requirements and schedules interviews with applicants. Another example is in the compensation and benefits function where chatbots respond to questions regarding benefits.
- *Augmented Intelligence* is AI systems that augment human decisions by efficiently collecting and analyzing vast droves of data and makes recommendations to the human decision maker. The system continuously learns from their interactions with humans and the environment. Returning to our examples from HR, in the talent acquisition process, the platform evaluates applicants based on their fit for the role they are being considered for and their readiness to change jobs and rank orders them for the manager who will make the final decision. In compensation and benefits, the system assesses past usage and profiles along with other data sets and recommends benefits.
- *Autonomous Intelligence* is AI systems that can adapt to different and changing situations and makes decisions without human involvement. As a talent management example, the platform would find, rank, interview, negotiate, and hire applicants. As a compensation and benefits example, the platform would autonomously personalize and offer benefits without HR or managerial review.

Two variables define each of these forms of intelligence; whether or not decisions are made by a human and if the system learns and adapts to new data, criteria, and contexts, or is hardwired and unable to adapt (Rao & Verweij, 2017; see Table 4.1).

*Assisted Intelligence* is hard wired, and humans make the decisions, *augmented intelligence* is adaptive systems and humans are involved, *autonomous intelligence* is adaptive systems and humans are not involved. These three forms of artificial intelligence are different from automation which is the automation of manual or cognitive tasks that are either routine or nonroutine and doesn't involve new ways of doing things. Examples are tracking systems for candidate applications in talent acquisition and sending automated benefit emails to employees. The system is hard wired and no humans are involved. The Conference Board defines AI as "technology that mimics human thinking by making assumptions, learning, reasoning, problem solving, or predicting with a high degree of autonomy" and categorizes automation as "not AI"

**Table 4.1**  The gradations of artificial intelligence adapted from Anand Rao and Gerard Verweij, *Sizing the Prize*, PwC, 2017

| | Assisted Intelligence | Automation |
|---|---|---|
| Hardwired—Specific Systems | | |
| Adaptive Systems | Augmented Intelligence | Autonomous Intelligence |
| | Humans Involved | Humans Not Involved |

(Young et al., 2019, p. 4). Rao and Verweij (2017, p. 1.) classify automation as automated intelligence although it can only do what it has been programmed to do. No machine or human actions are involved. Artificial Intelligence is itself an umbrella term encompassing a variety of technologies that mimic human intelligence. Most prominent are *Machine Learning* technologies such as computer vision that processes visual information, voice recognition, and speech recognition that continuously learns from new data and experience enhancing its capabilities over time; Deep Learning which is an advanced form of machine learning that can comprehend patterns and trends in big data and instantaneously adjust its models, and Natural Language Processing (NPL) that extracts meaning from the words say or write factoring in the context to capture nuances and subtleties of language being used in conversations. Human capital analytics teams in some companies now apply a form of NPL, sentiment analysis, to aggregated anonymous data extracted from online discussions for identifying employees' feelings and attitudes. While HRD professional don't need to be developers of these technologies they do need to understand their capabilities and limitations, and how to ethically apply them.

Having provided an overview of the AI, we turn now to applications in HR and HRD.

## 4.3    AI Applications in HRD Practice—Current and Potential

As presented in Chap. 1, HRD research and practices encompass the workforce planning aspects of human resource management, learning and development, organizational development. Strategic talent management can be effectively achieved through this integrated lens provided by HRD. Increasingly, these practices are becoming augmented by cognitive technologies. Chapter 3 provided a framework of the phases through which HR is transforming into a strategic partner in organizations. Progression through the phases involves gradations in applying technology. We know go deeper how digitalization and AI are being applied.

### 4.3.1   Adopting Emerging Technology in Human Resources

Enterprise adoption of emerging technologies has never been more critical, regardless of industry, from retail to transportation, healthcare to financial services, a suite of cognitive technologies like natural language processing, machine learning, and artificial intelligence are transforming the operations of every sector. Technology has become the center of every business and the Human Resources (HR) function is no exception. Major technology trends ranging from digital and cloud, to blockchain and cognitive are informing the nature of work—both the way we work today, and the way we will work tomorrow—and HR is at the center of these changes, with an opportunity to steward their organization's people agenda, including its human-machine collaboration model, in dynamic new ways.

Modernizing the core of the enterprise—including how the HR function operates—is not a new demand, but the current pressure reflects ongoing digitization requirements, user expectations, and the growing demand for data by algorithms. In an era of instantaneous, "always on," tailored interactions, organizations are looking for thoughtful approaches to modernizing their core technology, removing technical debt while reengineering legacy applications—and this includes the technology underpinning human resources administration.

The result for those stewarding human capital practices is twofold—a transformation of the underlying HR operational processes, through the continued evolution of automation, robots, and algorithms, and the ability to deliver more strategic talent practices. This chapter explores both aspects of the transformation underway within the HR function. Its operational transformation—the nuts and bolts of compensation and benefits, recruiting and succession planning, often leveraging cloud-based Human Capital Management (HCM) suites like Oracle HCM or Workday, as well as its strategic transformation supporting the organization navigate the new era of human-machine collaboration.

### 4.3.2   HR's Responsibilities as Stewards of Workforce Management

The traditional talent lifecycle enterprises often utilized to engage with their workforce often involves a handful of activities—from attracting, recruiting, and onboarding employees, to managing their ongoing performance, skill development, rewards, and ultimately their exit from the firm and any associated succession planning required for the organization. Oftentimes, HR also plays a role in broader business model transformation efforts, where organization design, role definition, and workforce strategy and required. While individual organizations define this talent lifecycle with some nuance, most follow a similar set of practices, and each of these dimensions is being affected by emerging technologies that are changing the art and science of talent management (Fig. 4.1).

### 4.3.3   A Brief Look Back: HR as Stewards of the Workforce Agenda

Starting in the 1920s up through the 1950s, the notion of "human capital" began to emerge with "personnel departments" established within organizations to manage the emotional and psychological needs of the workforce. These early personnel departments interacted with labor unions to address compensation and began internal investment in training (Marciano, 1995; Thornthwaite, 2012). By the 1960s, U.S. public policy matured to establish employment practices like the Equal Pay Act of 1963 and the Civil Rights Act of 1964 forcing companies to take seriously the notion of actively managing their workforces with deliberate policies and

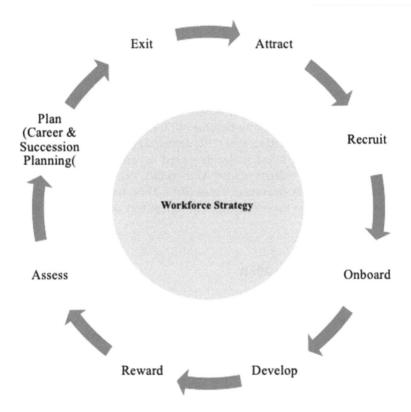

**Fig. 4.1**  Illustrative talent management lifecycle

practices. This compelled organizations to setup HR departments that at a minimum considered compliance. In parallel, the 1970s and 1980s was an era when organizational and industrial psychology emerged as academic fields, seeking to understand human motivation and self-determination. This led some HR departments to begin to consider the needs of employees, their need for achievement, advancement, and recognition (Marciano, 1995; Thornthwaite, 2012).

Modern HR departments have tended to focus on two primary goals: to drive efficiency in established operational disciplines, like benefits administration and recruiting, while enhancing the organization's talent, e.g., addressing skill gaps. Looking ahead to the next decade, HR will continue to operate in both realms—delivering increasingly sophisticated, seamless, tailored operational activities, while elevating their business through strategic talent practices.

The notion of task or process automation in HR has existed for about a century, evolving and maturing with each passing decade. Early phases of process automation involve taking what is a manual, high-volume, transactional business activity and applying a technical solution that is more efficient, and frequently more effective (e.g., eliminating human error which is common when performing repetitive tasks). Payroll administration is one of the earliest forms of HR applications of technologies. To date, much of this has been automation, but increasingly assisted AI is being applied.

The benefits of automation in HR have been extensive, from cost savings, to improved workforce experience, greater quality in the services offered, and improved accuracy. Self-service has been a huge trend, with predictive analytics. In recent years, process automation has evolved to include robotic process automation, cognitive technology use, and even more disruptive capabilities like augmented and virtual reality (AR/VR) (Benhamou, 2018).

According to 2019 research by Deloitte, 40% of organizations are using some form of AI in their Human Resources (HR) department. Companies looking to stay leaders in competing for talent realize they need to continue to pioneer emerging technologies—and this extends beyond AI to include augmented reality (AR), virtual reality (VR), and the internet of things (IoT). These tools are useful to reinvent how people work within the organization, as well as how new people are identified, sourced, and hired.

### 4.3.4  Fast Forward to 2030

As you enter the workplace, a network of cameras, microphones, ID readers, and sensors embedded throughout the workplace monitor your presence, facial expression, voice and the way you are interacting with the physical space and other workers in it. Analyzing the input in real time, the workplace—using voice recognition, machine learning, computer vision, and a host of other cognitive technologies—determines that you are getting angry or upset during a meeting. In response, these AI-powered tools lower the thermostat in the room to cool you down, while a conversational agent or chat bot suggests you take a break from the meeting for a quick stroll. A few hours later a colleague starts to doze off as they sit quietly on their computer diligently working on a project that has to be completed before the end of the day. The machine recognizes the lack of alertness and notifies a trusted co-worker to stop by with a fresh cub of your favorite coffee. These technologies are engaging you and those you trust—in human terms—by detecting your physical state, mood, and contextually engaging you in intuitive and emotionally appropriate ways. In this not so future world, the applications and use cases for HR are boundless.

The ability to relate to others recognizes ourselves in a storyline, and trust and feel complex emptions. Vision systems, natural language generation, sentiment analysis, voice recognition, voice stress analysis.

Ambient experience is a world where the physical and digital are intertwined with elegance and simplicity that we shift to natural and potentially even unconscious ways of engaging with complex technologies. Machine-to-machine interfaces, smart devices, internet of things, edge computing, 3D object modeling, spatial computing, brain–computer interfaces.

Exponential intelligence is able to build algorithms, confident predictions, and automated responses across complex, dynamic, and constantly evolving domains. This includes deep learning, neural networks, symbolic AI, reinforcement learning, advanced visualization, and semantic computing (Buchholz & Briggs, 2020, p. 117). The bridging of the physical and digital worlds is also affording an entire new realm to transform HR operations and strategic talent management. The opportunities to do sophisticated simulations and modeling, IoT, are making the data collected more dynamic and the types of decisions one can make that much more insightful.

## 4.4 AI in the Talent Lifecycle

We turn now to the role of AI in the eight stages in the talent lifecycle.

### 4.4.1 The Talent Lifecycle: Attraction and Recruiting

The front-end of the talent lifecycle involves identifying and sourcing desired talent. Talent attraction and recruiting have been one of the first use cases many organizations have already successfully applied AI, offering immediate, measurable results—for example, reducing time to hire and delivering superior candidate experience. For example, one leading financial services firm utilizes an AI to conduct candidate screening. The AI recruiting tool can shortlist candidates based on required skillsets, educational requirements and the like, sifting through a high-volume or applications in relatively no time. This same firm also utilizes a chatbot which has natural language processing (NLP) capabilities, and can actually handle direct exchanges with the candidates, answering basic questions and saving recruiters time to focus on higher-valued activities, like negotiating with highly sought-after talent Guenole & Feinzig, 2019).

### 4.4.2   The Talent Lifecycle: Onboarding

Customized and personalized experience. New employees don't know who to connect with, can get institutional information through AI. Providing new hires documents, containing useful information, like training requirements, policies, and paperwork. Introducing the new hire to his/her new team (e.g., in the phone book). Ample opportunities to automate onboarding payroll services, forms, and paperwork and employee time and attendance processes.

### 4.4.3   The Talent Lifecycle: Learning & Development

Advances in AI in recent years are often criticized for not having human-enough emotional qualities. This is changing. A growing class of AI often referred to as affective computing is redefining the way technology is experienced, as it better understands how to respond to humans more appropriately. Historically, computers have been unable to correlate events with emotional factors. Now an AI-powered chatbot understands when an employee calls a helpdesk and is frustrated, escalating the call immediately to another human to help. Emotional intelligence is building on current AI capabilities to deal with semantic and symbolic understandings, teasing out actual causality from correlation. Technology will increasingly be able to recognize and adapt to human emotion, eventually even getting close to the concept of personality.

### 4.4.4   The Talent Lifecycle: Rewards

One of the primary benefits of AI is the ability to analyze large data sets to find patterns and trends, unleashing additional insight to hopefully result in more informed decision-making. This has noticeable potential in the area of compensation, where organizations have traditionally been manually analyzing internal and external data points to make sense of the data and apply compensation practices that are appropriate. With AI, this data can be much more easily accessed, interpreted, and contextualized.

### 4.4.5   The Talent Lifecycle: Career Planning

AI is being utilized to visualize potential career tracks. Through the use of large data sets, it is now possible to identify possible career trajectories based on work experience, education, and skills developed. This helps navigate inconsistencies in title (e.g., Vice President does not always indicate consistent levels of responsibility) while offering multiple progression options for talent to further their contributions to the organization while continuing their own personal development. Machine learning technologies also have an impact in sifting through the unlimited set of possible career options to suggest the best potential choices. Data analysis reveals the difference between what is possible and what is likely, e.g., where movement from one field to another will yield positive results.

### 4.4.6   The Talent Lifecycle: Exit

The ability to use real-time data to monitor the employee experience, first and foremost allows organizations to proactively prevent employee attrition. By actively identifying, early signs employees are dissatisfied, organizations can engage employees to understand and evolve working practices.

## 4.5   Ethical Concerns in the Implementation of AI

In this age of pervasive digital everywhere, all aspects of an organization's operations are an opportunity to gain or lose trust with customers. In the context of the workforce, employee data and privacy are equally as critical as customers. The challenges become increasingly complex, ranging from hacking and inappropriate surveillance to the misuse of personal data, spread of misinformation, and algorithmic bias (Buchholz & Briggs, 2020). It would be inappropriate to conclude a discussion on the transformative opportunities for human resource practices in the age of disruptive technology, without also acknowledging the ethical terrain. The need for organizations to have clearly articulated values that guide technology deployment and use is critical to proactively ensure that the manner in which they are utilizing these capabilities is aligned with their purpose and mission (Albinson et al., 2019).

   Using talent identification and sourcing as an example, most organizations use intuition without objective and rigorous performance measures. These unconscious biases in recruiting influence how hiring managers make decisions, often citing things like cultural fit, when often they mean "is like me" or "seems like we'd get along." AI is currently not much better, given it is learning from mirroring human behavior. It is using large data sets (Chamorro-Premuzic et al., 2019). One critical capability of HR—talent management professionals is to be able to assess how an AI system has been trained. What data sets have been used and how have they been applied. When applied oversight needs to be in place. For example, when using an AI app in making hiring or promotion recommendations do white men consistently score higher than women or people of color. This is important for both initial assessment of the application and also being able to explain to others in the organization how the application functions. As AI continues to evolve doing more of the tradition tasks and making decisions, the traditional roles played by HR professionals will evolve into insuring transparency of the ethical actions taken by the systems.

## 4.6  Summary

As the descriptions above suggest, AI is increasing being applied across the talent life cycle, particularly assisted AI and increasingly augmented AI. Autonomous AI is also emerging. This is changing how HRM and L&D functions interact in developing and managing the workforce along with the culture of the organization. Being strategic in terms of with regard to attracting, reskilling/up skilling talent, and retaining talent is a core necessary of talent management in the age of the fourth industrial revolution. In addition to providing the resources necessary for addressing these talent management needs, the capacity for strategically repositioning the organization in a continuously changing competitive landscape and realigning functions across the organization is now central in the learning and development agenda. This includes facilitating necessary strategic conversations across the organization. One impact of AI is that it is playing a significant role in making the HR function a business partner in the operation of the organization.

## References

Albinson, N., Balaji, S., & Chu, Y. (2019). *Building digital trust: Technology can lead the way.* Deloitte Insights.

Anyoha, R. (2017). *Can machines think? Blog special edition on artificial intelligence. Science in the news.* Harvard University Graduate School of Arts and Sciences. Retrieved from https://sitn.hms.harvard.edu/flash/2017/history-artificial-intelligence/

Benhamou, J. (2018). *Robotic process automation is coming to HR—Here's what you need to know.* Forbes Human Resources Council. Retrieved from https://www.forbes.com/sites/forbeshumanresourcescouncil/2018/07/20/robotic-process-automation-is-coming-to-hr-heres-what-you-need-toknow/#13491ad37f6

Buchholz, S. & Briggs, B. (2020). *Executive Summary: Top Five Tech Trends, 2020.* Deloitte. https://www2.deloitte.com/us/en/insights/focus/tech-trends/2020/executive-summary.html.

Chamorro-Premuzic, T., Polli, F., & Dattner, B. (2019). *Building ethical AI for talent management.* Harvard Business Review.

Guenole, N., & Feinzig, S. (2019). *The business case for AI in HR.* IBM Smarter Workforce Institute.

Marciano, V. M. (1995, August). The origins and development of human resource management. In *Academy of Management Proceedings* (Vol. 1995, No. 1, pp. 223–227). Academy of Management.

Thornthwaite, L. (2012). The origins of personnel management: Reasserting the public sector experience. *Journal of Management History, 18*(3), 312–330.

Rao, D.A. & Verweij, G. (2017). Sizing the Prize: What's the Real Value of AI for Your Business And How Can You Capitalise? PwC Publication, Price Waterhouse Coopers.

Young, M.B., Abel, A.L., Yorks, L., & Ray, R.I. (2019). Artificial Intelligence for HR: Separating the Potential from the Hype. *The Conference Board.* New York: December

# Using Data and Analytics for Improved HRD Performance in the Age of Digital Technologies

The increased availability of data in the digital age provides Human Resources (HR) professionals with an even greater opportunity for driving business impact than ever before. The digitization of life in the twenty-first century has ushered in a period of "big data," with an astounding volume generated on a daily basis as part of the economic engine (Bersin, 2014; Daash, 2020; Dahlbom et al., 2019). Data resides both within an organization and about that organization—including customers, internal operations, and the workforce. This data, when managed effectively, can be leveraged for impactful analytical insight to inform policies, practices, and leadership decisions in more dynamic, real time, and systemic ways; for example, driving greater alignment of talent plans to change underway within the broader operating environment (Levenson, 2014; Fairhurst, 2014; Smith, 2013).

## 5.1 Situating HR in the Data Analytics Ecosystem

Traditional HR organizations have a defined set of functional responsibilities for the enterprise—responsibilities like recruiting, talent development, and employee relations. As a result of these core responsibilities, HR is privy to a large data set about how the organization—and particularly the workforce—are performing. From insights around absenteeism trends, to patterns related to evolving employee skill profiles, HR is situated at the epicenter of data around a whole host of individual domain areas, including benefits, compensation, performance management, learning and development, career trajectory, and succession planning. Each data set on their own offers powerful insights, yet collectively they also allow HR professionals to gain a unique understanding of the overall health of the business (Bersin, 2014; Dahlbom et al., 2019).

Furthermore, at the start pf the twenty-first century there are new data sets beyond these traditional sources emerging, in part due to advances in technology. Data from sources like the content of emails, internal networking platforms (e.g., Slack, Microsoft Teams), and external social media platforms (e.g., LinkedIn, Facebook) are available and offer unique opportunities to identify patterns from across these distinct sources which was previously unavailable.

The power of merging these traditional data sources with new data sets lies in their collective ability to improve overall enterprise decision-making, driving greater employee satisfaction and well-being, all while optimizing business

© The Author(s), under exclusive license to Springer Nature Switzerland AG 2022
L. Yorks et al., *Strategic Human Resource Development in Practice*, Management
for Professionals, https://doi.org/10.1007/978-3-030-95775-9_5

outcomes. Yet historically HR has not been recognized as the most proactive and strategic partner in utilizing the data available within its purview; with executives frequently believing this data has been underused or entirely unused (Angrave et al., 2016; Collins, 2015). For example, many HR organizations have produced diversity, equity, and inclusion (DEI) metrics in executive briefing packs at regular intervals, but the data is static and not grounded in a particular business process with clear actionable next steps for individuals and teams. This is an example of underused data that HR could instead be leveraging in different ways to inform and power the business toward action related to DEI goals, versus static reporting. The era of digitization during the first quarter of the twenty-first century has forced HR to confront this reputation—thrusting those in positions of leadership into a new frontier embracing big data to bring value to the business (Ben-Gal, 2019; Dahlbom et al., 2019; Edwards & Edwards, 2019; Momin and Mishra, 2015).

## 5.2    Value Proposition of Big Data—The Data-Driven HR Organization

A deeper understanding of the organization and its workforce—through useful data and insightful analytics—can help with a range of strategic and operational challenges. From helping to proactively predict when employees will leave, to better analyzing the talent pool in certain geographical locations to determine where to open a new office with the most suitable candidates, every aspect of traditional HR management has opportunities for data science techniques to be applied to improve outcomes (Marr, 2018). Recruiting, talent development, performance management, succession planning, compensation planning, benefits administration, and even often sensitive areas like employee relations are common HR responsibilities that are already being dramatically altered in the digital age (Smith, 2013; Momin & Mishra, 2015). By more effectively and proactively using data about the enterprise, its business, and its people, HR is becoming a data-driven steward of strategic value (Edwards & Edwards, 2019).

This value is two-fold. Changing both the efficiency and effectiveness of HRs operational activities—namely, how the HR organization becomes better and faster at providing its core services and changing the function's strategic impact to the business overall—namely, the kinds of workforce and people-related insights it produces. HR functions in a myriad of industries have started to rise to the occasion, well positioned to leverage the diverse data generated on a day-to-day basis into new analytic insights, allowing for advocacy around key people-related decisions while also enhancing the efficiency and efficacy of their own HR operations (Ben-Gal, 2019; Collins, 2015; Edwards & Edwards, 2019).

Given its database on the workforce, HR can provide predictive analytics on the organization and workforce; specifically, HR can forecast what will happen in the future based on what has happened in the past, Additionally, HR can offer more real time and dynamic monitoring of current realities so immediate action and perhaps even intervention can transpire. For example, what is employee morale and sentiment right now? The combination of predictive analytics and real-time monitoring offers powerful opportunities for HR to stand-out and add value for the enterprise by leveraging the large quantities of diverse data sets at its disposal to power the future of their business (Ben-Gal, 2019, Davenport, 2019; Marler & Boudreau, 2017; Marr, 2018).

## 5.3     The Evolution of HR in the Age of Big Data

Despite HR's historical track record of not traditionally leading from the front on data-driven analytics for decisioning, great progress has been made in the first quarter of the twenty-first century (Angrave et al., 2016; Fernandez & Gallardo-Gallardo, 2020; Fitz-Enz, 2010; Dahlbom et al., 2019). A 2019 Harvard Business Review survey of over 1500 senior leaders across the business, HR, and finance globally (23 countries) suggested 51% could perform predictive or prescriptive analytics on their workforce, whereas only 37% could undertake these more advanced forms of analytics on their financials (Davenport, 2019). In effect, this means HR is surpassing the finance function in identifying ways to use their existing data sets to the benefit of leadership to manage the business. Executives felt HR is coming to the table to provide more data-driven workforce management tooling and insight than finance is on topics like managing expenses, budgets, and forecasts.

In this same study, 89% of executives agreed or agreed strongly that their HR function is highly skilled at using data to determine future workforce plans (like the talent that the business needs), and only 1% disagreed; a strong showing of support for the progress HR has made in organizing its unique data sets, defining patterns and trends, and establishing meaningful models which can be utilized to inform the business on key trends (Davenport, 2019). These are promising indications of the evolving role HR playing within the enterprise as a trusted advisor and advocate for important organizational challenges—which often have a direct impact on people. Business leaders welcome enthusiastically the HR business partner who can serve as a true steward of a meaningful and relevant agenda informed by powerful workforce data (Momin & Mishra, 2015).

### 5.3.1     Understanding the HR Data & Analytics Landscape

HR plays a role in two related, but distinct, analytics spaces. HR analytics are the metrics of the HR function itself, like time to hire, or training expense per employee. These metrics are often referred to as "managed by HR for HR" and are critical to understanding the effectiveness and efficiency of the HR department in achieving its core operational responsibilities for the firm. There is a second supplementary space where HR plays an analytics role for the broader businesses and that is as it pertains to analytics about the workforce itself—namely, all the data generated by and about full-time employees, gig workers, contractors, consultants, and the like. This may involve data on productivity or employee experience. To expand upon these two distinct analytics domains, a combination of internal and external data is required. Internal data like employee tenure, compensation levels, reporting structure, and performance appraisals are needed. External data like the company's financial performance, organization-specific products/services, and historical data about economic, political, or environmental events are important data sets from which the HR organization must glean patterns to predict potential future outcomes (Fairhurst, 2014; Falletta & Combs, 2020). In the digital age, HR is expected to be stewards of both HR analytics—constantly driving the efficiency and effectiveness of their own function by having end-to-end command on their own operations and the data that matters—as well as leaders voicing the bigger picture as it pertains to broader workforce analytics trends and opportunities for the enterprise (Fernandez & Gallardo-Gallardo, 2020; Levenson, 2014; Momin & Mishra, 2015).

### 5.3.2   Levels of HR Analytics Maturity

How HR rises to the occasion manifests differently by industry and even within industries. However, there are some common building blocks to the process of identifying, organizing, and utilizing the enterprise's data resources that are relevant regardless of business (Fitz-Enz, 2010; Levenson, 2014). To determine where an organization is on the journey toward more mature HR analytics, having a framework is helpful to situate both the organization's current state and ambition for maturity. The Society for Human Resources Management (SHRM) collaborated with Bersin to establish a straightforward framework that identifies four levels of HR analytics maturity (Waters et al., 2018).

Level 1: Reactive Operating Reporting. Level 1 HR analytics is defined as a reactive approach to operational reporting on the HR function. By using existing data, the HR organization has access to leaders attempt to understand and reflect on what happened in the past to draw conclusions as to why past events played out in the ways they did. The fundamentals of this level of HR analytics are understanding already available data and eventually coming to an agreement as to what the data mean for the company (Collins, 2015; Fairhurst, 2014). The example alluded to earlier about static quarterly reporting on diversity, equity, and inclusion metrics fall into this category.

Level 2: Proactive Advanced Reporting. Progressing beyond level 1 to level 2 HR analytics involves moving toward more proactive, advanced reporting. The significant difference that separates Level 2 from Level 1 is the frequency of the data reporting. Level 2 is defined as being a proactive, routine, or even automated approach to benchmarking the organization by looking at relationships between key variables to decipher more nuanced meaning (Bersin, 2014). Organizations operating at this level.

of maturity may begin to forecast—for instance, that turnover at a particular time of year is likely to go up or down, based on historical experience.

Level 3: Strategic Analytics. For those organizations operating slightly more strategically, Level 3 analytics involve leaders that establish causal models to explore how changes in the relationships between variables effect outcomes. This may involve segmentation analysis, statistical analysis, and the development of advanced people-related workforce models (Dahlbom et al., 2019). Organizations will start to model how variables like geography, line of business, role, compensation, and the like impact performance—or vice versa—how does performance fluctuate based on geography or line of business? What do these trends tell us?

Level 4: Predictive Analytics. The highest level of the HR analytics maturity is defined by making predictions from the underlying data. HR departments functioning at Level 4 are gathering data and using it not only to predict what will happen in the future, but also to plan for it. This involves scenario planning, risk analysis, and mitigation as well as the integration of workforce planning models with the enterprise's broader business plan (Edwards & Edwards, 2019; Smith, 2013; Marr, 2018; Momin & Mishra, 2015). Firms operating at this level of maturity may use workforce trend data to collaborate with other parts of the business to address those trends proactively, mitigate risk and the like—for example, if it appears an accelerated set of employee relations issues are anticipated around a particular business issue underway.

When the framework was established and used to measure leading organizations across industries in 2014, less than 5% of organizations were operating at the most mature level 4, and less than 10% with Level 3 capabilities. Demonstrating very minimal success of HR maximizing the impact from their data to the benefit of the broader organization (Bersin, 2014). However, HR functions around the globe have made considerable progress in the years since, with the global pandemic of 2020 due to the Covid19 virus forcing acceleration at a pace and scale previous unprecedented. HR departments that were once reluctant to embrace the digital age were forced overnight to transform their operations to accept a new, fully digital reality. To the surprise of some, HR organizations around the globe and across industries, rose to the occasion immediately, successfully supporting their business and workforce with the urgent transition to a new way of working (Daash, 2020; Fernandez & Gallardo-Gallardo, 2020).

## 5.4   Making it Real

Prior to the Covid19 global pandemic one leading technology firm that had been voted a top company to work for over a period of five straight years leveraged analytics about their workforce to provide staff free meals, generous holiday allowances, and nap space for resting during the day. Each of these workforce policy changes was based on what the data suggested mattered most to employee satisfaction, e.g., they collected real-time data and acted on it to drive important outcomes, in this case to decrease staff turnover. This organization embraced the value of advanced workforce analytics before the Covid19 pandemic and was able to flex during the period of tumult by maintaining that alignment with their employees, through real-time data. The result was that they instituted flexible arrangements once the workforce moved to fully remote work in 2020, including childcare support, in explicit response to the needs expressed.

At another leading firm in the financial services industry, HR collected data on the recruiting process and noticed consistent aspects of hiring those managers were intentionally skipping due to their lack of perceived value. By a relatively straightforward modification in their approach, the organization was able to drop 2 weeks on average from the moment a requisition posted to the moment candidates started at their firm. These changes in employee experience, and in the operational time to hire, two distinct HR metrics, and demonstrate when HR organizations are performing HR analytics effectively, constantly monitoring their own operational data to drive efficiency and effectiveness outcomes.

These are two illustrative examples of the ways in which leveraging real-time data and insight about the HR function itself and the broader workforce for concrete action can add immense value to the enterprise. Additionally, the Covid19 global pandemic that caught the world economy by storm in early 2020 gave many HR organizations the opportunity to call for even bolder, expanded focus, extending HR's influence to address the changing market landscape (Daash, 2020). Workforce issues became central business issues overnight, with workers and leaders adopting entirely new ways of working and associated mindsets in the process. Many HR organizations stepped up, demonstrating agility and skill as they orchestrated the transformation of their business overnight. Companies from those in retail to those in healthcare had entirely new ways of operating in a matter of days. Changes that were not short-term, but lasted for months, if not more permanently as current fixtures of the business' operating practices, were navigated in part because of HR's leadership role.

According to a comparison between a 2020 Deloitte survey of 9000 executives (data collected in 2019 pre-pandemic) and an identical 2021 survey (data collected late in 2020 during the pandemic), non-HR business executives responded with 54% confidence in HR's ability to navigate the changes required in their business over the next 3–5 years. That's 12% greater confidence from the same set of stakeholders than pre-pandemic in 2020 when only 42% expressed that similar level of confidence. Similarly, HR's own confidence in themselves to conquer the challenges that will face their enterprise over the years ahead increased by the reality of how they coped during Covid19—with 74% of HR leaders having confidence postpandemic, compared to 58% prior (Volini et al., 2021). This bodes well for HR having both a maturing set of capabilities and a growing sense of confidence as leaders confront the new, fully digital operating environment.

## 5.5 Case Study in Action—Transforming Talent Acquisition & Internal Mobility

One large North American headquartered pharmaceutical organization has taken their enterprise into the new, digital era with capabilities like artificial intelligence—to transform their talent acquisition and internal mobility practices. By listening to employee engagement feedback, the organization identified an opportunity for improvement in the tooling that allowed external candidates and internal candidates to find available roles at the firm. Leaders were looking to simplify the experience for hiring managers, while streamlining the end-to-end talent acquisition and hiring process for recruiters. Furthermore, there was noticeable demand for a tooling ecosystem that could more dynamically support internal talent mobility. Historic offerings for career progression were happenstance, based on ad hoc knowledge sharing about opportunities and did little to match qualified internal talent with roles that were open requiring their skills. This organization was seeking to provide transparency to employees about how their current skills and experiences matched up against available opportunities. Finally, the organization wanted to remove bias from the hiring process—for example, with hiring managers unconsciously gravitate toward others with similar backgrounds due to familiarity or comfort.

By recognizing the power of data, and the rising role of AI to identify patterns and opportunities within large data sets, this HR organization leveraged a leading AI-powered technology platform to replace its existing talent acquisition and career mobility tooling suite. By sourcing data from a database of millions of past applications, and the profiles of current employees, the AI algorithms were able to identify matches between open roles and any of those individuals with requisite skills, rank them, and highlight by category where there are fits/mismatches in a matter of minutes or less. This has the added benefit of not only tapping into a talent pool that may be overlooked, e.g., legacy applications, but accomplishes this matching faster than any individual recruiter or team of recruiters could achieve. In the meantime, minimizing potential biases often inadvertently latent in the hiring process when humans are involved (Volini et al., 2021).

The value for this organization was immense. The average hiring manager or candidate has an enhanced end-to-end digital recruiting experience that is customized, fast, and accurate. Furthermore, employees seeking to progress their career by understanding other roles at the firm where their skills are of value, can quickly and immediately identify those opportunities for potential internal mobility. Ultimately, this reduces time to hire and leads to more engagement and commitment from employees while reducing turnover, as individuals can identify future career progression opportunities (See Table 5.1).

Hiring managers can open their dashboard every morning to quickly see any new candidates, provide real-time feedback on profiles that are rank ordered against their hiring criteria, and make decisions in a fraction of the time it used to take—while having access to a broader array of candidates. The impact has cut across key HR metrics, like reducing time to hire, while making dramatic improvements in more strategic goals for the firm—like maximizing the value of its existing workforce's skills by better pairing demand with supply.

**Table 5.1** Talent acquisition and career mobility reimagined

| Talent acquisition | Talent management | Talent diversity |
| --- | --- | --- |
| • Provides accurate AI-based matching, role calibration, and personalized career site<br>• Allows recruiters, candidates, and hiring managers the opportunity to identify talent and open roles in a much more effective manner<br>• Answers key questions for recruiters like who is the best fit for this specific job requirement?<br>• Answers key questions for candidates like what other positions do my current skills quality me for? | • Customized, easy-to-update talent profiles for all internal talent which automatically becomes part of searchable talent pool<br>• Enables internal mobility and career planning to elevate visibility of internal talent, offering more fluid career progression and retention of top performers<br>• Self-service for employee career planning to help employees match their skills and experiences to the most suitable positions | • Provides recruiters with visibility into the diversity of their pipelines and talent pools<br>• Candidate profiles mask key features to prevent unconscious bias<br>• Diversity analytics using pre-built dashboards identify where candidates fall out of the hiring process |

## 5.6   The Opportunity for Dynamic Workforce Development

Another area where HR analytics offers the most promise is in the realm of ongoing and continuous workforce development, reskilling, and upskilling. Due to the pace of digital transformation, with new technologies being introduced into the marketplace on a daily basis, the modern workplace has demanded an increasingly broad, varied and changing set of capabilities from its workforce. Supporting existing talent, and the broader labor market, through these periods of transition is challenging without effective analytical models that can describe what is happening, where, when, and how. Organizations that have been able to model both their own business' evolution, and the resulting demand for key capabilities over the next 2–4-6 years and compare that to the availability of skills in critical labor markets over similar periods, are best positioned to leverage these working models of reality, to guide and inform decision-making (Levenson, 2014; Shah et al., 2017).

Between 2010 and 2020, for example, many organizations in a battle for top engineering talent had models to recognize that unfortunately, relative to their compensation and incentive programs, they were not going to be able to compete in their primary corporate marketplaces for the kinds of skills they needed. By taking advantage of analytics of other marketplaces, with growing educational programs in critical science, technology, engineering, and mathematics (STEM) fields, these organizations were able to expand their technology centers into new satellite offices and hubs in second or third tier emerging cities that better matched their needs for talent while acknowledging their constraints around compensation and other benefits. Marrying the demand for skills with the supply of those skills and finding creative ways to grow the supply pool (e.g., through reskilling initiatives) is a powerful new frontier afforded through proactive workforce analytics.

One leading organization is meticulous about the integration of their workforce management framework with their operating practices on a day-to-day basis, epitomizing the potential new reality afforded in this digital era. Like many companies, their workforce of approximately 40 K employees are aligned to job families, with roles defined, grouped, and organized into a logical hierarchical leveling by capability domain area. Within technology, for example, there are job roles for architects, developers, security engineers, and infrastructure engineers ranging from beginners to more advanced. This form of categorization of the work that is underway within the firm is common for many firms, but what is unique about this organization is the use of these defined frameworks for dynamically managing the ongoing development of their existing talent. Everyone at the firm is not only aware of their job role, and how it fits into the broader job family ecosystem of the firm, but they know what that role encompasses, the skills that are required should they want to make a lateral move or progress from a level 1 infrastructure engineer to a level 2 infrastructure engineer. Furthermore, if they have doubts about their own skillsets relative to this domain, they can use the firm's learning and development platform which provides role-specific, curated content. By taking role-based assessments, individuals can precisely understand what parts of their current role's responsibilities they have mastered, as well as areas where they require further development to reach expert status.

Using these digital platforms—accessible anywhere and everywhere, on mobile devices, through company laptops or personal computers—to not only place oneself within one's area of expertise, but then based on the results of that role assessment profile has tailored recommendations for additional areas of study, is a new frontier of customized learning. Furthermore, the learning is modular and interactive. Perhaps a cloud architect is an expert on Amazon Web Services (AWS), but after answering several questions about Microsoft Azure's cloud platform, identified as being less familiar with architecting on Azure. Yet their firm is using both cloud providers and needs architects who can work on both platforms. The learning system can be precise about what exact questions were incorrect, and what domain areas this cloud architect should brush up on to become more familiar with architecting on the Azure cloud.

These customized, curated learning recommendations are bite sized. Perhaps a 10 min video, or a 15 min hands-on lab. In some cases, the assessment results may be a more extensive, indicating that an entire domain area was identified as being weak proficiency, so an entire 20-h learning journey of content is recommended to advance one's skills. In all cases however, the learning is framed relative to the organizations in-demand key capability framework, broken down into role profiles and job families, then translated into both an assessment of one's competence relative to those skills, and suggestions for how to develop them right now, should you choose. The power and autonomy are placed with the individual, the content available real time in a dynamic and engaging format. This is the future of ongoing talent development.

For those in HR, the ability to know anonymously at any given time, the proportion of the workforce that has certain proficiency levels (from beginner to expert) in every role within the firm's capability model is immensely valuable to pinpoint at the macro-level where the organization needs to invest, focus, and accelerate. If, for example, cloud computing remains a priority for that firm, and they are consistently identifying below average results with beginner and intermediate level proficiency from their technology workforce on cloud technologies, another strategy to acquire or accelerate development through more formal mechanisms may be required.

## 5.7    The Ethics of Big Data in HR

While the power and potential of big data in the context of human resources management is immense, equally important are the ethical considerations. Many organizations find themselves collaborating closely with internal legal and compliance groups to determine appropriate approaches to deploying these technologies in sustainable fashions and avoiding the often-unintended consequences of inadvertently exacerbating existing operational issues. For example, one organization that used historical performance data to form a predictive analytics engine, forecasting those in positions most likely to become promoted and/or overachieve in the upcoming performance year, realized that the underlying historical data set they were utilizing to feed the algorithm was filled with data already biased from years of human decision-making. Using that flawed and biased performance data as a predictor of future potential, would inevitably skew any perspective of the future.

Ultimately, there are four areas of ethical consideration for HR professionals stewarding their organizations forward through the digital age: bias, privacy, security, and people impact. Each should drive important questions, and implementation decisions, that are addressed not just for that point-in-time but for the ongoing lifespan of the business process—for example, an algorithm being used in recruiting over the next 12 months, should have ongoing controls and checks on each ethical domain area (Table 5.2).

**Table 5.2**  Key ethical considerations

| | |
|---|---|
| Bias | Is the data and algorithm fair? |
| | How will age, gender, race, etc. be used? |
| | Does it accurately reflect the performance or productivity data you are seeking to include without excluding, discriminating, or biasing the result? |
| Privacy | What information is captured? |
| | Is that information kept private and confidential? |
| | What happens if it is leaked/exposed? |
| Security | Is the data system and algorithm safe? |
| | Who has access and how do we audit its use? |
| | Is the information encrypted and are cyber protections in place? |
| People impact | How will this help people perform better? |
| | How will this help make people's life at work better? |
| | How will this make the workplace itself better? |

Adapted from Simbeck (2019)

## 5.8    What to Expect Next

Since the broader frameworks for governance in the digital era are still in their infancy, HR professionals will need to be stewards of sound management in the early twenty-first century. The legal protections for the digital age like Europe's Global Data Protection Regulation (GDPR)[1] are few and far between, leaving many gaps for those with ongoing management responsibilities. GDPR was the first of what one may describe as more expansive expectations for organizations operating around the world with respect to how they were treating the growing expanse of data about their customers, suppliers, employees, and the like. Yet there has been limited progress in this space since. Debate has ebbed and flowed due to public scandals— for example, the Facebook Cambridge Analytical events of the 2010s, where user's social media profiles and communication data were being stored, used, and sold without their consent.[2] Similarly cyber-attacks on companies within the United States that ramped up significantly in 2021 brought frenzy and concern.[3] However, there has been limited sweeping public policy reforms in the wake of these issues as one might expect. Albeit a period of heightened vigilance, one could argue in the digital age this is an area that's being significantly overlooked. For those in positions of HR leadership, the decades ahead involve acting on behalf of both their own organization and its workforce, and in the context of their broader nation, to protect, secure, and honor the underlying data about individuals being utilized. Ultimately, institutionalizing policies and operating standards that mitigate for risk and provide the privacy, bias, and security protections that future generations will appreciate.

## References

Angrave, D., Charlwood, A., Kirkpatrick, I., Lawrence, M., & Stuart, M. (2016). HR and analytics: Why HR is set to fail the big data challenge. *Human Resource Management Journal, 26*(1), 1–11.

Ben-Gal, H. C. (2019). *An ROI-based review of HR analytics: Practical implementation tools.* Personnel Review.

Bersin, J. (2014). *The datafication of HR.* Deloitte Review, Deloitte Insights.

Collins, L. (2015). *HR and people analytics: Stuck in neutral.* Deloitte Insights.

Daash, A. (2020). Importance of HR analytics in the era of 2020 post COVID-19. *Journal of Natural Remedies, 21*(3), 13–24.

Dahlbom, P., Siikanen, N., Sajasalo, P., & Jarvenpää, M. (2019). Big data and HR analytics in the digital era. *Baltic Journal of Management.*

Davenport, T. H. (2019). *Is HR the most analytics-driven function?* Harvard Business Review.

Edwards, M. R., & Edwards, K. (2019). *Predictive HR analytics: Mastering the HR metric.* Kogan Page Publishers.

---

[1] https://gdpr-info.eu

[2] https://en.wikipedia.org/wiki/Facebook–Cambridge_Analytica_data_scandal

[3] https://www.csis.org/programs/strategic-technologies-program/significant-cyber-incidents

Falletta, S. V., & Combs, W. L. (2020). The HR analytics cycle: A seven-step process for building evidence-based and ethical HR analytics capabilities. *Journal of Work-Applied Management, 13*(1).

Fairhurst, P. (2014). Big data and HR analytics. *IES Perspectives on HR, 2014*, 7–13.

Fernandez, V., & Gallardo-Gallardo, E. (2020). Tackling the HR digitalization challenge: Key factors and barriers to HR analytics adoption. *Competitiveness Review: An International Business Journal.* https://doi.org/10.1108/CR-12-2019-0163

Fitz-Enz, J. (2010). *The new HR analytics.* American Management Association.

Levenson, A. (2014). The promise of big data for HR. *People and Strategy, 36*(4), 22.

Marler, J. H., & Boudreau, J. W. (2017). An evidence-based review of HR analytics. *The International Journal of Human Resource Management, 28*(1), 3–26.

Marr, B. (2018). *Why data is HR's most important asset.* Forbes.

Momin, W. Y. M., & Mishra, K. (2015). HR analytics as a strategic workforce planning. *International Journal of Applied Research, 1*(4), 258–260.

Shah, N., Irani, Z., & Sharif, A. M. (2017). Big data in an HR context: Exploring organizational change readiness, employee attitudes and behaviors. *Journal of Business Research, 70*, 366–378.

Simbeck, K. (2019). HR analytics and ethics. *IBM Journal of Research and Development, 63*(4/5), 9:1–9:12.

Smith, T. (2013). *HR analytics: The what, why and how.* Numerical Insights LLC.

Waters, S. D., Streets, V. N., McFarlane, L. A., & Johnson-Murray, R. (2018). *The practical guide to HR analytics.* Society for Human Resources Management (SHRM).

Volini, E., Schwartz, J., Eaton, K., Mallon, D., Van Durme, Y., Hauptmann, M., Scott, R., & Poyton, S. (2021). *The social enterprise in a world disrupted: 2021 Deloitte global human capital trends.* Deloitte Insights.

# Strategic Learning for Sustainable Organization Performance

This chapter is titled "Strategic Learning" to make the point that learning is at the core of the strategy development process. Developing strategic learning capabilities has become an increasing focus of HRD practice at the individual, team, function, organizational, and institutional levels as organizations increasingly struggle with the challenge of the rapidly changing terrains of their competitive environment. While originally a military concept rooted in the Greek word *strategia*, meaning "generalship," as the concept has evolved and found application in virtually all-institutional contexts, there is no one agreed-upon definition of strategy (Freedman, 2013). One broad commonality in the literature is that strategic thinking is necessary under conditions of conflicting interests in which reaching resolution is necessary and outcomes cannot be predicted. Doing this requires ongoing learning and development at all levels of an organization.

Increasingly, writers on strategy are making a clear distinction between strategy development and planning (e.g., Fahey & Randall, 1998; Freedman, 2013; Pietersen, 2002, 2010). As Lawrence Freedman, Professor of War Studies at King's College London, has written "...strategy is much more than a plan. A plan supposes a sequence of events that allows one to move with confidence from one state of affairs to another. Strategy is required when others might frustrate one's plans because they have different and possibly opposing interests and concerns" (p. xi). Willie Pietersen (2002, 2010), Professor of Practice at the Columbia University Business School and a former senior executive running global businesses, distinguishes strategy formulation and strategic planning as separate phases in the process of developing and enacting strategy arguing that each is critical but mixing them is toxic.

These distinctions are growing in importance in a world characterized by rapid rates of change and increasing complexity as technology is not only intensifying competition among traditional competitors, but also enabling new entrants who transform the competitive landscape. The rise of Amazon, Uber, and Airbnb are obvious examples of the transformed competitive landscape for brick-and-mortar stores, the hospitality industry, and taxis. Walmart's entry into the online grocery market and Amazon's purchase of whole-foods are classic examples of a rapidly changing competitive terrain. While advancements in technology have always driven change, the emergence of artificial intelligence is increasing the pace and scope of change impacting a broader range of occupations including lawyers and doctors. In today's world, individual and organizational learning agility are central to establishing and sustaining competitive advantage, making HRD practices an essential part of the strategic positioning of organizations and the talent mix that comprises them.

This chapter explores core concepts of strategic learning. We frame this exploration with foundational strategic concepts and their connection with the learning process. The critical distinctions between strategic learning and strategic planning are discussed along with their necessary connection. Following discussion of the strategic frameworks, specific strategic learning practices are discussed along with the implications of mindsets for fostering strategic insight.

## 6.1 Foundational Models of Organizational Strategy

Numerous models and approaches to strategic management have emerged over the years (e.g., Mintzberg et al., 2005). From a practical standpoint, it's possible to classify three primary frameworks that have influenced strategic thinking in business over the past several decades: (1) The Planning and Design Strategic schools; (2) The Positioning Strategic School; and 3) The Disruptive Innovation and Blue Ocean Strategy Schools. These schools have each provided a framework for how strategists can think through the challenges of strategy development. The sequential emergence, and the relative waning, of these frameworks has paralleled the increasing pace of change in the socio-economic environment. To contextualize the changing role of HRD practices, we begin with a brief overview of the foundational theories for these schools. The evolution of the schools reflects how the competitive landscape has been evolving, driven in large part by the impact of technology.

### 6.1.1 The Design and Planning Schools

The design school, grounded in the work of Philip Selznick (1957) and Alfred Chandler Jr. (1962), and the Planning School, founded by Igor Ansoff (1965) and also influenced by Chandler's work, came into popularity in the 1960s, a time of relative stability and predictability in terms of the complexity of the socio-economic context. Although many executives in companies experienced the market expansion of the 1960s and 1970s as a time of uncertainty, this period was essentially level one and two in terms of Courtney et al.'s (1997) levels of uncertainty described in Chap. 1. However, as the shift from level 1 (a clear enough future) to level 2 (alternative futures) became common across industries, a shift in strategic mindset was needed. These schools provided methods still used in the strategic thinking process (Ansoff is widely called in the literature as "the father of strategic management"). Reflected in the words widely linked to these schools, "planning" and "management," neither school provided the focus necessary for the strategic agility needed in eras of rapid change requiring real-time creative strategy making (Mintzberg et al., 2005).

During the 1980s, Henry Mintzberg made the distinction between deliberate and emergent strategy. Deliberate strategy referred to what was the traditional way of thinking about strategy beginning with forming a mission, goals, and objectives. In contrast, emergent strategy was embryonic, growing through allocation of resources and taking actions prior to formalized mission or goals. Mintzberg (1994a, 1994b) characterized the necessary evolution of the process for strategy development as "the rise and fall of strategic planning" arguing that strategy cannot be planned because planning is about analysis while strategy is about synthesis and is emergent. While critiqued by Mintzberg for his highly analytical approach to strategy, Ansoff was aware of the potential problems of over engaging in analysis, coining the term "paralysis by analysis" in his book *Corporate Strategy: An Analytic Approach to Business Policy for Growth and Expansion* (1965). However, his focus remained on analysis. So, while many of his tools, such as the Ansoff Matrix, remain in use in various stages of the strategy development and implementation process, his overall theory is not often taught in business schools or widely referenced by consultants.

## 6.1.2   The Positioning School

With the introduction of Michael Porter's five forces model in 1979, the Positioning School became a dominant framework for strategic thinking through the 1980s and remains influential in strategic thinking practices today. Porter's five forces (Porter, 1979);

- The bargaining power of suppliers;
- The bargaining power buyers;
- The threat of new entrants;
- The threat of substitutes;
- Industry rivalry.

place a focus on the competitive environment, providing a general framework for assessing what tactical and strategic adaptations need to be taken. In the twenty-first century, digitalization and AI are exponentially increasing the *threat of substitutes* and *new entrants* as forces in the strategic environment needing ongoing review.

The positioning school highlighted the need for responding to changes in the external organizational environment, an emphasis that was relevant for the time, as the pace of change was becoming a key interest for executives in most businesses. Analysis of the dynamics of changes within the competitive environment was seen as important forerunner of planning. Porter's model provided the basis for situation analysis; a process of learning through the implications of divergent trends seeking new insights for strategic positioning. Willie Pietersen (2002) reframes the five forces as (1) customers, (2) competitors, (3) the firm's own realities, (4) industry dynamics, and the (5) broader environment, emphasizing "the key to a successful situation analysis is to ask the right questions—those that probe and explore the deeper trends at work in relevant areas..." with the goal of arriving at valuable new insights (p. 72) (see Table 6.1 for questions for probing trends adapted from Pietersen and used in working with clients). The learning challenge is deciding what are the most relevant questions to pursue in one's setting and answering them better and ahead of one's competitors, current or potentially emergent.

**Table 6.1**  Five sectors for strategic trend analysis. Adapted from Pietersen (2002)

**Customers**

How are our customers' expectations trending from the past to today and the future? What changes in customer behaviors and values are occurring?

What are the most and less important customer needs, including hidden needs they are unaware of and we must understand before they do?

How well do we currently serve those needs? (S = Strong, M=Moderate, P = Poor)

**Competitors**

What distinctive ways are our most significant competitors serving the market? How do customers compare how effective we are in serving the market compared to our competitors?

What new competitors are emerging, including from outside our traditional market space and what is unique about what are they offering customers? Who is the major new threat to us, and in what way?

What will be the next major disruption in how customer needs will be served? Will we launch it or a competitor?

**The firm's own realities**

What inferences, suppositions, and necessary decisions are implied by the trends measured on our performance measures during the last two to five-years.

Considering our cash flow by customer, product/service, and region, where do we make money and where don't we make money.

What key strengths can we leverage for enhancing our competitive advantage? What weaknesses do we have that are blocking us from improving our performance?

**Industry dynamics**

What trends in our industry and the emerging economy are the most important to respond to in terms of our future and how will they change are strategy and how we need to reshape our strategy?

What initiatives/actions are we taking to leverage these developments that will produce greater value for our customers?

What obstacles and challenges must we address to overcome these obstacles and challenges to profitably leverage these trends and what are the priorities?

**Broader environment**

What is happening around us that will impact our business in regard to the following factors?

Socio-economic changes

Socio-cultural changes

Technologies including new applications of artificial intelligence

Demographics

Regulations

Politics

### 6.1.3 Disruptive Innovation, and Blue Ocean Strategy

In the 1990s and early 2000s, disruptive innovation (Bower & Christensen, 1995; Christensen, 1997) became a popular concept in management. While the term disruptive innovation gained popularity, Christensen has argued that "the theory's core concepts have been widely misunderstood and its basic tenets frequently misapplied" (Christensen et al., 2015, p. 46). Christensen's concept of *disruptive innovation* is a strategic process through which a product or service is strategically introduced into the bottom of an existing market, then persistently moves up the market stream displacing established competitors. As businesses that are successful in their market continue to pursue sustaining their product line through innovations making their products and services more sophisticated than many of their customers need, and more expensive than many of their customers can afford, they increasingly target the higher tiers of their market. Targeting the higher ends of the market is more profitable, but also opens the door for new entrants willing to have lower profit margins to target segments of the market comprised of customers who are comfortable with more basic versions of the product or service that cost less. If successful, these new entrants gradually improve their products and push upmarket increasingly becoming competitors of the previously established players in the market. The new entrants may also be incorporating new technologies or methods that initially appeal to a particular, or even new, market segment.

Christensen, Raynor, and McDonald's disruptive innovation model provides a strategic management process through which new entrants target specific market segments, either low-end/marginal in existing markets or newmarket footholds, essentially overlooked by established incumbent businesses. They argue that disruptive innovation is distinct from new entrants into existing markets such as Uber. Uber entered into the Taxi market serving people who "were generally already in the habit of hiring rides" (p. 47). Uber, they argue, has transformed the market through its business model, but is not a disruptor because it did not originate in a low-end or newmarket foothold. Rather Uber immediately targeted mainstream customers of the taxi industry. In Porter's terms, it was a new emergent competitor.

The late 1990s saw the emergence of Kim and Mauborgne's concept of *Blue Ocean* strategy (2004, 2005) reframing the strategic conversation from positioning an organization within its strategic context to transforming the strategic context itself. Kim and Mauborgne used the term Red Ocean to characterize traditional defined market space within which competitors within their industry competed using a positioning mindset to achieve competitive advantage. Red Ocean was a metaphor for shark-infested oceans in which sharks are fighting each other for the same prey, with blood turning the water red. Blue Ocean was a metaphor for uncontested market space created by reconstructing market boundaries that makes the competition irrelevant. Four questions regarding the company's product or service offering in the current "Red Ocean" are asked for creating this Blue Ocean:

Given the current competitive positioning strategies in our industry:

1. What aspects of our product or service should be eliminated?
2. What aspects of our product or service should be reduced?
3. What aspects of our product or service should be enhanced? and;
4. What can be created that currently doesn't exist in the industry that opens a new "blue ocean" space? (Kim & Mauborgne, 2005, p 11).

Working through these questions requires thinking about what aspects of one's company's products and services that are part of the industry standard that don't really provide any value to the customer (Question 1); have the company's products or services been over designed as part of the race to beat the competition (Question 2); what can be done to eliminate compromises customers are having to make in receiving and/or using the company's products and services (Question 3); and how can the company break out of its traditional boundaries to open new space apart from its traditional competitors (Question 4).

## 6.2 From Enhancement and Adaptation to Generative Disruption—The Pattern Is Clear

The way strategic thinking has been evolving since the 1960s clearly reflects how the socio-economic landscape has been evolving as a function of technological innovation. Disruptive change and strategic innovation are the new normal and the classic statement "if it isn't broke, don't fix it" needs to be restated as "if it's broke it may be too late to fix it." Of necessity, strategic thinking has to shift from continually enhancing one's products and services in the race to the upper end of the market with periodic adaptations to shifts in the competitive space, to anticipating how the competitive space may/will be disrupted or ideally being the disruptor. From the mid-1950s to the present, strategic thinking has been evolving from essentially a planning process focused on analysis of what's working (and not) with the goal of improving competitive advantage to a need for continually reassessing the strategic positioning of the organization in response to disruptive innovation (or being the disruptor).

Taking this changing landscape of strategic thinking further, in her book *The End of Competitive Advantage,* Rita McGrath describes the need for strategically escaping the competitive advantage trap by embracing the need for fostering transient advantage. McGrath describes transient advantage as involving continuous morphing, looking for new opportunities and "freeing up of resources from old advantages in order to fund the development of new ones" (p. 28). As new opportunities are being ramped up, the organization has to go through reconfiguration in terms of allocation of resources and reassignment of people. At the other end of the transient advantage, continuum is disengagement; disposing of the assets and capabilities supportive of successful products or services when their returns begin to decline either by "selling them, shutting them down, or repurposing them" (p. 14). Essentially, seen through the lens of transient advantage, competitive advantage is temporary and not sustainable—the need for sustainable advantage requires strategic agility for launching, ramping up, exploiting, and reconfiguring the organization for new products or services, while disengaging from stagnating or downward trending products and services in terms of returns.

Artificial intelligence has taken this reconfiguring into a new competitive territory being driven by what Harvard Business School professors Marco Iansiti and Karim Lakhani (2020) call the AI Factory, their term for software algorithms that makes decisions through analytically converting "internal and external data into predictions, insights, and choices, which in turn guide and automate operational workflows" (p. 63). Examples of the decisions being made include cars ride offers on Lyft, Uber and other ride services, prices for some products on Amazon, running floor cleaning robots at some Walmart stores, fidelity customer service bots, and interpreting X-rays at Zebra Medical. AI technologies are now at the heart of strategic thinking. Returning to the five forces landscape depicted in Table 6.1, technology needs to be extracted from the broader environment category and become its own category creating a six forces framework (see the core question guide for situation analysis at the end of this chapter). As Iansiti and Lakhani note the traditional approach to strategy that focused on analysis with the traditional boundaries of one's industry is outdated. AI enables new, non-traditional competitors to cross traditional boundaries essentially disrupting traditional competitive markets. Further, AI enables companies to compete in disparate markets as Amazon has done. Diverse industries increasingly all share comparable technology foundations.

It is obvious that this shift toward technology providing the strategic foundation for an organization has significant HRD implications. In the words of Iansiti and Lakhani, "Machine learning will transform the nature of almost every job" (p. 66). Even the executive search process is being affected. "When Uber looked for a new CEO, the board hired someone who had previously run a digital firm—Expedia— not a limousine services company" (p. 66). Additionally, realignment of functions and departments must occur as a result of data sourcing and analysis capabilities. All these impacts reflect the need for coordination between HRM, L&D, and OD as described in Chaps. 1 and 7 (see Figs. 1.1 and 7.2) in HRD practice.

Adapting to this world of continuous strategic transition requires continuous learning agility at the organization, function, team, and individual levels of virtually all enterprises (the impact Amazon has had on the brick-and-mortar bookstores and the recording industry is an obvious example). As has already become evident, the accelerating development of artificial intelligence will intensify this need, making the role of coordinated HRD practices critical for sustainable performance. Strategically learning at the organizational, functional, and cross-functional, and individual levels is required.

## 6.3  Strategy Development as Learning

We have been arguing the point that learning is at the heart of the strategy development process. Strategic learning is a process of recognizing emergent patterns in the socio-economic environment seeking new insights through mapping trends, seeking viewpoints that differ from one's own, exploring diverse scenarios, and asking uncomfortable questions about what might emerge in the future. This requires self-awareness of one's own habitual reactions to ideas that differ from one's own. Everyone sees and interprets the world through their own frames of reference that are shaped by their past experiences. The essence of strategic learning is about generating new ideas and insights. Albert Szent-Gyorgyi, winner of the 1937 Nobel Prize for Biochemistry, once said, "Discovery consists of seeing what everybody has seen and thinking what nobody has thought." While insights can emerge from a spontaneous thought often generated by hearing a comment or coming across information that connects to an issue one has been thinking about, we argue when a person is intentionally engaging in a strategy development process, new insights are a function of a person's competency and capacity as expressed in the following equation:

$$\text{New strategic insight} = f\left(\text{Competency}\right) \times \left(\text{Capacity}\right)$$

New strategic insight is a function of competency and capacity. *Competency* is defined as (1) understanding the ability for working with strategic frameworks and concepts and (2) applying strategic learning practices for facilitating strategic conversations and assessing emerging insights. *Capacity* is defined as one's way of making meaning and taking action in terms of action inquiry and action logic. These two components of the equation have important implications for management and executive development that will be explored further below.

## 6.4    Core Competencies for Strategic Learning

The strategic frameworks described above are useful as mental models for organizing one's own thinking and providing a scaffolding for strategic learning conversations. These frameworks can be triangulated drawing on insights from each by matching them with the state of the socio-economic context of the organization and rigorously applying strategic learning practices. For example, the porter positioning framework focuses on socio-economic context and the distinct trends external to the organization. When considering the potential force of new entrants, the disruptive innovation framework expands the scope of considerations for organizations that have been pushing their products to the top end of the competitive market through upscaling and making them more expensive. It can also trigger new insights regarding decisions maintaining the organization's competitive space. Following an C suite executive training workshop with Clayton Christensen in which Intel's CEO Andy Grove learned of how the steel industry had ceded the low-end of the market to minimill that began producing low-end cheap rebars and then began moving into higher end products. Grove announced "If we lose the low end today, we could lose the high-end tomorrow" and had the company more aggressively promote its low-end processer into the low-end market (Gavetti & Rivkin, p. 56). McGrath's transient advantage model is also relevant with regard to the pitfalls of continuing to focus extracting profits through exploiting existing advantages.

Conducting trend analysis within each of the five forces (or in today's world of AI, the six forces) is basic to mapping the dynamic external context of the organization. In today's world of the so-called fourth revolution of the competitive space by digital technology and AI, particular attention needs to be paid to how these trends are being disrupted and how competitors and customers are responding. As we are all aware, technology has disrupted the hospitality industry, hotels in particular. It has also enabled new competitors entering and disrupting the taxi industry.

The possible trajectories and disruptions of each of the six forces, with particular attention to intelligent technologies, need to be explored through a process of inquiry initially seeking possibilities not answers. As previously mentioned above, this process best begins by asking questions, not advocating outcomes. Initially brainstorming the questions to be answered helps avoid the common trap of immediately moving to answers through our existing frames of reference and opens diverse avenues for inquiry (Gregersen, 2018). Seeking diverse viewpoints in answering the questions leads to new deeper questions opening the door for new insights. The goal is to map the industry or service sector dynamics addressing which trends in the "new and emerging economy" are most important in shaping the future of the organization. How will the rules of success be changed and what, if anything, is the organization doing to exploit emerging developments to produce greater value for key customers and stakeholders? What new opportunities are possible? New strategic direction involves disengagement with what has been working in the past and resistance to letting go is often the first response. Strategic learning practices can be applied for countering this natural resistance to letting go and surfacing new strategic opportunities. In particular, engaging in action inquiry, mapping analogies, creating value curves, and scenario thinking are ways of navigating through uncertainty.

## 6.4.1   Action Inquiry

As described in Chap. 2, action inquiry involves presenting awareness of one's own reactions and the reactions of others in the conversation providing balance for listening to and exploring diverse perspectives. Integrating the practices of action inquiry into strategy development meetings is useful because generating new insight requires exploring diverse perspectives with mindful awareness of one's own feelings about what others are saying and paying attention to the patterns of speech that unfold. Bill Torbert (2004) describes action inquiry as "a kind of behavior that is simultaneously productive and self-assessing" (2004, p. 13). This behavior is particularly valuable for gaining strategic insight into possible options in the context of a disruptive socio-ecosystem driven by continuously emerging AI technologies. Attention to what Torbert, the four parts of speech described in Chap. 2, (1) framing, (2) advocating, (3) illustrating, (4) inquiring, is enabling for holding dialogue about the meaning different people make of the disruptive trends in the external environment. Framing one's intention before advocating for a direction of action along with examples, and then inquiring into what others think fosters strategic dialogue.

### 6.4.2   Gaining Insight from Analogies

Drawing on analogies is basic humans thinking. When we draw on our prior experience to address a challenge that is confronting us, we are using analogies. In their article *How Strategists Really Think,* Gavetti and Rivkin (2005) provide examples of how analogies have been the source for making strategic choices. They note that the supermarket has been an analogy used by several innovative entrepreneurs including Charlie Merrill drawing on his experience as an executive in a supermarket in creating Merrill Lynch as a financial services supermarket, Charles Lazarus using the supermarket as a model for Toys R Us, and Thomas Stemberg beginning the creation of Staples with the analogical question "Could we be the Toys R Us of office supplies?" Steve Job's saw that "the digital 'desktop' developed but unappreciated at Xerox PARC", was an analogy with the potential to make computers accessible to millions of people. Creative insight using analogies steams from creatively re-categorizing what we observe from sometimes surprising sources. Today we see how Airbnb and Uber are models for any number of starts ups leveraging online marketing.

However, successfully using analogies requires systematically mapping the differences along with the similarities between the source analogy and the new application. As Gavetti and Rivkin write, using superficial similarities can lead to making bad decisions. They cite the example of how Ford initially looked at Dell's strategy of virtual integration as an analogy worth following when the auto company was overhauling its supply chain. However, while the computer and auto assembly resemble each other in terms of producing a vast number of different models from fairly standard components, closer examination of difference such as how fast prices of material decline much faster in the PC industry revealed that the analogy was not appropriate (p. 58). Avoiding the pitfall of superficial similarity involves understanding the analogy being used and actively searching for differences between the analogy situation and the intended adaptation. That includes understanding the differences between the context (market, supply chain, customer chain, regulatory environment, etc.) of the analogy and what was the value proposition and the strategic concept being developed. It is useful to talk to sophisticated barbarians, trusted knowledgeable contacts that will provide critical assessments. Surface the assumptions that are being made regarding the similarities between the analogy and the strategic idea. Make changes in the idea in response to glaring differences.

### 6.4.3   Creating Value Curves and Identifying the Most Important Customer/Stakeholder

Value curves describe the value of an organization's offerings and those of the competition to its most important customer. The more divergent the organization's curve is from the competition, the more distinct its offering. This assessment begins with identifying the most important customer (MIC) in the organization's demand side customer chain and asking three questions:

1. If there's a problem/issue with our product or service, who is responsible for taking the necessary immediate action to rectify the situation?
2. Who stands to lose the most financially (and/or reputation) if there's a problem/issue with my product or service?
3. Who is the most likely to recognize the value provided by my product or service?

If the answers to all three or two of the questions identify the same link in the customer chain, then that's the most important customer. For example, consider a company manufacturing replacement automobile parts. The manufacture's customer chain is comprised of distributors, who sell, to jobbers, who in turn sell to auto repair shops, who put the replacement parts in cars brought in for service. When we initially ask participants in executive education workshops who is the most important customer the majority of them answer the distributor or the person whose car is being worked on. This is a natural response. Most executives think of their direct customer (in this case, the distributor) or the final user (in this case, the person in whose car the project will be inserted). Once they consider the three questions, they immediately see it's repair shop. If the replacement part fails or breaks down after it installed the repair shop has to replace it eating the cost of both the new replacement part and the cost of time required to do so. This also can impact their customer's impression of the quality of their work. Additionally, over time they will recognize which manufacturer's products are of higher quality and less likely to break down.

Once the most important customer has been identified it's time for the strategist to put on their anthropologist hat and learn what elements of their product and service are most important or useful to them, less important, not important and can be eliminated, or what new elements could be added. This involves engaging in field research that essentially explores what is keeping representative MIC's "up at night." The scope of this inquiry will vary depending on the business involved, but the purpose is to understand the experience of MIC in using the organization's produce or services and assessing their experience with competitor or alternative products and services. These inquiries can be carried out through site visits, association meetings, or other venues. For example, returning to the example of the auto repair shops a primary need that emerged was having a better understanding of how to manage aspects of their business. The auto parts manufacturer created a way of meeting this need that was provided to repair shops. Consequently, the repair shops began requesting their product line from the distributors and they went from being a minor player in the market to the dominant one.

When there is more than one most important customer, similar research needs to be done with each of them. Also, the description above is on the demand side value chain. Some organizations such as not-for-profits and educational institutions also have to apply the same three question analysis to their supply side value chain such as not-for profits, some educational institutions, and community groups. The supply side can consist of funders, foundations, or referral organizations.

The results of the research can be used to for creating value curves to help visualize potential strategy. Value curves consist of the elements that the organization provides to the most important client. Elements are not a product or service but a descriptor the organization invests in to provide enhanced value to the customer. Based on the information gathered in through the inquiries with MICs, the elements most important to them should be identified and used to develop the value curve. One's value curve can be either comparing the organization with competitors or an "as is" and "to be" case for the organization.

This process is applicable in a wide range of institutional sectors. An example in the business school executive education sector is the use of value chains and value curves at the LSU College of Business Executive Education Program. From the 1960s through the early 1990s, the Senior Executive Program was very profitable, attracting participants from fortune 500 companies for a six-week program that met for 2 weeks at a time. While there was slight erosion in attendance in the late 1990s, a significant decline in attendance followed the 2001 downturn in the economy with companies dropping out. By 2008, attendance had declined by more than 80 percent. Travel expenses for visiting faculty coupled with the drop-in revenue had turned the program into a loss. The program was moved from the office overseeing the MBA and EMBA program to newly created executive education institute with the directive that the program had to be self-sustaining within 3 years. From the external trends in the executive education sector across the country, it was clear that sustaining and building a profitable and self-sustaining program would require strategic repositioning of the program if it was going to survive. The new Program Director initiated a learning process to identify "the most important stake holders" (MIS) in the program's value chain with the intention of creating value curves to visualize possible strategic changes in the program's design.

After constructing the value chain that consisted of the companies/organizations which sent participants, past participants, the HR/Management Development Department in the Organizations, the Business Division/or Department in which participants where situated, and current participants the three questions were applied to determine the MIS. As seen in Table 6.2, the MIS was the HR Department, which surprised the executive education staff who were used to considering previous participants and program participants as the MIS. After conducting a series of interviews with various heads of HR departments, the executive education leadership team created an "*as is*" value curve representing the value currently being provided (Table 6.3) that became the basis for a series of strategic conversations. Table 6.4 illustrates the "*to be*" value curve emerged from those conversations based on the perceived needs of the MIS derived from the interviews. The specific changes depicted in the curve led the strategic repositioning and reorganization of the executive education programs. Within a year Executive Education returned to being profitable. The next step was continuing to use value curves to differentiate the program from its primary competitors. Executive education was, and is, largely a "red ocean" with programs relying on the name of the University.

For another example of the process for facilitating the application of value curves in practice see the McMains Children's Developmental Center case in the final section of this book.

**Table 6.2** The value chain depicting the most important stakeholder (MIS) for the executive education program (Penton, 2015)

| Value Chain | Question 1 | Question 2 | Question 3 |
|---|---|---|---|
| **Executive Education** | | | |
| Companies / Organizations | | X | |
| Past Participants | | | X |
| HR Dept. / Mgt, Development | X | X | X |
| Business Div / Dept. | | X | |
| Current Participants | | | |

**Table 6.3** The "as is" value curve for the executive education programs (Penton, 2015)

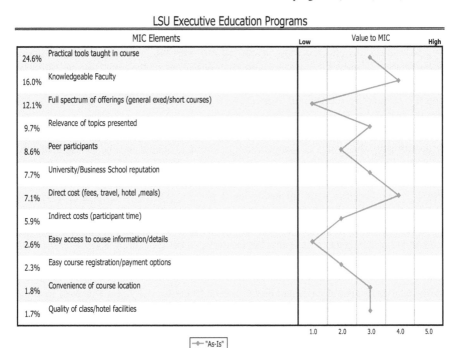

**Table 6.4** The "as is" and "to be" value curves for executive education (Penton 2015)

### 6.4.4   Scenario Learning

Working with scenarios is a method for learning about the future by understanding the nature and impact of the most uncertain and important driving forces affecting the future of one's organization, function or team, or career. Scenario learning is a process of imaging future states, each of which is possible but unsure and identifying potential risks and red flags. If carried out with the practice of engaged action inquiry, the scenario learning expands understanding of the situation, highlighting new possible strategic directions and reframing existing decisions. The scenario matrix, created by Illbury and Sunter (2011), is a useful tool for structuring the discourse (see Table 6.5).

Taking the strategic challenge being addressed through the matrix begins by brainstorming the "rules of the game" (Quadrant 1). These are the givens that can't or won't be changed such as legal requirements, policies, and financial constraints. These are the boundaries within which the strategy will have to be implemented. Next is brainstorming the uncertainties that exist (Quadrant 2). Determine what driving forces behind the trends analysis are unlikely to change and which are uncertain. The driving forces unlikely to change can be treated as predetermined and added to the rules of the game but continue to be monitored. Rank the uncertain driving forces by level of uncertainty and importance. The top 2 that are most uncertain and important are defined as the critical uncertainties. Present each as an axis with polar extremes at each end and combine to create a 2X2 matrix with four different quadrants of future uncertainties and implications regarding these uncertainties (See Table 6.6). Create a story line that presents the implications of each quadrant as a scenario that might unfold. Based on the scenario in each quadrant identify options for each (Quadrant 3) (See Table 6.7). Based on the likely hood of

**Table 6.5** A scenario learning matrix. Adapted from Mind of the Fox, C. Ilbury & C. Sunter (2011)

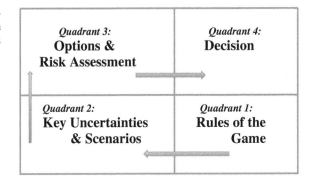

| *Quadrant 3:* **Options & Risk Assessment** | *Quadrant 4:* **Decision** |
|---|---|
| *Quadrant 2:* **Key Uncertainties & Scenarios** | *Quadrant 1:* **Rules of the Game** |

**Table 6.6** Scenario matrix for Quadrant 2

| | **Quadrant 3: Options & Risk Assessment** | **Quadrant 4: Decisions** |
|---|---|---|
| **Quadrant 2: Uncertainties & Scenarios** *Identify Two Key Uncertainties and the Opposite Ends of Each* | | **Quadrant 1: Rules of the Game** |

*Key Uncertainty 1*

| Scenario 1 | Scenario 2 |
|---|---|

*Key Uncertainty 2*

| Scenario 3 | Scenario 4 |
|---|---|

**Table 6.7** Identify options for each scenario & assess risk

Lorem ipsum

**Quadrant 3: Options-Identify Strategic Choices for Each Scenario & Assess Risk**
[Based on the Scenario & Implications, Identify Strategic Options & Risks for Each]

*Key Uncertainty 1*

| Options for Scenario 1 | Options for Scenario 2 |
|---|---|

*Key Uncertainty 2*

| Options for Scenario 3 | Options for Scenario 4 |
|---|---|

**Quadrant 2: Key Uncertainties and Scenarios**

| Scenario 1 | Scenario 2 |
|---|---|
| Scenario 3 | Scenario 4 |

**Rules of the Game**

each scenario and the level of risk for each move toward creating strategic action steps (Quadrant 4). Also, identify early warning signals that indicate possible future directions and the likely emergence of one scenario rather than others. Additionally, the exercise can be repeated with another uncertainty replacing one of the two initially used or two other uncertainties to create alternative matrixes.

The scenario matrix can be incorporated into executive development initiatives purposively intended to develop mindsets prepared to deal with the unpredictable disruptions that will emerge in the future.

While in the past learning initiatives focused on drawing lessons from the past experience, as Peter Scoblic (2020) has highlighted "At the very moment when the present least resembles the past, it makes little sense to look back in time for clues about the future" (p. 41). Rather organizations need to be consistently and robustly learning from possible futures, not with the belief they can predict the future, but rather to create the capability for exploiting new possibilities that emerge and not being locked into the past.

As an example, Scoblic (2020) describes how the U.S. Coast Guard, working with the consultancy Futures Strategy Group (FSG), brought together a group of leaders from different parts of the organization, with different points of view based on different experiences. Participants articulated and reflected on the assumptions underlying their current strategy, the future they expected it to produce, and treated their expected future as a projected scenario that is only one of other possible futures that might result. They then reflected again on their assumptions and which ones might be changed. In doing so participants separated environmental forces they could influence from those they could not and how combinations of those forces might produce other possible futures, perhaps 5 or 10 years in the future. In doing so participants created "artifacts from the future such as fictional newspaper stories and video clips" that help to challenge existing frames of reference. Teams were created to inhabit each of the possible far future realities and address the question what the Coast Guard should be presently doing that would enable the organization to operate effectively in each particular future. The teams then shared their strategies and singled out commonalities and plans and investments that would help prepare for a range of futures. These strategies were then implemented. Over time, the process became an iterative cycle.

This process got leaders to think about the future in a way that prepared the organization for agility in the present. One leader who went through the program began developing bilateral relationships with counterparts in other nations and government agencies to prepare for possible threats in the Pacific. The agility that was created in the organization has been evident in a number of crises requiring immediate shifts in operations that have been experienced over decades, including 9/11. Longview and Evergreen in the Coast Guard is a synchronist L&D and OD intervention, developing both the ability of individual leaders to think differently and also changes the culture of the organization as participants develop the ability to take actions at the unit level.

It also illustrates the need for enhanced developmental capacity. Scoblic (2020) notes that imagining dramatically different, but plausible futures was "the most difficult part of the exercise, particularly for those used to more analytical thinking" (p. 46). This doesn't negate the value of analytical thinking but does demonstrate how one must be able to put it aside to avoid being trapped in the present when confronted with uncertainty or ambiguity. Practicing scenario learning facilitates growth in cognitive development. We turn now to considering the capacity element of the equation for strategic insight.

## 6.5    Capacity

Capacity is a function of one's way of making meaning and taking action that is shaped by a person's state of cognitive development. As described in Chap. 2, adult development theory has evolved substantially over the past several decades through the work of Robert Kegan (Kegan, 1982, 1995; Kegan & Lahey, 2001), William Torbert (Torbert, 1991; Rooke & Torbert, 2005), and John Heron (1992) demonstrating that development potentially continues throughout adulthood. In the words of Kegan (2000) transitioning to a more complex mindset stage is a process of transformative changes in "*how* we know," which in turn shapes and enhances "*what* we know" (p. 50). Developmental growth, if and when it occurs, takes place through a gradual transitional process.

As developmental capacity grows, it has an exponential impact on the potential for fostering insights. This is particularly true in contexts of complexity, high uncertainty or ambiguity and change. Such settings require those participating to engage in the process of developmental action inquiry described in Chap. 2, while they are sharing, listening, and inquiring into diverse viewpoints and exploring alternative interpretations of the implications of emerging changes for the future.

As previously stated, all of the practices presented in this chapter can be applied in a range of ways, most often as part of off-sight strategy sessions, workshops, and action learning programs. This is increasingly necessary in an environment of complexity and rapid change with the intention of creating a mindset of awareness of possibilities. Using them over time results in not only more effective strategy development initiatives, but also becomes a way of thinking integrated into the meaning-making mindsets throughout the organization and by extension creates an organizational culture of agility.

While the design and sequencing of the discussions will vary from organization to organization, the sequencing of topics needs to consist of four essential conversations:

- 1st Conversation—What have we been doing?
- 2nd Conversation—What are we capable of doing?
  - Situation assessment of trends
  - Value Chain Analysis
  - What's our winning value proposition based on analysis from the scenario matrix?
  - Our strategic intent?
- 3rd Conversation—Testing our converging strategy against;
  - Our core competencies—What developmental changes are needed?
  - Political realities—What changes are needed in the dominant coalition and influence patterns
  - What alternative futures might emerge (returning to the scenario matrix—high light possible red flags?)
- 4th Conversation—Allocation of resources and facilitating alignment

   – Develop plans and continually assess progress across the transition process from feelings of loss to commitment. These conversations can be conducted over the course of an off-site retreat or as a sequence of meetings. Either way attention needs to be paid to the need for having access to necessary data, getting right mix of people in the room, and recognition of the relevance of timing; as Rita McGrath has phrased it, we live in a world of transient strategy.

These conversations can be conducted in off-site retreats or as a sequence of meetings with each conversation occurring over more than one meeting. Essentially, these conversations are segments of the strategic learning process and can be implemented with each segment comprised of sub-topics. Either way attention needs to be paid to having the necessary data, getting the right mix of people in the room, and timing; as Columbia Business School Executive Education Professor Rita McGrath has phrased it, "we live in a world of transient strategic advantage" (2013). Due to the continuing impact of new technologies driving change, even as existing strategy is being implemented executives need to be exploring new possible strategies. And in the 4IR, this includes AI, which can inform these conversations by providing assisted, augmented, and autonomous intelligence. Additionally, these conversations need to consider how technologies across the organization need to be coordinated, or centralized, as AI becomes a major driver of changes in the competitive marketplace. Figure 6.1 integrates these conversations with strategic learning practices and Willie Pietersen's four phase strategic learning cycle: *Learn, Focus, Align*, and *Execute*. As previously described, strategic learning is an iterative process and takes into account the political economy of the organization, or in the case of self-employed and gig-contract workers the political economy of their socio-economic context. At the end of this chapter, we provide a core questions guide for situation analysis for personal reflection and having a dialogue with colleagues to generate new insights about the socio-economic context.

## 6.6   Summary

Strategy development is a process involving learning, with the goal of generating new insights that can then be focused and articulated into a strategy. This involves developing and applying strategic learning competencies with awareness of how one's developmental capacity is in play and can be further developed.

Strategic Insight = *(F)* Competencies     X     Capacity

Applying Strategic Frameworks ⟺ Applying Learning Practices     Awareness of
                                                                    Developmental Stages

        Positioning                 Action Inquiry            Action Logics
        Blue Ocean              Mapping Analogies
        Transient             Creating Value Chains
                              & Value Curves
                              Scenario Matrixes

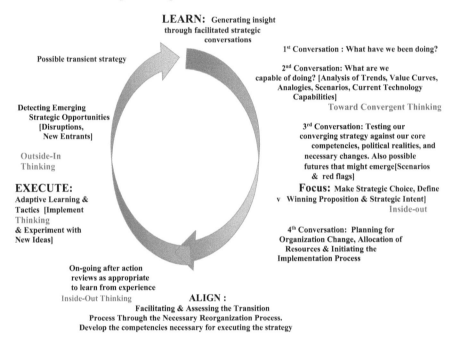

**External Political Economy**
Industry Dynamics
New Entrants
Emergent Technologies
Capital Markets
Shifting Distribution Channels
Labor Costs and Availability
Changing Customer Tastes
Social/Cultural Habits & Attitudes
Demographics
Potential Legislation & Govt. Policies
Subsidies & Trade Restrictions

Outside-In
Divergent Thinking

**Internal Political Economy**
Core Competencies
Technology & Organizational Capabilities
Dominant Coalitions & Influence Patterns
Administrative Processes
Return on Investment (Products & Programs)
Wage & Salary Structures
Budget Allocations
Capital Investment including Human Capital
Organizational Demographics
Organizational Culture—Norms, Values, Factions

Continuing Divergent Thinking

**LEARN:** Generating insight through facilitated strategic conversations

Possible transient strategy

1st Conversation : What have we been doing?

2nd Conversation: What are we capable of doing? [Analysis of Trends, Value Curves, Analogies, Scenarios, Current Technology Capabilities]

Detecting Emerging Strategic Opportunities [Disruptions, New Entrants]

Toward Convergent Thinking

Outside-In Thinking

3rd Conversation: Testing our converging strategy against our core competencies, political realities, and necessary changes. Also possible futures that might emerge[Scenarios & red flags]

**EXECUTE:**
Adaptive Learning & Tactics [Implement Thinking & Experiment with New Ideas]

**Focus:** Make Strategic Choice, Define Winning Proposition & Strategic Intent]
Inside-out

4th Conversation: Planning for Organization Change, Allocation of Resources & Initiating the Implementation Process

On-going after action reviews as appropriate to learn from experience
Inside-Out Thinking

**ALIGN :** Facilitating & Assessing the Transition Process Through the Necessary Reorganization Process. Develop the competencies necessary for executing the strategy

**Fig. 6.1** The strategic learning cycle process and practices. Based on and adapted from W. G. Pietersen (2002)

Putting together strategy development processes that utilize these competencies along with an awareness of the action logics of those involved in a critical part of the HRD role. This requires providing learning opportunities for executives and managers across the organization, designing and implementing strategy development initiatives, and applying them to the HRD functions as well is a significant responsibility in the twenty-first century.

**A Core Question Guide for Situation Analysis Generating Questioning Insight Customers**:

What underlying trends are reflected in their purchasing actions?
What markets are they choosing to participate in?
What problematic challenges are confronting them?

### Competitors:

What are their distinctive core competencies?
What is their business model?
How do they make money?
What are their distinctive performances trends?
How are they perceived by their customers/clients?
What are the underlying trends impacting their business model?
What do these trends suggest about emergent needs?

### Technologies:

What technologies are disrupting our markets?
What new competitors are using emerging technology to enter our business?
In what ways are emerging technologies being used in different industries that are
    potentially analogous for our industry (both threats and opportunities)?
What new disruptive technologies can enhance our performance and in what ways?

### Dynamics of the Industry:

What trends are apparent in our industry and what forces are driving these trends?
What might disrupt these dynamics?

### Our Own Realities:

What are our distinctive core competencies and how do they compare to the answers
    to our customer and competitor analysis and what are the implications for our
    business or livelihood model?
When, where, and how do we make money (or achieve the most impact)?

### The Broader Context:

What are the current socio-economic trends?
What cultural dynamics are driving trends exist in social attitudes?

Derived and adapted from Pietersen (2002).

# References

Ansoff, H. I. (1965). *Corporate strategy: An analytic approach to business policy for growth and expansion*. McGraw-Hill.

Bower, J. L., & Christensen, C. M. (1995). Disruptive technologies: Catching the wave. *Harvard Business Review, 73*(1), 43–53.

Chandler, A. D., Jr. (1962). *Strategy and structure: Chapters in the history of the industrial enterprise*. MIT Press.

Christensen, C. M. (1997). *The innovators dilemma: When new technologies cause great firms to fail*. Harvard Business School Press.

Christensen, C.M., Raynor, M.E., & McDonald, R. (2015). What is disruptive innovation? *Harvard Business Review, 93*(12), 44–53.

Courtney, H., Kirkland, J., & Viguerie, P. (1997). Strategy under uncertainty. *Harvard Business Review, 75*(6), 67–79.

Fahey, L., & Randall, R. M. (Eds.). (1998). *Learning from the future: Competitive foresight scenarios*. Wiley.

Freedman, L. (2013). *Strategy: A history*. Oxford University Press.

Gavetti, G., & Rivkin, J. W. (2005). How strategists really think: Tapping the power of analogy. *Harvard Business Review, 83*(4), 54–63.

Gregersen, H. (2018). Better brainstorming: Focus on questions, not answers for breakthrough insights. *Harvard Business Review, 96*(2), 64–71.

Heron, J. (1992). *Feeling and personhood: Psychology in another key*. SAGE.

Iansiti, M., & Lakhani, K. R. (2020). Competing in the age of AI: How machine intelligence changes the rules of business. *Harvard Business Review, 98*(1), 60–67.

Illbury, C., & Sunter, C. (2011). *The mind of a fox: Scenario planning in action*. Human & Rousseau.

Kegan, R. (1982). *The evolving self: Problem and process in human development*. Harvard University Press.

Kegan, R. (1995). *In over our heads: Mental demands of modern life*. Harvard University Press.

Kegan, R. (2000). What "form" transforms? A constructive developmental approach to transforming learning. In J. Mezirow (Ed.), *Learning as transformation: Critical perspectives on a theory in progress*. Jossey-Bass.

Kegan, R., & Lahey, L. L. (2001). The real reason people won't change. *Harvard Business Review, 79*(10), 84–92.

Kim, W. C., & Mauborgne, R. (2004). Blue Ocean strategy. *Harvard Business Review, 82*(10), 76–84.

Kim, W. C., & Mauborgne, R. (2005). Blue Ocean strategy: From theory to practice. *California Management Review, 47*(3), 105–121.

McGrath, R. G. (2013). *The end of competitive advantage: How to keep your strategy moving as fast as your business*. Harvard Business Review Press.

Mintzberg, H. (1994a). *The rise and fall of strategic planning: Reconceiving roles for planning, plans, planners*. The Free Press.

Mintzberg, H. (1994b). The fall and rise of strategic planning. *Harvard Business Review, 74*(1), 107–114.

Mintzberg, H., Ahlstrand, B., & Lampel, J. B. (2005). *Strategy safari: The complete guide through the wilds of strategic management* (2nd ed.). FT Publishing.

Penton, H. (2015). Power points from *strategic agility in practice* workshop at Teachers College, Columbia University and other Executive Education Workshops including LSU.

Pietersen, W. (2002). *Reinventing strategy: Using strategic learning to create and sustain breakthrough performance*. Wiley.

Pietersen, W. (2010). *Strategic learning: How to be smarter than your competition and turn key insights into competitive advantage*. Wiley.

Porter, M. E. (1979). How competitive forces shape strategy. *Harvard Business Review, 73*(2), 137–145.

Rooke, D., & Torbert, W. (2005). Seven transformations of leadership. *Harvard Business Review, 83*(4), 66–76.

Selznick, P. (1957). *Leadership in Administration: A Sociological Interpretation.* New York: Harper & Row.

Scoblic, P. J. (2020). Learning from the future: How to make robust strategy in times of deep uncertainty. *Harvard Business Review, 98*(4), 38–47.

Torbert, B. and Associates. (2004). *Action inquiry: The secret of timely and transforming leadership.* Berrett-Koehler Publishing.

Torbert, W. R. (1991). *The power of balance: Transforming self, society, and scientific inquiry.* Sage.

# Aligning Strategic, Tactical, and Operational Level Learning for Performance

**7**

Strategic HRD interventions integrated with intelligent technologies initiatives can provide an architectural framework for addressing strategic, tactical, and operational performance issues across organizational levels. We describe this framework as the HRD pyramid. In the age of Volatility, Uncertainty, Complexity, and Ambiguity (VUCA) continuously reassessing the strategy of an organization is critical for surfacing potential threats to organizational performance and sustainability. The strategic responses to these potential threats then require planning for and implementing necessary realignments of operations as previously depicted in Willie Pietersen's strategic learning cycle. As the strategic changes are executed, performance needs to be continuously assessed and, as always, performance problems need to be addressed through HRD interventions. This chapter provides a framework for addressing performance problems that emerge during the execution of strategy at the tactical and operational levels of the organization.

## 7.1 Implications of Strategic Change for the HRD Agenda

Strategy making as a learning process in today's environment of uncertainty and rapid change widens the HRD agenda to initiating strategic learning conversations while also fostering individual development of both competencies and capacity of participants. The executive development process includes both development of embedded skills for triangulating one's thinking through the strategic frameworks and using the strategic learning practices as a way of being in the face of new emergent challenges. This requires initiatives for both horizontal and vertical development on the part of managers and executives. Horizontal development is acquiring competencies in using strategic thinking frameworks and strategic learning practices; vertical development involves recognizing how one's mindset is shaping how one is able to listen to diverse viewpoints and consciously seeking to develop enhanced capacity for how one learns. These two interconnected dimensions of

© The Author(s), under exclusive license to Springer Nature Switzerland AG 2022
L. Yorks et al., *Strategic Human Resource Development in Practice*, Management for Professionals, https://doi.org/10.1007/978-3-030-95775-9_7

development apply when addressing the learning needs across, and at various levels of, the organization. This interconnectedness can be visualized in the metaphor of the HRD pyramid.

## 7.2    The Metaphor of the HRD Pyramid

The metaphor of the HRD pyramid (see Fig. 7.1) visualizes the relationship between strategy, tactics, and operations and how they are increasing becoming interconnected with each other. Although the focus of this book has been on strategic learning, tactical and operational learning are essential for the successful execution of strategy and for potentially revealing new potentialities and impediments. While the designs of learning initiatives vary between the strategic, tactical, and operational levels of the pyramid, the levels have to be aligned with learning initiatives not restricted in particular to the formal hierarchical organization structure. Although the strategic level initiatives are typically targeted at the senior levels of the organization, in today's world midlevel managers need to be included in strategic conversations. Developing a capacity for strategic thinking has to occur early in careers. Conversely, senior executives often need to be developing new competencies for understanding the operational challenges facing the business and utilizing new technologies. While strategy development is a process of defining the gap between where an organization is and where it needs to be in the future and tactics are steps taken to implement the strategy, tactical decisions and actions are taken all levels of an organization and must be aligned with strategy. Some tactical decisions are imbedded in the plans that are created once the strategy has been decided; others need to be made in the process of execution as actions are taken.

**Fig. 7.1**  The HRD pyramid

Senior management makes tactical decisions regarding capital investments, restructuring the organization, and final choices around new product lines. Upper and midlevel managers have to make staffing changes, make pricing decisions, reorganization of facilities, and promotion decisions. At the same time they have to be thinking strategically about the potential realignments that may take place within the organization and how to position their division, department, or function (and self) for the future. So while at the macro-level of conceptualizing the organization, these three levels depict the over-all hierarchy of the management structure, all three are relevant for each level of the organization although with different emphasis and implications.

The patterns of tactical adaptions that need to be taken in turn become data points for the ongoing discussions of assessing the next strategic decisions that will need to be made. Tactical moves, either offensive in nature such as bypassing or outflanking competitors or defensive such as creating structural barriers through exclusive agreements with suppliers or lobbying for favorable trade policies, will produce reactions from competitors, adversaries, and stakeholders who are adversely affected. These responses are themselves elements of trends that should be captured and used for future strategic analysis. Learning from the tactical decisions that are made can eventually result in reframing of a poor strategic idea or become the basis of insights for making a transient move (McGrath, 2013a) beginning a process of disengaging from an existing strategy and launching a new one.

Operational effectiveness is both a component and derivative of strategy. Porter's (1996) definition of strategy involves creating a unique, sustainable position of providing value through performing activities in a distinctive pattern that cannot be easily duplicated or imitated by competitors without compromising their existing strategic position. Operational effectiveness involves performance activities better than competitors in terms of speed of delivery, level of quality, and/or cost effectiveness. Operational performance and strategy are complementary in that both are required for sustained superior performance, although most operational performance advantages can be imitated and adapted. Sustainable competitive advantage is dependent on strategic positioning. That said strategic shifts invariably require changes in operational competencies across the organization and at various levels, a requirement that is becoming even more necessary in the age of strategy being driven by continuous technological innovation.

Although the HRD pyramid suggests alignment with the traditional hierarchical structure in organizations, it is important to remember that the structure depicted is about the learning challenges of each category and the kind of learning that addresses them. Although there is a loose correspondence between formal organizational structure and the primary learning challenges of each, the learning hierarchy doesn't strictly map onto formal organizational structure. In today's world of rapid change and horizontal lean management processes, strategic learning is needed up and down the formal structure. Depending on the organization and industry, strategic learning may be necessary at several levels of an organization and senior managers may need operational level learning in certain new competencies required by the organization. Getting learning to the right people at right time is a talent management responsibility.

## 7.3    Aligning Individual Competencies, Core Competencies (Functions and Teams), and HRM Systems for Executing Strategic Performance

While formulating strategy is an outside-in process leveraging diverse perspectives on the implications of various trends, mapping any emerging analogies and assessing possible scenarios with the process converging on a strategic focus, once a new strategic focus is articulated, thinking shifts to inside-out thinking, addressing the changes necessary for effective execution. As Thomas Edison famously said, "vision without execution is hallucination." Execution requires planning and aligning the organization for effective performance. Strategic change invariably produces gaps between the organization's capabilities for delivering on its new value proposition and the competencies necessary for effectively executing its strategy. The extended role of HRD professionals involves facilitating the third and fourth conversations described in Chap. 6 to identify these gaps.

Through the conversations outlined in the strategic learning cycle presented in Chap. 6 (Fig. 6.1), three sets of HRD related needs must be aligned for the direction of the organization to be successfully derived: (1) the individual and organizational core competencies necessary for successfully implementing and sustaining the strategy, (2) individual and organizational connections and focus, and (3) the HR management systems that position and focus people for organizational performance. Each of these three is imperative for successful execution of the strategy and must be aligned with the other. Realizing this alignment requires learning and development (L&D), organizational development (OD), and human resource management (HRM) interventions, including:

- L&D interventions to develop necessary individual level competencies in support of the strategy (e.g., targeted learning journeys to upskill the workforce on emerging technology like cloud and blockchain);
- L&D and OD interventions to address gaps in organizational and group core competencies (e.g., team learning skills and compatible cultural norms facilitating the formation of horizontal cross-functional teams for efficient coordination of developing new product development systems);
- OD interventions to align key organizational functions (e.g., structural reorganization for enhancing applications of sales related technologies being made available to customers);
- OD/L&D interventions to address team learning and aligning individuals;
- HRM/Talent Management interventions to align the organization and individuals in support of implementing the strategy (e.g., modifying reward and talent acquisition practices.

These interventions involve the systemic interplay of L&D, OD, and HRM as described in Chap. 1. This coordination can increasingly be supported through AI applications described in Chap. 4, Digitalization, Artificial Intelligence, and Strategic HRD.

### 7.3.1   Building Core Competencies as Part of Strategic Alignment

At the organizational level of the HRD pyramid, core competencies and functional alignment are often highly interdependent of one another. Organizational core competencies are typically embedded in the culture of the organization becoming evident in the interactions between members in particular situations. The reorganizations that typically accompany strategic changes may disrupt existing core competencies as new work roles and relationships evolve informal working relationships between members of the organization. Strategic change often involves changes in the formal organizational structure as well. Existing capabilities are thought about in new ways, often becoming segmented into new pieces and redistributed to different parts of the organization to form new capabilities, unintentionally creating new barriers to cooperation. The complexities of these reorganizations are illustrated by a conversation that one of the authors had many years ago with a design engineer following a major restructuring at General Motors. He stated that one problem he still had involved:

> "...to follow the organizational chart...It used to be I could call over to [technical]...and get what I needed; now they don't even exist as a unit any more...they have been absorbed elsewhere. All I can do is follow channels; it takes forever and going back and forth several times to get the information or change I need."

Although the engineer hadn't thought of it in these terms, as we explored his experience it became clear that the reorganization had not only changed the formal structure of the company, but also it had disrupted informal ways of operating. In this particular instance, core competencies around product development were embedded in the relationships, between product design engineers, and those who developed the manufacturing system. Through his experience in working on past product design projects, questions would emerge in his mind about the capacity of the manufacturing system and he would collaborate informally with his colleagues in that area. The answers for these questions were not provided in formal training materials or production documents, but they were important for keeping the process working efficiently. Having cross-functional conversations such as these were an importance competency. In most organizations, performance is a product of both formal and informal relationships. Further, while core competencies are organizational attributes, they are built on the foundations of individual competencies that are directly related to exercising organizational core competencies. Many of these competences are learned informally through individuals being socialized into the organization. As an L&D executive said to one of the authors during a discussion on the impacts of people leaving the organization, many times important knowledge and capabilities that they have learned over time are not documented in formal descriptions of skills sets necessary for effective job performance. One lesson from this is that during the alignment phase, and following execution, talent management professionals need to continue monitoring the impacts of the change process on formal as well informal relationships.

Another key intervention is establishing learning groups for facilitating the development of necessary core competencies. Developing core competencies requires intensive interaction over time—often developing the individual level competencies in concert with establishing the holding environment and conceptual framework within which organizational level core competencies emerge. These learning-oriented interventions can be forms of what Popper and Lipshitz (1998) have called "dedicated organization learning mechanisms" simultaneously developing both individual competencies and organizational core competencies or, returning to Popper & Lipshitz's terminology, "learning in organization" and "learning by organization." Action learning programs and cross-functional task forces framed as tasks and learning groups are examples of these learning interventions. Particular attention needs to be paid to facilitating transfer of learning (discussed in Chap. 8) from the group experiences in the programs to their groups when back in the workplace. Consistent with effective transfer of learning practices, many of these interventions need to precede execution of the strategy and be initiated early in the alignment process.

Equally important to note is that developing core competencies requires more than L&D and OD programs. Support from HRM systems such as Reward and Performance Evaluation systems are important for both reinforcing desired behavior and sending informal messages about what is considered important. These changes in HRM systems can require supporting learning interventions if managers are going to use them appropriately in practice for these informal messages are going to be communicated. Just as training alone is insufficient for changing behavior so is just changing these systems if managers don't have the appropriate skills for implementing them.

Additionally, strategic change often requires changing job profiles to allow recruiting to bring the necessary new competencies into the organization. However, often times, new staff acquisition processes that bring desired skills into the organization, must still be supplemented by developing the core competencies needed for effectively executing the strategy internally among the existing workforce. Although the mix of competencies will have changed, people and teams must learn how to work together. The capability for exhibiting core competencies needs to take place through embedding them into the organization's culture.

### 7.3.2   Gaps in Strategically Critical Individual Skills and Competencies

In addition to core competencies, organizations typically need to build new skills and competencies at the individual employee level that are not linked to organizational level capabilities but are still required for the success of the new strategy. This is particularly true in the age of the fourth industrial revolution (4IR) in which disruptive new technologies are central to repositioning businesses to serve clients, deliver products/services, and do so in an efficient and resilient manner. So organizations undertaking strategic changes—driven by emerging technologies or other internal/external marketplace factors—typically translate into new competency profiles for the kind of talent required. Sourcing that talent profile is often satisfied in part through recruiting new staff, and in part through reskilling and upskilling existing staff, so they are able to execute new/modified tasks in accordance with the performance criteria defined as part of the new business strategy.

Conducting a needs analysis that links skills and competencies to role and job requirements driven by a strategic change is a specific HRD talent management initiative with the purpose of surfacing existing gaps that need to be addressed. Assisted and augmented AI can help target some of these gaps through connecting staff performance with work history profiles, again another point of coordination between HRD practices and IT. Addressing these gaps is imperative for successful execution of strategy. These analyses begin when entering the alignment phase and continue through the initial execution process. We turn now to the tactical and operational levels of the HRD Pyramid and the learning needs that emerge as strategy are executed.

## 7.4   Emerging Learning Needs Through Tactical and Operational Actions

Execution of strategy provides three particular opportunities for learning from the tactical and operational actions taken. First is conducting after-action reviews following the initiation of any major initiatives derived from the strategy while the experience is fresh in everyone's mind. Facilitated with a diverse group of staff from different groups and levels of responsibility, with rank and prestige put aside and the focus being on listening and dialogue, such reviews can increase the effectiveness of future initiatives. These after-action reviews should also conclude with a process of reflection and dialogue on how the review itself went. Second is conducting periodic reviews of leading and lagging indicators of performance across the organization. These too should be focused on learning, and explore what's behind the numbers, initially surfacing divergent explanations for what is driving the results, then testing these attributions with others and with additional data and making adjustments. This learning can be captured for the organization as best practices. The third learning opportunity, also from systematic reviews of performance, is the emergence of previously unrecognized skill deficiencies adding to previously conducted needs analysis. When a more systematic needs assessment determines, the performance issues are linked to lack of competencies, knowledge, and experience and a learning solution can be developed and proposed or changes in staffing profiles for recruitment put in place.

Surfacing and addressing each of these three sources of performance related learning needs follow the principles of the Kolb learning cycle presented in Chap. 2. This cycle needs to be followed by engaging members of the organization as process of collaborative action inquiry, capturing and documenting the learning for the organization that guides subsequent actions. Figure 7.2 provides an elaborated version of the learning cycle—learning from tactical and operational action. One learning outcome that can result from reflecting on tactical and operational actions

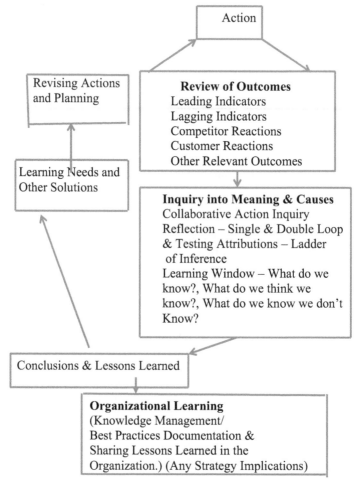

**Fig. 7.2** The elaborated learning cycle: learning from tactical and operational actions (Yorks, 2005, p. 232)

is the identification of additional gaps or needs in the skills of organizational members. Also, independent of the reflection process managers may approach the L&D or OD functions for assistance in addressing performance issues at either the organizational or the individual level. In either case, it is important that the HRD/talent management professional engages the participants in a process of inquiry around the causes of discrepancies between expected and actual performance. We turn now to a diagnostic framework for addressing performance issues.

## 7.5    A Framework for Diagnosing Performance Issues

Managers and others often approach talent management professionals requesting training for staff to address some pressing problem in their workforce. Although training may be the right solution often it's not. The manager's request can be of function of their seeing training as the only solution, or as a "safe" solution providing evidence that the manager took action and that the responsibility for changing the performance of the staff member, or members, now lays with L&D. When approached with this request, HRD professionals need to apply a diagnostic framework to systematically work through the problem and to discuss with the managers involved. HRD professionals can also take the initiative to begin such conversations with management when they observe a recognized performance problem in the organization using the diagnostic framework as a basis for the conversation.

When conducting these conversations, it is important to avoid confusing symptoms and problems. A symptom is a set of events or behaviors associated with poor performance like low productivity, poor service ratings, late reports or response time, quality issues, or morale-related issues such as attendance or general deportment. These performance issues might manifest at the organizational level, group level, or with a particular individual. Initial investigation into the performance issue typically reveals poor communication, planning, self or group disorganization, or skills and competencies. While managers often refer to these types of issues as problems, i.e., "we have a communication problem" or "a planning problem," they are typically *symptoms* of more fundamental *problems* that must be addressed by *appropriate solutions* if performance is going to improve. Figure 7.3 presents a diagnostic sequence for guiding the conversation consistent with the Kolb learning cycle.

The first step in the cycle is inquiring into the problematic situation and then continuing to work through the symptoms (step two), identifying the underlying problem (step three), and matching the problem with a solution. As the solution is implemented, outcomes in terms of the impact on the problem situation are tracked for any new insights regarding symptoms and necessary reframing of the problem and changes to the solution. Using this framework requires field research skills, for descriptively identifying symptoms, connecting the symptoms to problems, and the problems to relevant solutions. Attention validity issues around personal bias given that the researcher is embedded in the organization and has his or her own preferences regarding how work is being conducted in the problematic performance

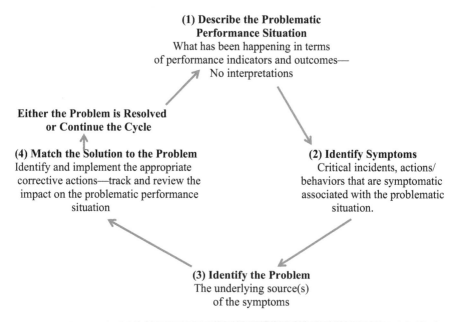

**Fig. 7.3** A diagnostic learning cycle sequence for addressing problematic performance

situation and personal preferences for solutions. In some ways, this is potentially an action research process, especially when the initial implementation of solutions leads to additional symptoms being surfaced. The capability for using the diagnostic framework is an important management skill that should be included in management development initiatives. We will return to the process of linking the stages, especially symptoms with problems. First, however we turn

to step three of the process, identifying the problem.

### 7.5.1   Identifying the Problem

As previously stated above, it is important not to confuse symptoms with the underlying problem; symptoms are essentially manifestations of the underlying problem. Six categories of underlying problems have been identified (Yorks, 2005) based on both the literature and extensive experience:

**Systems:** Problematic performance can be a function of the capacity and alignment of the systems, processes, and formal structures within which individuals and functions work. These include technology-based systems that are not aligned in ways necessary for completing processes that are cross-functional, lack of access to or sloppy communication networks, digitally intelligent systems that inappropriately make changes that are wrong, or the need for structural organizational change in reporting relationships and/or job design for improving productivity or quality of service or products.

**Others:** A performance problem on the part of one person, group, or function may actually be rooted or caused by performance problems on the part of another person, group, or function. As anyone working within a sequential process where they are building on or carrying forward work initiated by others knows, the quality of their work depends on the performance of those who are passing down information or components down the line. In some instances, symptoms of poor performance can be the result of poor supervision or management. When "others" emergences as the source, or part of the source, of the problem, the diagnostic process needs to switch to the other for identifying the problem. Many times this also requires management interventions.

**Knowledge and/or Experience:** Lack of formal training and/or relevant experience for adequately performing certain role and task responsibilities. Scheduled training, either online or in person workshops, or coaching are common ways of addressing this problem. When appropriate setting up peer partnerships can work to for learning and development; also providing access to information sources. When appropriate, setting up peer partnerships can be a very useful and effective way for providing learning and development. Also, access to information sources for self-directed learning can be effective for addressing this problem.

**Motivation:** Is a function of how interested a person or group is in their work (intrinsic motivation) and/or their desired outcomes (extrinsic motivation), typically the rewards they are or will be receiving. Generally, both are in play, although often one is dominant over the other. Some people work at tasks they don't find particularly interesting, but chose to do the work because they need the income it provides, or are able to pursue activities they are interested in because of their income. In other situations, people aren't necessary pleased or motivated by their rewards, but enjoy or are committed to the work. Addressing this problem can be complex and also often requires HR interventions such as reassigning people, dismissing them or changes in policy. Also, motivation issues are sometimes interconnected with the other problem areas. We will discuss this in more detail following our description of the final two potential problem areas.

**Personality:** This problem is mostly one at the individual level in most conventional work situations. Personality problems arise when a person has a trait or personal characteristic that is negatively influencing his or her interactions with others. These might be co-workers, customers, key providers in other areas of the organization, to identify a few. His or her behavior could be a function of their cognitive style, habits, and or personal beliefs. Sometimes these traits are only problematic in certain aspect of their job but contribute to their effectiveness in other aspects. Either way it is an issue related to their personal fit for the job. Although typically an individual problem, it can manifest in groups where a particular function has been biased by the personality preferences of the manager and his or her personal selections.

**Aptitude:** A lack of the innate ability for doing the job. This problem is most relevant at the individual level of performance although it can emerge across numerous people in a function or across functions as a result of

organizational restructuring or the implementation of new technologies changing the content of jobs. This particularly can happen as new artificial intelligence technology is applied across organizations. In addressing these
situations, careful diagnostic assessment needs to be made between lack of
training or experience vs. aptitude.

As previously written by Yorks (2005, p. 235), these six categories extend Victor
Vroom's seminal theoretical framework that a person's performance ($P$) is a function ($f$) of ability ($A$) × motivation ($M$) stated as $P = f(A \times M)$ as follows:

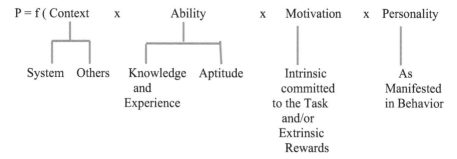

This extended framework can be applied for assessing performance problems at
both the individual and group level.

As implied above, sometimes poor performance is related to the interconnectedness between a couple of the problems. For example, motivation can be
related to how tasks are structured or processes are aligned in the larger system.
While the initial diagnosis might point toward motivation, addressing it might
require changes in organizational systems or processes, particularly if it is an
issue for more than one individual. Hence the underlying problem is systems,
which are impacting people's motivation; a problem requiring solutions dating
back to the job enrichment movement in the 1960s and 1970s. On the other
hand, the systems may be well designed with innovative technologies requiring
changes in staffing. Another connection to systems can be problems regarding
knowledge and/or aptitude that are not attended to as continuous changes occur
over time.

With regard to the implementation of AI technologies this framework provides a
lens through which pre-planning for the possible impact of implementating a system change might initially have on people's performance. Implementation of AI is
increasingly changing the context and required abilities of those whose roles are
being changed by augmented, and eventually autonomous, intelligence. AI obviously changes the system, but also leads to changes in required abilities, and possibility motivation as roles are changed. These are the most likely problem categories
to be interactively impacted by AI although these interconnections will vary across
different work settings and among individuals. The diagnostic framework to depict
this interconnectedness is

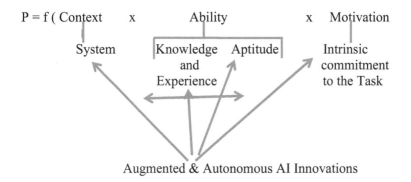

$$P = f (\text{ Context} \quad x \quad \text{Ability} \quad x \quad \text{Motivation}$$

System        Knowledge   Aptitude        Intrinsic
              and                          commitment
              Experience                   to the Task

Augmented & Autonomous AI Innovations

Of course, while this interconnectedness of problem categories often is created as a result of implementing new digital intelligences, sometimes the problem is connected to one of the categories, particularly motivation or knowledge and experience. For example, new technology may have been well designed and tested for enhancing performance, and training and technical support has been successfully applied, but some employees might not be as motivated as a result of how it has impacted their role. In another instance, there is no problem with the design of the new digitally intelligent system and the employee is very motivated, but the training and support has been inadequate.

## 7.5.2   Connecting Problems with Solutions

As the narrative above makes clear, diagnosing the problem is the pivotal step in the learning cycle for addressing problematic performance (Fig. 7.3—Step 3). Once the problem has been identified, then the pathway to solutions has been opened. The process of developing workable solutions points back to the three sectors of HRD practice: (a) Human Resource Management, (b) Learning and Development, and (c) Organizational Development, described in Chap. 2, The Scope of Human Resource Development (Fig. 1.1), and how these disciplines are becoming increasingly interconnected. Depending on the situation, a system problem can require coordination between HR talent management and technology functions anticipating any talent acquisition and learning and development needs. For some performance problems, the need for additional or different kinds of training is given emphasis, but what is overlooked is the need for systemic changes in organizational culture.

An example is the emphasis being given to the need for additional police training as a result of the disclosures of racially charged brutalities by police in the United States. While additional training for using alternative tactics when engaged in an emotionally charged event, the question is what kinds of training, how will it be delivered, and what systemic changes need to be made for facilitating training transfer. Also, the role of motivation needs to be considered. Moreover, as some proposals for change have noted, what structural changes need to be made such as moving some responsibilities to other social institution settings and changing the scope of the kinds of events to which police are expected to respond. Equally, attention needs to be paid to the culture of law enforcement agencies and the broader culture that has shaped them which by extension also impacts motivation.

While policing is a broad and complex societal issue, it compasses the kinds of interconnections that need to be addressed regarding many behavioral based performance problems. As previously mentioned, going through the learning process depicted in Fig. 7.3 can be considered a process of action inquiry. If the first time through the cycle the problem is resolved, then one can move on. However, if the performance issue has not been resolved, then there is a need for assessing what can be learned from the process and the action inquiry process is repeated. This starts with description of what, if anything has changed, document what has been learned and dig deeper into the diagnostic process.

These inquiries can be carried out by the HRD professional or in collaboration with line managers working as a project team. This process may evolve as the learning cycle is implemented. Initially, HRD professionals may collect data inquiring into the problematic performance situation and clarifying the symptoms, then collaborate with line management for identifying the problem. In the case of a performance problem with an individual manager, this collaboration would be one on one, but when addressing a function level performance problem, a team may be created. As discussed in Chap. 5, analytics and metrics are often an important part of this process, especially for addressing performance problems at the functional or department levels of the organization. However, qualitative field research skills are important as well for gaining a deeper understanding of the dynamics underlying the metrics. This includes good questioning and listening skills, probing by asking open ended questions for descriptions of what has been happening and surfacing the assumptions being made. Double loop learning is an important part of steps 1 and 2 of the learning cycle. Additionally, both the HRD professional and managers should be engaging in triple loop learning for surfacing awareness of their own interactions with the situation and how unintended bias may be impacting the process or their interpretation of it. As Bill Torbert and Associates (2004) have described, this is an important part of the action inquiry process. Building the skills of the action inquiry process into management development processes is an important part of the leadership development process.

## 7.6    Examples of HRM, L&D, and Organization Development in Action for Strategically Leveraging AI

A global, leading asset, and wealth management firm developed an equities platform to perform portfolio research and quantitative analysis for portfolio construction, leveraging the latest in artificial intelligence, specifically natural language processing (NLP). By combining cutting-edge natural language processing technology with 30+ years of historical data, including micro- and macro-economic data, the capability provides a single launch point for investment professionals at the asset management firm, setting them apart from their peers by enabling access to real-time market data and marrying that with a vast set of embedded analytics, supporting capabilities for a myriad of investment strategies, and an extensive set of dashboards. It generates ~1500 daily reports covering ~3000 securities using 300+ industry benchmarks and indices.

The value to the business is multiple fold, in terms efficiencies saved from what would be traditionally human analysis hours, as well as the speed and pace at which analytics can be performed and turned into powerful insights for action (e.g., minutes vs. days or weeks). New, richer data sets can be used as source materials, scanned and interpreted almost seamlessly, and integrated into the overarching portfolio construction suggestions. Investment professionals can also begin to be measured on their efficacy in leveraging the new equities NLP enabled platform to scale their decision-making and timeliness, e.g., they should be more accurate and more insightful in their insights due to the broader data set, and more real-time in their decision timeframes. The build out of this capability alone is a prime example of strategic HRD principles at work. The global equities platform was designed by bringing together deep technical engineering talent, with experienced investment advisors and portfolio managers—forcing a reconstruction of how teams operate to build out new firm-wide capabilities and maintain/enhance them over time. It is a prime example of organizational strategic change, to deliver on a cutting-edge business strategy, and operate that platform, month over month, for clients around the world.

## 7.7 Summary

This chapter has described how learning and development competencies are foundational for strategy development and learning for tactical and operational changes. The strategic learning process is contextualized within the political economy of the organization and necessary core competencies for initiating strategic learning have been presented. Interconnections between HR based policies, learning and development interventions, and organization development initiatives comprise the essence of HRD practice, along with increasing coordination with the technology function in organizations. Especially in the age of the fourth industrial revolution in which artificial intelligence has created a continuously changing workplace HRD professionals must be strategically engaged in anticipating and addressing potential performance problems being triggered by these changes as the workforce has to adjust. In particular, changes in systems, new competencies, and impacts on the motivation of the workforce need to be assessed. Using the diagnostic framework $P = f$ (Context $\times$ Ability $\times$ Motivation $\times$ Personality) provides a pathway for addressing potential and existing performance problems and thinking through appropriate solutions as organizations continue to further develop augmented intelligence and roles in the workforce continue to evolve.

# References

McGrath, R. G. (2013a). Transient advantage. *Harvard Business Review, 91*(6), 63–70.

Popper, M., & Lipshitz. (1998). Organizational learning mechanisms: A structural and cultural approach to organizational learning. *Journal of Applied Behavioral Science, 34*(2), 161–179.

Porter, M. (1996). What is strategy? *Harvard Business Review, 74*(6), 61–78.

Torbert, B. and Associates (2004). Action Inquiry: The Secret to Timely and Transforming Leadership. Berrett-Koehler Publishers.

Yorks, L. (2005). *Strategic human resource development*. Thompson South-Western.

# Transfer of Learning: The Path that Connects Learning to Performance

Providing learning interventions is at the heart of HRD practices, from onboarding people joining the workforce to continuing to develop them for advanced productivity and career progression. If learning interventions are going to provide value to the organization, they must translate into improved individual and organizational performance. Learning transfer refers to the extent to which the individual or team applies their learning beyond the learning event itself. This learning can be changed in knowledge, insight, understanding, meaning, attitudes, competencies, behaviors, and they may or not be connected depending on the goal/purpose of the learning intervention. Ultimately, the returns on investment for these learning and development interventions depend on whether the individual or team is able to transfer their learning to their workplace practices.

Learning transfer is an especially challenging issue for executive and management development because as Dennis Laker (1990) noted there is "tremendous leeway in what a manager or supervisor needs to know and the contexts in which he or she might apply that knowledge" (p. 219). While true in the 1990s, it's even more so in today's complex world with broader-scale and more complex technology in use across the workplace. Creating the conditions that facilitate learning transfer is a critical part of HRD practice. Doing so requires going beyond the design of learning interventions per se although these designs impact if and how learning is transferred. It involves constructing larger scaffolding around learning events and processes, by broadening how learning design is conceptualized, and integrating design of learning events with the larger workplace context. While the way learning and development is delivered has also evolved and expanded from primarily classrooms to online technologies, action learning programs, and coaching, so has the understanding of learning transfer evolved. Additionally, the incidental learning employees experience can be leveraged through paying attention to how that learning can be transferred to other situations in the workplace.

Originally transfer of learning was conceptualized as "training transfer," defined as the extent to which what is learned in training is applied to the job and enhances

L. Yorks et al., *Strategic Human Resource Development in Practice*, Management for Professionals, https://doi.org/10.1007/978-3-030-95775-9_8

job-related performance (Wexley & Latham, 1981). Timothy Baldwin and Kevin Ford (1988) argued that transfer of learning from a training program involved learned behavior being "generalized to the job context and maintained over a period of time on the job" (1988, p. 63). While these points are still valid for learning taking place in classrooms and workshops, the term training is used in a more limited way today as traditional training programs have become less used for many kinds of learning initiatives and replaced by more experiential and personalized learning initiatives. Concurrent with this use of different ways of providing developmental learning through a growing emphasis on mentoring, coaching, and various forms of experiential learning, the focus on transfer expanded in the 1990s with transfer being framed as a process (Foxon, 1993, 1994), not a singular occurrence. Rather the learning transfer process was being defined and researched "as a case of related activities occurring before, during, and after training" (Yelon & Ford, 2016, p. 201). This transition is being accelerated by the applications of technologies providing for learning in "real time" on the job (Marsick et al., 2022). We return to these processes further below, but first we begin with a description of the foundational conceptualizations of learning transfer.

## 8.1   Defining Learning Transfer

While the definition of learning transfer is rather straightforward, there are a number of dimensions to the concept of learning transfer. In 1989, Gavriel Salomon and David Perkins made the distinction between low-road transfer and high road transfer. Low-road transfer involves the learners being trained in a very specific set of skills/behaviors such as computer skills, legal aspects of administrative work, or brainstorm practices for solving problems, which can then be applied on the job with little if any modification. For example, low-road transfer is the intention of some forms of supervisory and customer service training that is focused on behavioral practices and actions to keep interactions and conversations on target and avoiding legal problems. These include disciplinary conversations with employees in which supervisors learn the "broken record" technique to stay focused on the problem at hand and avoid arguing over the difficulties in an employee's life and repeat saying "Ok, but what do you need to do to get to work on time?" no matter what excuses the employee offers.

Salomon and Perkins contrast this kind of transfer with high road transfer where the learner applies a generally known principle to a new situation through mindful abstraction from the learning context to other situations. Management and supervisory development programs, in which the intention is the cultivation of cognitive and interpersonal skills for managing higher level and more complicated problems, require high road transfer. They further differentiate between "forward reaching high road transfer" and "backward reaching high road transfer." Forward reaching high road transfer involves setting aside time and specific experiences; "the principle is so well learned in the first place as a general principle that it simply suggests itself appropriately on later occasions" (1989, pp. 118–119). In backward reaching high road transfer, the learner mindfully looks backward into his or her past experiences for matches. Backward reaching high road transfer has several characteristics of what Earl Butterfield and Gregory Nelson (1989) describe as "far transfer"; the ability to think and take action in diverse, complex, and uncertain contexts. Holton III and Baldwin (2003) build on the notion of transfer distance, describing it as a six-step process: the first three steps, the learner moves from "knowing that" to "know how," to building capability through practice; in the second three steps that involve work-based processes, the learner applies the learning to maintaining and generalizing (far transfer).

With these distinct kinds of learning transfer established, research and modeling of the transfer process became the focus of attention for understanding how transfer could be more contextually understood. The distinction between low-road and high road transfer became refined further as result by the differences in the kind of skills or competencies that are being transmitted to the learner; "hard skills (technical skills that involve working with equipment, data, software, etc.) and soft skills (intrapersonal personal skills such as one's ability to manage oneself as well as interpersonal skills such as how one handles one's interactions with others)" (Laker & Powell, 2011, p.112). For reasons that will be discussed, hard skills are more likely to be transferred to the job than soft skills. Further, these different kinds of skills influence the extent to which learning is being provided through technology in the workplace.

## 8.2 Learning Transfer from a System Perspective

Three streams of research supported the ongoing development of conceptual distinctions between kinds of learning transfer during the 1990s (Holton III & Baldwin, 2003). The first stream focused on training design factors that influence transfer. The second stream focused on how the organizational context impacts the ability of learners to apply what they learned. The third stream focused on the individual characteristics that the learner brings to the learning event.

Connecting the three streams, Holton and Baldwin developed a model to depict the points in the process that facilitate learning transfer:

- The learner's individual characteristics that comprise their personal readiness for learning—*motivation, existing abilities,* and *prior experience;*
- The two organizational level intervention points—(1) *pre-program orientation of learners to the learning event* (how the learning event is framed in terms of purpose and rational) and (2) *post-program support and leveraging of their learning*;
- The two individual level intervention points—(1) *pre-program preparation* (prework) and (2) *post-program follow-up and maintenance* (activities).
- The final factor in their model is the *content* and *design* of the learning event itself. Holton and Baldwin's model illustrates how the overall context and design constitute the process that eventually determines the outcome in terms of the *learning* that actually occurs, subsequent *application* of the learning, and *performance results.*

The learning transfer system frames the broader learning ecosystem that needs to be considered when planning for learning interventions to enhance individual and organization performance. While content and design of the learning event remain important, it is one of several elements that learning and development professionals need to address for the delivery of successful learning that translate into improved performance through learning transfer. The model also shifted the focus from solely on the learner and the design of the training program to the learner's journey through the systematic process. The motivation of the learner is a significant factor underlying this journey.

### 8.2.1   Motivation to Transfer—The Learner Characteristic Driving Transfer of Learning

Particular attention has been given to the learner's motivation to apply what he or she learned and how the larger context influenced his or her motivation. As initial research into particular elements in the transfer system was being conducted (e.g., Egan et al., 2004; Velada et al., 2007), motivation to transfer was coming to be seen as an essential element for transfer to take place (Burke & Hutchins, 2007; Gegenfurtner et al., 2009) playing a mediating role between the components in the transfer system (Grohmann et al., 2014; Massenberg et al., 2015).

Building on the research identifying motivation as central to learning transfer, and the need for examining the impact on learning transfer of the pre- and post-training transfer system elements (Grossman & Salas, 2011), Ann-Christine Massenberg, Eva-Maria, Schulte, and Simone Kauffeld (2017) did studies on the effect of transfer system factors on motivation to transfer *before* and *after* training programs. Conducted as part of a mandatory manager-training program for line managers in the headquarters of a German-speaking financial and insurance company. Comprised of two parts, each lasting 2 days, with the second part taking place 3 months after the first part. Part I focused on their roles as supervisors, including making the most of the resources they had available to them, basics in coaching employees for success, and knowing and managing themselves. Part 2 expanded on coaching practices, their interactions with employees, managing difficult situations, growing the talent in their teams, and maximizing team performance. The variables were statistically analyzed using the German Learning Transfer System inventory (GLTSI) (Bates et al., 2007; Bates et al., 2012; Kauffeld et al., 2008). Consistent with prior research studies (e.g., Quinones, 1995; Weissbein et al., 2011) among the findings that stood out was that time spent before the training started was important for the trainees developing motivation to transfer before attending the sessions. Also, "different factors have a positive impact on motivation to transfer before the training than after" and "surprisingly, more learning transfer system factors before the training (6 of 13 factors) than after the training (3 of 15 factors) predicted motivation to transfer, which underpins the importance of taking the time before the training starts into account" (Massenberg et al. p. 74). Specifically and consistent with prior research (Broad, 2005; Chang & Chiang, 2013; and Tannenbaum et al., 1991), readiness, self-efficacy, and supervisor support emerged as "important factors before the training program" (Massenberg et al., 2017, p. 75).

The implications for practice are significant in that they draw attention to the need for talent management professionals to work with learners before the formal program to have them think about the opportunities for applying what they will be learning and how it can benefit them. "Opportunity to use and transfer effort-performance expectations before the training program showed positive relationships with motivation to transfer" (Massenberg, et al. 2017, p. 75). Also spend time having the learners clarify their goals and objectives in terms of what they want to take away from the training and be able to apply in their job. This stream of research also points to the value of post-program review and providing supervisor and peer support. Post-program review should take place beyond right at the conclusion of the training event; anywhere from 2 or 3 months to longer in order to assess the extent and sustainability of how learning is being transferred. While pre-program support is highly influential on motivation to transfer, this doesn't negate the importance of post-program support as well. Managers of those having participated in learning programs and initiatives have to be supportive of the learners' efforts to apply their learning after the program.

Research into the various pre- and post-program variables needs to continue as there is still much to learn about the interconnections between the various factors that comprise the learning transfer system and how these interconnections vary with regard to different kinds and topics of learning interventions. Additionally, a range of data collection methods need to be used including a more human "consumer-centric inquiry" (Baldwin et al., 2017), that focuses on understanding the context and lived experience of the learners. While in no way diminishing the value of statistical analysis demonstrating the predictability of outcomes derived from the correlations, regression, and path & structural equation analysis, they "propose the need to examine 'how' to enhance or optimize transfer, rather than simply describing the 'what' of relationships between the predictor and transfer constructs" (p. 21). Their argument in many ways parallels the points made in the Harvard Business Review article by Christian Madsbjerg and Mikkel Rasmussen (2014), *An Anthropologist Walks into a Bar,* demonstrating the value of qualitative field research for understanding drops and/or up-ticks in performance outcome measures, by understanding the dynamics behind the numbers. Assessment of the impact of learning interventions should use mixed methods using qualitative methods for fostering understanding of the enablers and impediments of how learning is being transferred.

Additionally, Baldwin et al. (2017) also raise the importance of further research (and by extension supervising practitioners) considering the motives of trainers. "…in most extant transfer studies, it is unstated what, if anything, trainers are held accountable for—satisfaction of the trainees, learning standards, transfer outcomes, or just filling seats" (p. 19). How the trainers assess the "accountability demands" they must meet also shapes the way in which they focus and deliver their training which, by extension, influences the degree of learning transfer that takes place.

## 8.2.2   Learning Content—Hard or Soft Skills/Competencies

Returning to the distinction between "hard" and "soft" skills, as previously mentioned hard skills are more likely to be transferred. Laker and Powell (2011) present 10 differences between hard and soft skills training that impact the prospects of learning transfer as:

> Trainees learning soft skills, as compared with learning hard skills, are more likely to be adversely affected by (a) prior learning and experience, (b) their own resistance, (c) organizational resistance, (d) less managerial support and greater managerial resistance, (e) difficulty in identifying training needs and objectives, (f) less immediate and less salient feedback and consequences, (g) less similarity between training and work or work environment, (h) a lesser degree of immediate and subsequent proficiency in using their training (mastery), (i) a lesser degree of self-efficacy, and (j) differences in the trainers and methods of instruction (p. 114).

Even if some learners are not enthusiastic, or even upset, about changes being made in technology or machines and work processes, they can see the need for learning necessary hard skills as they directly relate to the ability to execute their job. As a consequence, the motivation to learn exists regardless of their level of enthusiasm for the changes. Additionally, the learning needs and objectives are clearly focused and defined. The learning process itself typically involves hands on practice overseen by instructors who are well skilled themselves. Feedback is immediately experienced through successful or failed application, and managers of the participants also see the need for the training. Transfer back on the job is typically "low-level transfer." These conditions are in contrast to learning interventions focused on soft skills that essentially involves working with humans and introduces or advocates for responses that may differ from the habits and beliefs of the learner. Further, immediate needs may be unclear from the perspective of the learner, even if formal objectives are set. Additionally, the settings in which the content of the learning is to be applied can vary which has implications for both the design of the learning experience and how outcomes are assessed. As previously mentioned, this is especially true in the case of managers and executives who typically must apply influencing and conflict resolution, collaboration, team and group process, constructive feedback, and other skills in a wide range of diverse settings with subordinates, superiors, customers, external stakeholders, and the like requiring high road transfer. Even when the learner is highly motivated, developing embedded competence in the skills requires long term practice to overcome one's habitual patterns of behavior.

## 8.2.3   An Adapted Learning Transfer System Model

Returning to Holton and Baldwin's model of the learning transfer system, the importance of post-program support is often problematic. If the skills and approaches being developed are not appreciated and even modeled by the learner's manager, the likely hood of transfer is reduced as the skills and practices are devalued in the learners work setting. Research conducted into transfer also identifies peers as having an impact on transfer (Burke & Hutchins, 2008; Chiaburu & Marinova, 2005; Jellema et al., 2006). More broadly, the workplace climate is a factor in determining the degree of transfer that occurs (Martin, 2010). Climate, which is driven in part by HRM practices and various elements of an organization's culture Kontoghiorghes, 2001; Lim & Morris, 2006) including what behaviors are valued or accepted, shapes how the learners' supervisors and peers respond to the learners' efforts to apply their learning on the job. This is consistent with research on the work environment being a support for learning transfer (Gaudine & Saks, 2004; Lim & Morris, 2006), particularly supervisor support (Gaudine & Saks, 2004).

Based on a survey of 139 professional training associates or managers, along with a comprehensive integrative literature review, Lisa Burke and Holly Hutchins (2008) have proposed a model of transfer that integrates their findings with existing training transfer models, particularly the Baldwin and Ford (1988) and the Broad (2005) models (see Fig. 9.1). In their model, the design and content of the learner's work and jobs, the training content that is being provided, and the size and structure of the organization are contextual moderating variables shaping five distinct categories influencing learning transfer: *Learner characteristics*, *Trainer Characteristics*, *Design/Delivery of the Learning Material*, the *Work Environment*, and *Evaluation*. Based on these five distinct categories, their model identifies five groupings of stakeholders whose interactions shape the degree of support that exists for learning transfer: These stakeholders impact learning transfer throughout the process.

- *Peers*—co-worker/colleague reinforcement and participation;
- *Trainer*—knowledge of both content and teaching practices combined with professional experience and flexibility in working with different learning styles;
- *Trainee*—learner's ability, motivation, experience;
- *Supervisor*—supportive providing feedback on applications;
- *Organization*—broadly influences transfer through the climate: situations and consequences that inhibit or facilitate use of what has been learned either directly or indirectly.

In addressing the temporal dimensions in their model, Burke and Hutchins argue that transfer strategies "go beyond the classic before, during, and after phases to reflect that transfer strategies can work across all these phases (Broad, 2005) and thus are not time-bound" (p. 121). Support for transfer is not a matter of a specific time point in the process but is "iterative and pervasive" throughout the design, delivery, post-program process with the stakeholders interacting throughout. They write:

> This proposed extension to transfer models is consistent with a growing systems perspective on transfer, which suggests transfer should be considered throughout the entire instructional design process (see Holton III et al., 2000; Kontoghiorghes, 2002; Russ-Eft, 2002). It is also compatible with the workplace learning literature that acknowledges a blurred line between training and continuous on-the-job learning (Baldwin-Evans, 2006; Clarke, 2004).

As the above literature suggests, in many ways the learning transfer system is comprised of interacting subsystems that themselves involve interacting variables that need to be brought into alignment. Realizing this alignment points to the need for integrating selective HRM initiatives and OD with L&D in HRD practices for facilitating learning transfer. In short, facilitating learning transfer involves aligning a complex set of subsystems. This is particularly true with regard to executive and management development practices and the soft skills needed for effective leadership.

### 8.2.4   The 70:20:10 Framework and the Challenges of Alignment for Transfer

The need for aligning these subsystems is made clear by Samantha Johnson, Deborah Blackman, and Fiona Buick's (2018) study of the 70:20:10 framework that emerged during the 1980s and is generally attributed to research conducted at the Center for Creative Leadership by Morgan McCall Jr., Michael M. Lombardo, Ann Morrison, and colleagues, (McCall Jr., 1988). Proposing that 70% of employee, management, and executive development takes place through experiential learning on the job, 20% through social learning involving interactions with supervisors, mentors, peers, and others, and 10% through formal learning programs, the framework has become popular among L&D practitioners in various institutional sectors around the world. Johnson, Blackman, and Buick studied the framework in the Australian public sector. Their research provided examples of all three types of learning, experiential, social, and formal, having made important contributions to the learning and development of middle managers who participated in the study. However, "Participants recognized that for effective transfer of learning of managerial skills into everyday work practices, the formal, experiential and social elements of the 70:20:10 framework should work together and not be undertaken in isolation...their integration is critical for the effective transfer of learning" (Johnson et al., 2018, p. 394). Their research also revealed four misconceptions regarding the framework's elements that obstructed learning transfer:

1. *Assuming that unstructured experiential learning automatically results in developing capability;*
2. *Defining social learning very narrowly, failing to recognize the role social learning has in integrating the three elements;*
3. *Expecting that formal training and development will automatically change the behavior of managers without any active support pre-during-post the formal training process;*
4. *Not recognizing the need for a plan integrating the relationship between experiential, social, and formal learning for learning transfer back to the workplace to occur.*

The importance of establishing processes that integrate these elements and conceptualizing social learning as playing a pivotal role is important given that it occurs beyond networking with co-workers and other peers, social networking, and being mentored. Drawing on Bandura (1977), they note that social learning also occurs outside of these activities through everyday observations of others, imitating and modeling them. When observing managers who the learner respects and considers successful and seeing behaviors that are the contradict what is being taught in formal learning sessions transfer can be "compromised due to managers adopting the behaviors observed in the workplace, rather than the desired behaviors espoused in formal training programs" (Johnson et al., 2018, p. 395). This points to the need for taking a systems perspective when creating a development plan for staff and managers, taking into consideration what HR practices need to be changed or created, changes needed in organization's culture, and what learning and development practices need to be adopted.

Beyond the need for coordination and integration among the three elements of the 70:20:10 framework, its growing popularity has stimulated debates between researchers regarding the generalizability of the formula. All three factors are important elements for an effective workforce development strategy, but their relative percentage needs to vary by industry, occupation, and specific jobs. Tom Whelan, director of corporate research at training industry, Inc., introduced an alternative framing, OSF [O—on-the-job, S—social, F—formal] (2018a, 2018b), arguing that while "there are companies where 70-20-10 is the right mix—but such companies are not the average. For some companies, the numbers may be 48-23-29 or 56-27-17 or some other combination" ((2018a, 2018b). The right mix changes from company to company and role to role within a company. "There is no single ratio of learning sources that is best for everyone" (Whelan, 2018a, 2018b).

Getting the right mix is important. To make his point Whelan poses the question, "Do you want your surgeon to be learning most of what he or she knows with a scalpel in hand while patients lie on the table? Or would you prefer the surgeon to have undergone extensive formal training in surgical techniques before ever going into the operating room?" With this and other examples, such as airline pilots learning to take off and land the plane or accountants balancing budgets in compliance with regulations, also argues that, again while all three elements are important, sometimes formal education is the most important in preparing people for work [FSO—not OSF in terms of the ratio-based equation]. That point being said, Whelan's examples are addressing the core "hard skills" that are basic to the role, not the development of high-level soft skills. Fostering transfer of high-level soft skills is particularly complex, requiring alignment among the elements of the transfer system regardless of the mix.

## 8.3 Connecting with the Learning Paths of the Learners

While research into the learning transfer system must continue, the concept of the learning paths employees create adds another dimension to the issue of learning transfer. Noting that the learning transfer issue is essentially connected to formal learning initiatives created by the organization that separate the learning from the workplace and makes it hard to be relevant to the daily work situation, Rob Poell and Ferd J. van der Krogt (2010) have called for a pivot that focuses on the learning paths created by the learners. People can, and for the most part do, learn all the time (Billett, 2001; Lave & Wenger, 1991) apart from formal learning initiatives, both informally and incidentally. First introduced by Van Der Krogt in 2007, the learning path concept refers to "a set of learning activities that are both coherent as a whole and meaningful to the employee" (Poell & Van Der Krogt, 2010, p. 217). They use the concept for describing and understanding "how each individual employee makes sense of the multitude of work-based and intentional learning experiences as they move from one such experience to the next in their organizational context" (Poell, 2017, p.11). Even a casual comment from a colleague or customer can be a learning event if the employee attaches meaning to it and reflects on it, or informally seeks additional information or advice from a supervisor, a more experienced employee, go online or register for a formal learning event. Employee learning paths make clear the central role played by social learning

The concept of the learning path connects with the learning transfer system, specifically the motivation to learn in order to improve one's performance or career advancement. The education literature (e.g., Kember et al., 2008) has documented the importance of relevance to the learner's motivation for retention and transfer of learning. The same is true for managers and employees in the workforce. When the content and delivery of learning content, either formally provided or resources that can be informally accessed, are designed to connect to certain skill development needs or various future career opportunities with self-selection possibilities, relevance connects learning content with learning paths. For example, Schneider Electric, a multinational company with 135,000 employees in over 100 countries launched its internal mobility platform in late 2018 to help develop and retain talent. Through this AI-driven platform, employees can access job postings, mentors, training, and temporary projects. Once employees create a talent profile to describe their background (e.g., education, experience, skills) and indicate career aspirations, the platform uses algorithms to match employees with courses and mentors to help close skills gaps, enhance learning, and expand their network within the company (augmented intelligence). Although the tool initially aimed to assist employees with skills development and permanent internal moves, the shifting business priorities caused by the COVID-19 pandemic also helped the company realize the value of this tool to match employees with company-wide short-term projects (aka creating an internal gig economy). The platform allows the company to (re)deploy talent for temporary projects with high speed and agility. Schneider has now rolled out the platform in multiple languages (e.g., English, French, Spanish, and Mandarin), with a goal of reaching approximately 90 percent of its employees in their preferred language across the world.

Consistent with the need for qualitative data regarding the *how* of learning transfer discussed above, conducting periodic or annual discussions with staff of their concerns, challenges and interests in performing their jobs and their role in the organization, can provide insight into desired learning paths. AI can also provide patterns of what initiatives members take to access learning opportunities providing possible insights into learning paths across the workforce, including those who choose to leave. These kinds of data gathering initiatives can inform what learning resources should be made available.

## 8.4    Technology and Learning Transfer

For the past couple of decades, technology has been having an impact on both informal self-directed learning and learning transfer (Hester et al., 2016). The emergence of the web based connected world enables workers to access online training options as needed, information and solutions relevant to challenges confronting them, and connect with peers based on distant locations, expanding opportunities for social learning. The ability to pursue and access these opportunities through various web based options allows individuals to obtain additional support following formal learning interventions, providing post-training support. This access provides opportunities for people to pursue their personal learning paths. More specifically, technology is increasing the opportunity for people to learn while working. With the emerging spread of the electronic performance support systems (EPSSs) in the early twenty-first century, workers (and others) could find answers for problems or address job-related learning needs through help systems provided through the technology. These systems clearly provide support for post-program learning transfer. Internal employee portals also provide increased opportunity for social learning to occur, including peer learning. However, it is also decreasing the issues regarding learning transfer in another way, companies are investing less in formal on-site training program and workshops, replacing them with digital online training for addressing training-relevant issues in the workplace while the employees are working on the job. In short, they are applying their learning immediately on the job and can repeatedly access needed information as they are working.

Returning to the 70:20:10 and OSF frameworks discussed above and the need for getting the mix right, the availability of digital technologies is also changing the ratio in terms of how training is distributed. In their study of 21 senior learning officers in 19 different companies, Abbie Lundberg and George Westerman (2020) found that a privately held food and agriculture business, Cargill, which had allocated its budget ratio in terms of 80% in-person training and 20% digital training was flipping that ratio the other way. A matrix developed by the telecommunications company Deutsche Telekom is designed to help leaders determine whether a training content is best delivered through face-to-face instruction, through digital, or a blended face-to-face and digital delivery. The matrix suggested provides two sets of content related factors be taken into consideration in making the choice:

- Hard skills, simple topics, mandatory training, and durable, reusable material;
- Soft skills, ad hoc training, complex topics, and material that changes frequently.

Purely digital formats are best suited for factors in the first bullet above, while face-to-face or blended formats for the second bullet. Of course, some trainings will involve a mix of the factors, for example, mandatory soft skills training for sales representatives being trained in handling customer services. The matrix also addresses the target audience in terms of its size and geographic distribution (Lundberg & Westerman, 2020, p. 90).

As previously discussed, learning transfer is more challenging when providing learning for soft skills. However, existing technologies are increasingly providing opportunities for designing blended learning experiences that enable spreading the learning across time periods allowing for periods of practice and reflection on the effectiveness of a learner's application of the skills being trained. These include mobile apps the provide leadership questions throughout the day. Some companies are "even exploring the use of artificial intelligence to de develop recommendation engines that, guided by individual and peer behavior, will suggest tailored learning activities to employees" (Lundberg & Westerman, 2020, p. 89). This kind of application of augmented intelligence systems is an example of how machine–human interaction will increasingly be becoming part of the learning & development space in organizations in organizations.

Increasingly, AI will be part of the learning transfer system being integrated into the pre-program, delivery, and post-program phases of learning events. We note however that motivation to learn on the part of the learner will remain a major factor determining the engagement and commitment to applying the learning in the workplace. Digital intelligence systems need to be designed to make clear the need for the learning being provide. In additional to interaction with supervisors and coaches describing the need for the learning, virtual reality presentations can simulate the need for the learning by putting the learner in either "existing situations" or "the workplace of the future" to experience the need for the learning. This will accelerate with the transfer of learning that is taking place in technology.

## 8.5   Transfer Learning: Another Dimension of the Learning Workplace

This chapter is titled *transfer of learning*, a term, along with *training transfer* and *learning transfer,* imbedded in the HRD and education literature. However, drop the *of* and transfer learning is now a popular headline phrase in the world of technology. And it is not used to refer to technology professionals learning, but rather, for the technology itself. In his blog posting "A gentle Introduction to Transfer Learning with Deep Learning" Jason Brownlee defines transfer learning as "a machine learning technique where a model trained on one task is re-purposed on a second related task" (2019). In their book, *Deep Learning* (2016) Ian Goodfellow, Yoshua Bengio, and Aaron Courville write "transfer of learning and domain adaptation refer to the situation where what has been learned in one setting…is explored to improve generalization in another setting" (p. 526). While these technologies are still in the early phases of development and application, there is growing consensus that transfer learning is giving rise to collaborative artificial intelligence (Gilles Wainrib, interviewed at the Deep Learning in Healthcare Summit, London, 2017); transfer learning is machine learning's next frontier (Ruder, 2017).

Lundberg, A., & Westerman, G. (2020). The transformer CLO: The role of the chief learning officer isn't just about training anymore. *Harvard Business Review, 98*(1), 84–93.

Madsbjerg, C., & Rasmussen, M. A. (2014). An anthropologist walks into a bar…to understand what makes your customers tick, you have to observe them in their natural habitats. *Harvard Business Review, 92*(3), 80–88.

Marsick, V. J., Fichter, R., & Watkins, K. E. (2022). From work-based learning to learning-based work: Exploring the changing relationship between learning and work. In *The Sage handbook of learning and work.* Sage Publications.

Martin, H. J. (2010). Workplace climate and peer support as determinants of training transfer. *Human Resource Development Quarterly, 21*(1), 87–104.

Massenberg, A., Spurk, D., & Kauffeld, S. (2015). Social support at the workplace, motivation to transfer and training transfer: A multilevel indirect effects model. *International Journal of Training and Development, 19*(3), 161–173.

Massenberg, A.C, Schulte, E.M., & Kauffeld, S. (2017). Never too early: Learning transfer System factors affecting motivation to transfer. *Human Resource Development Quarterly, 28*(1), 55–85.

McCall, M. W., Jr., Lombardo, M. M., & Morrison, A. M. (1988). *The lessons of experience: How successful executives develop on the job.* Free Press.

Poell, R. F. (2017). Time to 'flip' the training transfer tradition: Employees create learning paths strategically. *Human Resource Development Quarterly, 28*(1), 9–15.

Poell, R. F., & van der Krogt, F. J. (2010). Individual learning paths in the context of social networks. In S. Billett (Ed.), *Learning through practice: Models, traditions, orientations, and approaches* (pp. 197–221). Springer.

Quinones, M. A. (1995). Pretraining context effects: Training assignment as feedback. *Journal of Applied Psychology, 80,* 226–238.

Ruder, S. (2017). *An overview of multitask learning in deep neural networks.* Retrieved from https://ruder.io/multi-task/

Ruder, S. (2019). *Neural transfer learning for natural language processing.* Ph.D. Thesis, National University of Ireland, Galway, February.

Russ-Eft, D. (2002). A typology of training design and work environment factors affecting workplace learning and transfer. *Human Resource Development Review, 1*(1), 45–65.

Salomon, G., & Perkins, D. N. (1989). Rocky roads to transfer: Rethinking mechanisms of a neglected phenomenon. *Educational Psychologist, 24*(2), 113–142.

Torrey, L., & Shavlik. (2010). Transfer learning. In E. S. Olivas, J. D. Guerro, M. M. Sober, J. R. M. Benedito, & A. J. S. Lopez (Eds.), *Handbook of research on machine learning applications & trends: Algorithms, methods and technique.* IGI Global.

Tannenbaum, S.I., Mathieu, J.E., Salas, E. and Cannon-Bowers, J.A. (1991) Meeting Trainees' Expectations: The influence of training fulfillment on the development of commitment, self-efficacy, and motivation. *Journal of Applied Psychology, 76*(6), 759–769.

Van Der Krogt, F. J. (2007). *Organiseren van leerwegen:Strategieen van werknemers, Managers en leeradviseurs in dienstverlenende organisaties {Organizing learning paths: Strategies of workers, managers, and consultants in service organizations}.* Performa.

Velada, R., Caetano, A., Michel, J. W., Lyons, B. D., & Kavanagh, M. J. (2007). The effects of training design, individual characteristics and work environment on transfer of training. *International Journal of Training and Development, 11*(4), 282–294.

Wainrib, Gilles, (2017). *Interviewed at the Deep Learning in Healthcare Summit, London.* Retrieved from https://videos.re-work.co/videos/395-interview-with-gilles-wainrib-owkin

Weissbein, D. A., Huang, J. L., Ford, J. K., & Schmidt, A. M. (2011). Influencing learning states to enhance trainee motivation and improve training transfer. *Journal of Business and Psychology, 26*(4), 423–435.

Wexley, K. N., & Latham, G. P. (1981). *Developing and training human resources in organizations.* Scott Foresman.

Whelan, T. (2018a). *70-20-10 and the concept of the OSF ratio.* Retrieved from https://trainingindustry.com/blog/strategy-alignment-and-planning/70-20-10-and-the-concept-of-the-osf-ratio/

Whelan, T. (2018b). *Research report: Deconstructing 70-2010.* Training Industry. Retrieved from https://trainingindustry.com/content/uploads/2018/07/Deconstructing_702010_Preview.pdf

on the frontiers of machine learning
ay humans process learning and trans-
ceptualization, the process mirrors the
ir chapter on Transfer Learning in the
g Applications and Trends, Lisa Torrey
s of transfer learning in which informa-
has been trained in flows to the target
plore for accomplishing this is mapping
mans often think when seeking to trans-
potential opportunity (e.g., Gavetti &
ws on neurophysiological and psycho-
ins learn to recognize objects. His work
drawing on the pathways of the brain
out programming algorithms for learn-
es pedagogical literature (Brown & Lee,
ctive, we often learn tasks first that pro-
lore complex techniques. This is true for
l arts as much as learning a language."
elong learning that "can also be seen as

of how, although the substance of the
s, the language of human learning has
development of collaborative technolo-
ained to function in one circumstance to
is in the future. While Wainrib's use of
ce" refers to machines collaborating, in
llaborating. Its already happening with
ling suggestions for action. With regard
els will include AI.

lopment and performance of individuals
ied from the learning experience into the
s, especially learning that requires "high
volves continuing to further development
ning event. Understanding the systemic
cess and taking action to facilitate trans-
and development function's role. This
re the facilitates the process. While ini-
ing from formal programs such as semi-
nuch learning is being embedded into the
managers who share their experience and
bsites. While the way in which learning is

delivered has shifted, paying attention to the systemic dynamics o... cess remains important to be monitored. An employee may obtai... mation and examples from the site, but this learning must still be ... supervisor and peers.

Accessing learning from websites goes beyond obtaining info... current role; it is also sought for obtaining learning resources t... providing a basis for pursuing one's intended career path. Augm... can provide employees with opportunities for accessing this lea... tracking and supporting their next steps. The patterns that emerge... ing opportunities are being accessed are important information f... ment professionals to enhance workforce engagement and retenti... provide talent management with learning opportunities for anticip... ing talent development challenges.

## References

Baldwin, T. T., & Ford, J. K. (1988). Transfer of training: A review and ... research. *Personnel Psychology, 41*, 63–105.

Baldwin, T. T., Ford, J. K., & Blume, B. D. (2017). The state of transfer ... Moving toward more consumer-centric inquiry. *Human Resource Dev*... 28(1), 17–28.

Baldwin-Evans, K. (2006). Key steps to implementing a successful blende... *Industrial & Commercial Training, 38*, 156–163.

Bandura, A. (1977). *Social learning theory*. Prentice-Hall.

Bates, R., Holton, E. F., & Hatala, J. P. (2012). A revised learning transfe... Factorial replication and validation. *Human Resource Development I*... 549–569.

Bates, R., Kauffeld, S., & Holton, E. F. (2007). Examining the factor stru... ability of the German-version of the learning transfer systems inventory. J... *Industrial Training, 31*(3), 195–211.

Billett, S. (2001). *Learning in the workplace: Strategies for effective practice.*

Broad, M. L. (2005). *Beyond transfer of training: Engaging systems to improve*...

Brown, H. D., & Lee, H. (1994). *Teaching by principles: An interactive ap*... *pedagogy* (Vol. 1). Prentice Hall Regents.

Burke, L. A., & Hutchins, H. M. (2007). Training transfer: An integrative litera... *Resource Development Review, 6*(3), 263–296.

Burke, L. A., & Hutchins, H. M. (2008). A study of best practices in training tr... model of transfer. *Human Resource Development Quarterly, 19*(2), 107–1...

Butterfield, E. C., & Nelson, G. D. (1989). Theory and practice of teaching for t... *Technology Research and Development, 37*, 5–58.

Chang, J., & Chiang, T. (2013). The Impact of Learner Characteristics on T... *Journal of Information Technology and Application in Education, 2*(1) 16-...

Chiaburu, D. S., & Marinova, S. V. (2005). What predicts skill transfer? An ... goal orientation, training self-efficacy and organizational supports. *Inter*... *Training and Development, 9*(2), 110–123.

Clarke, N. (2004). HRD and the challenges of assessing learning in the work... *Journal of Training and Development, 8*, 140–156.

...& Barlett, K. R. (2004). The effects of organizational learning culture and ... motivation to transfer learning and turnover intention. *Human Resource* ...*rterly, 15*(3), 279–301.

...process approach to the transfer of training: Part 1: The impact of super-... transfer maintenance. *Australian Journal of Educational Technology, 9*(2),

...process approach to the transfer of training: Part 2: Using action planning to ...fer of training. *Australian Journal of Educational Technology, 10*(1), 1–18. ...14742/ajet.2080

...ks, A. M. (2004). A longitudinal quasi-experiment on the effects of post-... interventions. *Human Resource Development Quarterly, 15*(1), 57–76.

...n, J. W. (2005). How strategists really think: Tapping the power of analogy. ...*Review, 83*(4), 54–63.

...ermans, K., Festner, D., & Guber, H. (2009). Review: Motivation to trans-... integrative literature review. *Human Resource Development Review, 8*(3),

...er, J., & Kauffeld, S. (2014). Exploring the critical role of motivation to ...ining transfer process. *International Journal of Training and Development,*

...as, E. (2011). The transfer of training: What really matters. *International* ...*ng and Development, 15*(2), 103–120.

...s, H. M., & Burke-Smalley, L. A. (2016). Web 2.0 and transfer: Trainers' use ...support employees' learning transfer on the job. *Performance Improvement* ...231–255.

...aldwin, T. T. (2003). Making transfer happen: An action perspective on learn-...ms. In E. F. Holton III & T. T. Baldwin (Eds.), *Improving learning transfer in* ...). 3–15). Jossey-Bass.

...ates, R., & Ruona, W. E. A. (2000). Development of a generalized learning ...ventory. *Human Resource Development Quarterly, 11*(4), 333–360.

...A., & Scheerens, J. (2006). Measuring change in work behavior by means ...edback. *International Journal of Training and Development, 10*(2), 121–139.

...man, D. A., & Buick, F. (2018). The 70:20:10 framework and the transfer of ...*Resource Development Quarterly, 29*(4), 383–402.

...R., Holton, E., & Müller, A. C. (2008). Das deutsche Lerntransfer-System ...: psychometrische Überprüfung der deutschsprachigen version [The German ...Learning Transfer System Inventory (GLTSI): psychometric validation]. ...*rsonalpsychologie, 7*(2), 50–69.

...& Hong, C. (2008). The importance of establishing relevance in motivating ...*Active Learning in Higher Education, 9*(3), 249–263.

...(2001). Factors affecting training effectiveness in the context of new technol-...e study. *International Journal of Training and Development, 5*(4), 248–260.

...(2002). Predicting motivation to learn and motivation to transfer learning ...n a service organization: A new systemic model for training effectiveness. ...*provement Quarterly, 15*, 114–129.

...). Dual dimensionality of training transfer. *Human Resource Development* ...209–223.

...ell, J. L. (2011). The differences between hard and soft skills and their relative ...g transfer. *Human Resource Development Quarterly, 22*(1), 111–122.

...E. (1991). *Situated learning: Legitimate peripheral participation.* Cambridge

...ris, M. L. (2006). Influence of trainee characteristics, instructional satisfac-...zational climate on perceived learning and training transfer. *Human Resource* ...*uarterly, 17*(1), 85–115.

# The Future of Work

As is evident from previous chapters, the 4th IR is changing the terrain of the workplace, including how both repetitive and non-repetitive tasks are being done, services are being provided, decisions are being made, and the relationship between humans and technology as work is being done. These changes have given raise to the popular question "What is the future of work?" Underlying this question are questions regarding the essential components of the relationship between humans and intelligent technologies. However, a number of factors are contributing to how the future of work will evolve. These include how remote learning necessitated by the Covid pandemic has changed how employees and employers have developed new preferences regarding how work is managed, the changing mix of generations composing the workforce and their expectations, globalization of industries, the acerating pace of innovation and change, and pressures regarding environmental sustainability.

In short, the dynamics determining the future of work are complex as these various factors not only evolve themselves, but also interact among and shape each other. Returning to the acronym at the beginning of Chap. 1, the future of work is evolving in a world of VUCA: Volatility, Uncertainty, Complexity, and Ambiguity. That said, it doesn't mean it's not possible to identify necessary skills and practices for learning, adapting/transforming, and performing through the uncertainty and ambiguity regarding the future of work. It should be noted that addressing the future of work is an issue facing both employees and organizations. For employees, and students preparing for careers, the challenges are trying to plan for much more fluid career paths that are less secure and require changing skill sets. For organizations, the challenges are creating processes for managing a workforce that is capable of performing in this world of VUCA and is also very fluid in terms of continuously seeking new employment opportunities. Perhaps ironically these challenges provide a foundation for integrating talent management/HRD practices with aspirations and needs of the workforce even as everything changes.

L. Yorks et al., *Strategic Human Resource Development in Practice*, Management for Professionals, https://doi.org/10.1007/978-3-030-95775-9_9

However, to execute this foundation, members of the workforce will need to be prepared for navigating through uncertainty. Developing this capacity is not easy but doing so needs to be a priority on the talent management agenda. As previously noted, people don't resist change, they resist loss. Anticipating and preparing for change in the workplace trigger fears of loss of security, identity, status, relationships, and lifestyle. Change in the workplace can be interconnected with other segments of the socio-economy complex, especially as the pace of change accelerates. This accelerated pace change comes with increasing levels of uncertainty in terms of work which in turn can raise fears of change among members of the workforce.

Additionally, as noted in Chaps. 7 and 8 how learning is provided to the workforce has changed with more emphasis placed on self-directed, informal learning. Of course, the implications of this will transition as generational changes take place in the workforce with younger members having grown up with new technologies and shifting career options being the new normal. However, there are important implications for the education industry having to include learning experiences that focus on developing competencies for applying strategic learning practices (practices that will continue to evolve as technologies and work/living venues continue to evolve) and a more "post conventional" mindset.

## 9.1    The Future of Work

Although the title of this chapter (and this section of the chapter) has been a popular one for several years, making a conclusive declaration about the future of work for most occupations is not possible. The uncertainty of what the workplace and workforce will be like over the course of the next 5 years and beyond is too high for specific predictions to be made. A review of existing studies and surveys of talent management executives suggests that a majority of members of the workforce (around 70–85 percent) are in occupations with uncertain prospects (Schwartz et al., 2019). This uncertainty is being driven by advances in AI. However, at least initially the changes in the workplace in terms of AI causing job elimination as not been dramatic as the initial hype suggested. A final report in November 2020 by the MIT Task Force on the Work of the Future stated, "In the two-and-a half years since the task force set to work, autonomous vehicles, robotics, and AI have advanced remarkably. But the world has not been turned on its head by automation, nor has the labor market" (Davenport & Westerman, 2021). More on this later in the chapter.

However, even given the difficulty of predicting precisely what changes will happen and when, it is possible to identify some of the challenges that lay ahead that will need to be addressed along with general guidelines for addressing them. Crowd sourcing of more than 250 C-suite and senior level executives attending *The Future of Work: The Strategic HR Joint Council Meeting* held in Chicago by The Conference Board in May 2018 (Mitchell et al., 2018). Three of the themes that emerged and are increasing reflected in how work is being organized were an emphasis on (1) teams and horizontal cross-functional work, (2) continuous learning for addressing skill deficits for developing the organization's existing talent, and (3) effectively balancing and leveraging contingent and full-time workers.

### 9.1.1   Teams and Horizontal Cross-Functional Work

One of the major themes that emerged from the Conference Board's joint council meeting of senior executives was that HR systems, and by extension HRD practices, need to support collaboration by placing value on work done in teams. Traditionally, rewards have been based on individual performance. However, increasingly work is being organized around cross-functional project teams brought together for specific projects and then disbanded with the team members moving on to other diverse projects. "As teams become a centerpiece of human capital strategy, companies need to emphasize the collaborative aspects of culture. The challenge is developing a rewards system that values work in teams" (Mitchell, Young, & Popiela, 2018, p. 13). This challenge reflects the need for aligning HRM functions such as compensation with systemic cultural change as depicted in systemic interplay of HRM, L&D, & OD framework (Fig. 9.1).

This trend toward transient teams has significant implications for the role played by managers in organizations. With the shift from structured hierarchies to collaborative work done by fluid and often self-managed teams, the role of managers will

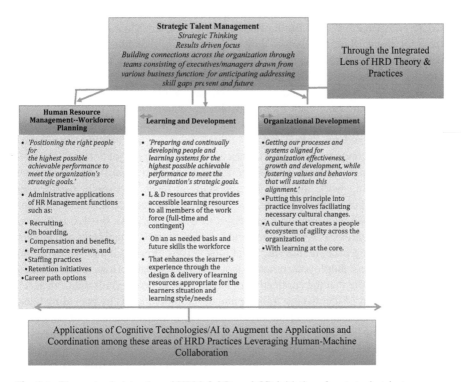

**Fig. 9.1** The systemic interplay of HRM, L&D, and OD initiatives for strategic talent management in HRD practice facilitated by technological innovation involving human–machine interaction

shift from being a monitor of work to that of being a performance coach for teams. "But its more like coaching an improvising jazz band than a football team with well-defined roles and a structured playbook." Mitchell et al. (2018, p. 14) raising the need for HRD practitioners to develop and facilitate learning and development processes that train managers how to train teams through coaching. Connecting both compensating team performance and coaching teams is the need for assessing performance not only in terms of what teams achieve, but also how the team achieved it. In the words of one participant in The Conference Board Joint Council Meeting:

We still have to assess an individual's impact and award compensation. But now are trying to get away from individual achievement and include more collaborative measures, such as, how did you contribute to other people's performance? (p. 19)

### 9.1.2 Continuous Learning for Addressing Skill Deficits for Developing the Organization's Existing Talent

As AI is changing the roles people play in organizations, it is necessary to provide members of workforce with the access and time for learning new skills. This access can involve options such as AI supported learning through individually accessed systems, reverse mentoring, and periodic webinars. As one of the presenters at The Conference Board session on the Future of Work stated "digital skills today stay fresh for about 18 months before they are outdated … individuals need to become continuous learners because there is a chance their job now won't be the same in six months" (Mitchell et al., 2018, p. 16).

As Revin Jesuthasan and John Boudreau wrote in early January 2021 "Organizations are held back by the obsolescence and stubborn inertia of a traditional work operating system that was built for the Second Industrial Revolution with *work* defined as 'jobs' and *Workers* defined as 'job-holding employees'" (Jesuthasan & Boudreau, 2021, p. 6). They argue this focus on "jobholders" obscures specific skills gaps because it takes the focus away from identifying connections between changing work and the "specific skills of those who might perform the work." (p. 6). Their proposed alternative is a process of deconstruction of jobs into discrete tasks and adopting agile processes in which work can involve collaborations across functions as work is conducted. And as digital technologies are adopted at an accelerating pace, identifying what jobs will be eliminated and what training will keep existing employees relevant is a necessary aspect of the talent management role. We note that the application of augmented AI on the skills data can accelerate the process of identifying training and development needs by providing talent management professionals in the organization with needs analysis and suggested training options for employees while also providing career options to the employees.

Jesuthasan and Boudreau make the case that a focus on what skills are becoming obsolete and what skills are increasingly necessary provides a database for organizing learning content and also bringing the attention of the workforce on both the need for and the opportunity to develop new skills. For example, "a global telecommunications company is transparent about what jobs will evolve with technology advancements and helps employees develop the skills they will need to shift to a new role" (Mitchell et al., 2021, p. 8). Consistent with this argument is a McKinsey Blog posting (Field et al., 2020)) that organizations should assess candidates for jobs based on their skills, rather than past job titles, as a way for filling critical roles with the best talent. Field et al. advocate for skills-based matching as "an approach that assesses candidates based on their holistic set (including adjacent skills across industries) rather than just industry experience or certain educational credentials. Assessing candidates based on skills, instead of their last job title, can help fill critical roles with the best talent." Their blog demonstrates how skills-matching is effective for assessing external talent candidates and for assessing, allocating, and developing internal talent as well. Companies such as IBM, Cisco, and Unilever are at the forefront of this transition to a skills-based approach (Devine, 2021). The focus on skills, not jobs also provides for transitioning to a third major theme that surfaced during The Conference Board's joint council meeting on the future of work, the need for balancing and leveraging contingent and full-time workers.

### 9.1.3   Effectively Balancing and Leveraging Contingent and Full-Time Workers

Terms like contingent workers, the gig economy, and nonpermanent talent have become widespread during the second decade of the twenty-first century, creating the view that the future of employment is workers and organizations having to construct a tangential set of employment relationships. There is no question that many workers will be part time in the future; that is already the case. In the words of one participant in the joint council meeting, "All this adds a new layer to the workforce, such as crowd-sourced workers and project-based data scientists, which can be found on online platforms such as Kaggle. These individuals never actually come into your organization, but they are part of your workforce." Another participant noted that this means that organizations will need to keep good data on the nonpermanent talent they use, not just on their full-time talent and "to expand its view on who we serve. Contingent workers need financial security just as much as full-timers do."

This evolving shift in the configuration of the workforce comes with its own challenges. "Both CEO's and other C-suite executives foresee major problems in finding enough workers with appropriate high-demand skills within the contingent, nontraditional workforce pool. They also believe the greater use of contingent workers will make it even more challenging to engage and retain not only the part-time and project workers needed to fill the mushrooming talent and skills gaps but also existing full-time employees" (Mitchell et al., 2018). Returning to the need for keeping good data on the workforce, organizations need to understand their permanent talent base and their freelance talent, building engagement with both groups. Some companies are beginning to consider what kind of benefits to offer to their contingent workforce, while also creating opportunities for understanding the future career paths that exist, or are emerging, for full-time members of the workforce. Although currently there is a growing focus on contingent workers, there is also the realization that reskilling and adapting full-time workers are important for addressing the increasing challenges of obtaining contingent workers on an as-needed basis. Another factor in play in both providing benefits and reskilling options for both contingent and full-time workers are the needs for building an engaged workforce that is available when needed and emerging societal concerns.

As previously stated above, all three themes demonstrate the need for effective coordination between the administrative applications of:

(a) HR management functions such as recruiting, on boarding, compensation and benefits, performance reviews, and staffing practices;
(b) L & D resources that provide accessible learning resources to all members of the workforce (full-time and contingent) on an as-needed basis and future skills of the workforce;
(c) A culture that creates a people ecosystem of agility across the organization.

Given the need for focusing on skills and the increasing pace of technological change making some existing skills less relevant, even obsolete, with new skills being necessary, we turn now to the skilling of the workforce for the future, which needs to be a fundamental focus for strategic HRD.

## 9.2    Skilling the Workforce for the Future

As the content throughout this book implies, learning & development functions have had to transform over the past couple of decades to stay relevant for meeting the needs of their organization and the people who are populating them. While traditionally L&D functions have been largely siloed in various parts of the organization, in the world of VUCA, AI driven change, the need for continuing reskilling and/or upskilling members of the workforce is an integral part of sustaining organization performance and realizing strategic objectives. In this context, L&D functions have to be strategically aligned with the organization's goals and change initiatives which requires breaking through the silos and having an enterprise-wide L&D function. Accomplishing this aligns L&D across the talent management functions and the business. In 2015, a research working group (RWG) convened by the Conference Board comprised of "human capital practitioners, researchers, and other experts in the field" to identify ways organizations could "break down these silos in an effort to build future capabilities" was formed (Abel & Nair, 2015, p. 4). The RWG adopted the concept of an environmental ecosystem comprised of organisms that continually interact with one another and their environment, exchanging energies enabling the emergence of system level processes as an analogy for a "People Ecosystem" in organizations that develops "structures, tools, and capabilities for anticipating disruptive changes and respond with maximum agility." They used the

Interestingly, the technologists working on the frontiers of machine learning through cognitive intelligence draw on the way humans process learning and transfer it to other settings. First, in terms of conceptualization, the process mirrors the concept of reasoning from analogies. In their chapter on Transfer Learning in the Handbook of Research on Machine Learning Applications and Trends, Lisa Torrey and Jude Shavlik (2010) describe the process of transfer learning in which information from the source task that the program has been trained in flows to the target task. Among the potential processes, they explore for accomplishing this is mapping by analogy, which has parallels with how humans often think when seeking to transfer experience from one setting to another potential opportunity (e.g., Gavetti & Rivkin, 2005). Sebastian Ruder (2019) draws on neurophysiological and psychological studies for theorizing into how humans learn to recognize objects. His work is representative of how technologists are drawing on the pathways of the brain revealed through neuroscience to theorize about programming algorithms for learning transfer in machine learning. He also cites pedagogical literature (Brown & Lee, 1994) writing: "From a pedagogical perspective, we often learn tasks first that provide us with the necessary skills to master more complex techniques. This is true for learning the proper way of falling in martial arts as much as learning a language." Additionally he relates to the concept of lifelong learning that "can also be seen as an online form of multi-task learning."

The above are provided as illustrations of how, although the substance of the work is in the development of technologies, the language of human learning has been adopted to provide frameworks for the development of collaborative technologies. Transfer learning enabling machines trained to function in one circumstance to apply that learning in another circumstance is in the future. While Wainrib's use of the term "collaborative artificial intelligence" refers to machines collaborating, in the future, machine and humans will be collaborating. Its already happening with assisted and augmented intelligence providing suggestions for action. With regard to learning transfer for humans, future models will include AI.

## 8.6    Summary

For learning to positively impact the development and performance of individuals and teams, it has to be transferred and applied from the learning experience into the work itself. Additionally, in many instances, especially learning that requires "high road" transfer, the transfer process itself involves continuing to further development what has been learned in the initial learning event. Understanding the systemic issues that impact the learning transfer process and taking action to facilitate transfer is an important piece of the learning and development function's role. This includes fostering an organizational culture the facilitates the process. While initially developed around transferring learning from formal programs such as seminars and workshops, in the current world much learning is being embedded into the flow of work with learning from peers and managers who share their experience and learnings through postings on learning websites. While the way in which learning is delivered has shifted, paying attention to the systemic dynamics of the transfer process remains important to be monitored. An employee may obtain important information and examples from the site, but this learning must still be supported by their supervisor and peers.

Accessing learning from websites goes beyond obtaining information for one's current role; it is also sought for obtaining learning resources that are viewed as providing a basis for pursuing one's intended career path. Augmented AI systems can provide employees with opportunities for accessing this learning along with tracking and supporting their next steps. The patterns that emerge from what learning opportunities are being accessed are important information for talent management professionals to enhance workforce engagement and retention. In short, it can provide talent management with learning opportunities for anticipating and addressing talent development challenges.

## References

Baldwin, T. T., & Ford, J. K. (1988). Transfer of training: A review and directions for future research. *Personnel Psychology, 41*, 63–105.

Baldwin, T. T., Ford, J. K., & Blume, B. D. (2017). The state of transfer of training research: Moving toward more consumer-centric inquiry. *Human Resource Development Quarterly, 28*(1), 17–28.

Baldwin-Evans, K. (2006). Key steps to implementing a successful blended learning strategy. *Industrial & Commercial Training, 38*, 156–163.

Bandura, A. (1977). *Social learning theory*. Prentice-Hall.

Bates, R., Holton, E. F., & Hatala, J. P. (2012). A revised learning transfer system inventory: Factorial replication and validation. *Human Resource Development International, 15*(5), 549–569.

Bates, R., Kauffeld, S., & Holton, E. F. (2007). Examining the factor structure and predictive ability of the German-version of the learning transfer systems inventory. *Journal of European Industrial Training, 31*(3), 195–211.

Billett, S. (2001). *Learning in the workplace: Strategies for effective practice*. Allen & Unwin.

Broad, M. L. (2005). *Beyond transfer of training: Engaging systems to improve performance*. Wiley.

Brown, H. D., & Lee, H. (1994). *Teaching by principles: An interactive approach to language pedagogy* (Vol. 1). Prentice Hall Regents.

Burke, L. A., & Hutchins, H. M. (2007). Training transfer: An integrative literature review. *Human Resource Development Review, 6*(3), 263–296.

Burke, L. A., & Hutchins, H. M. (2008). A study of best practices in training transfer and proposed model of transfer. *Human Resource Development Quarterly, 19*(2), 107–128.

Butterfield, E. C., & Nelson, G. D. (1989). Theory and practice of teaching for transfer. *Educational Technology Research and Development, 37*, 5–58.

Chang, J., & Chiang, T. (2013). The Impact of Learner Characteristics on Transfer of Training. *Journal of Information Technology and Application in Education, 2*(1) 16–22.

Chiaburu, D. S., & Marinova, S. V. (2005). What predicts skill transfer? An exploratory study of goal orientation, training self-efficacy and organizational supports. *International Journal of Training and Development, 9*(2), 110–123.

Clarke, N. (2004). HRD and the challenges of assessing learning in the workplace. *International Journal of Training and Development, 8*, 140–156.

Egan, T. M., Yang, B., & Barlett, K. R. (2004). The effects of organizational learning culture and job satisfaction on motivation to transfer learning and turnover intention. *Human Resource Development Quarterly, 15*(3), 279–301.

Foxon, M. (1993). A process approach to the transfer of training: Part 1: The impact of supervisor support on transfer maintenance. *Australian Journal of Educational Technology, 9*(2), 130–143.

Foxon, M. (1994). A process approach to the transfer of training: Part 2: Using action planning to facilitate the transfer of training. *Australian Journal of Educational Technology, 10*(1), 1–18. https://doi.org/10.14742/ajet.2080

Gaudine, A. P., & Saks, A. M. (2004). A longitudinal quasi-experiment on the effects of post-training transfer interventions. *Human Resource Development Quarterly, 15*(1), 57–76.

Gavetti, G., & Rivkin, J. W. (2005). How strategists really think: Tapping the power of analogy. *Harvard Business Review, 83*(4), 54–63.

Gegenfurtner, A., Veermans, K., Festner, D., & Guber, H. (2009). Review: Motivation to transfer training: An integrative literature review. *Human Resource Development Review, 8*(3), 403–423.

Grohmann, A., Beller, J., & Kauffeld, S. (2014). Exploring the critical role of motivation to transfer in the training transfer process. *International Journal of Training and Development, 18*(2), 84–103.

Grossman, R. & Salas, E. (2011). The transfer of training: What really matters. *International Journal of Training and Development, 15*(2), 103–120.

Hester, A. J., Hutchins, H. M., & Burke-Smalley, L. A. (2016). Web 2.0 and transfer: Trainers' use of technology to support employees' learning transfer on the job. *Performance Improvement Quarterly, 29*(3), 231–255.

Holton, E. F., III, & Baldwin, T. T. (2003). Making transfer happen: An action perspective on learning transfer systems. In E. F. Holton III & T. T. Baldwin (Eds.), *Improving learning transfer in organizations* (pp. 3–15). Jossey-Bass.

Holton, E. F., III, Bates, R., & Ruona, W. E. A. (2000). Development of a generalized learning transfer system inventory. *Human Resource Development Quarterly, 11*(4), 333–360.

Jellema, F., Visscher, A., & Scheerens, J. (2006). Measuring change in work behavior by means of multisource feedback. *International Journal of Training and Development, 10*(2), 121–139.

Johnson, S. J., Blackman, D. A., & Buick, F. (2018). The 70:20:10 framework and the transfer of learning. *Human Resource Development Quarterly, 29*(4), 383–402.

Kauffeld, S., Bates, R., Holton, E., & Müller, A. C. (2008). Das deutsche Lerntransfer-System Inventar (GLTSI): psychometrische Überprüfung der deutschsprachigen version [The German version of the Learning Transfer System Inventory (GLTSI): psychometric validation]. *Zeitschrift für Personalpsychologie, 7*(2), 50–69.

Kember, D., Ho, A., & Hong, C. (2008). The importance of establishing relevance in motivating student learning. *Active Learning in Higher Education, 9*(3), 249–263.

Kontoghiorghes, C. (2001). Factors affecting training effectiveness in the context of new technology—A U.S. case study. *International Journal of Training and Development, 5*(4), 248–260.

Kontoghiorghes, C. (2002). Predicting motivation to learn and motivation to transfer learning back to the job in a service organization: A new systemic model for training effectiveness. *Performance Improvement Quarterly, 15*, 114–129.

Laker, D. R. (1990). Dual dimensionality of training transfer. *Human Resource Development Quarterly, 1*(3), 209–223.

Laker, D. R., & Powell, J. L. (2011). The differences between hard and soft skills and their relative impact on training transfer. *Human Resource Development Quarterly, 22*(1), 111–122.

Lave, J., & Wenger, E. (1991). *Situated learning: Legitimate peripheral participation.* Cambridge University Press.

Lim, D. H., & Morris, M. L. (2006). Influence of trainee characteristics, instructional satisfaction, and organizational climate on perceived learning and training transfer. *Human Resource Development Quarterly, 17*(1), 85–115.

Lundberg, A., & Westerman, G. (2020). The transformer CLO: The role of the chief learning officer isn't just about training anymore. *Harvard Business Review, 98*(1), 84–93.

Madsbjerg, C., & Rasmussen, M. A. (2014). An anthropologist walks into a bar...to understand what makes your customers tick, you have to observe them in their natural habitats. *Harvard Business Review, 92*(3), 80–88.

Marsick, V. J., Fichter, R., & Watkins, K. E. (2022). From work-based learning to learning-based work: Exploring the changing relationship between learning and work. In *The Sage handbook of learning and work*. Sage Publications.

Martin, H. J. (2010). Workplace climate and peer support as determinants of training transfer. *Human Resource Development Quarterly, 21*(1), 87–104.

Massenberg, A., Spurk, D., & Kauffeld, S. (2015). Social support at the workplace, motivation to transfer and training transfer: A multilevel indirect effects model. *International Journal of Training and Development, 19*(3), 161–173.

Massenberg, A.C, Schulte, E.M., & Kauffeld, S. (2017). Never too early: Learning transfer System factors affecting motivation to transfer. *Human Resource Development Quarterly, 28*(1), 55–85.

McCall, M. W., Jr., Lombardo, M. M., & Morrison, A. M. (1988). *The lessons of experience: How successful executives develop on the job.* Free Press.

Poell, R. F. (2017). Time to 'flip' the training transfer tradition: Employees create learning paths strategically. *Human Resource Development Quarterly, 28*(1), 9–15.

Poell, R. F., & van der Krogt, F. J. (2010). Individual learning paths in the context of social networks. In S. Billett (Ed.), *Learning through practice: Models, traditions, orientations, and approaches* (pp. 197–221). Springer.

Quinones, M. A. (1995). Pretraining context effects: Training assignment as feedback. *Journal of Applied Psychology, 80,* 226–238.

Ruder, S. (2017). *An overview of multitask learning in deep neural networks.* Retrieved from https://ruder.io/multi-task/

Ruder, S. (2019). *Neural transfer learning for natural language processing.* Ph.D. Thesis, National University of Ireland, Galway, February.

Russ-Eft, D. (2002). A typology of training design and work environment factors affecting workplace learning and transfer. *Human Resource Development Review, 1*(1), 45–65.

Salomon, G., & Perkins, D. N. (1989). Rocky roads to transfer: Rethinking mechanisms of a neglected phenomenon. *Educational Psychologist, 24*(2), 113–142.

Torrey, L., & Shavlik. (2010). Transfer learning. In E. S. Olivas, J. D. Guerro, M. M. Sober, J. R. M. Benedito, & A. J. S. Lopez (Eds.), *Handbook of research on machine learning applications & trends: Algorithms, methods and technique.* IGI Global.

Tannenbaum, S.I., Mathieu, J.E., Salas, E. and Cannon-Bowers, J.A. (1991) Meeting Trainees' Expectations: The influence of training fulfillment on the development of commitment, self-efficacy, and motivation. *Journal of Applied Psychology, 76*(6), 759–769.

Van Der Krogt, F. J. (2007). *Organiseren van leerwegen:Strategieen van werknemers, Managers en leeradviseurs in dienstverlenende organisaties {Organizing learning paths: Strategies of workers, managers, and consultants in service organizations}.* Performa.

Velada, R., Caetano, A., Michel, J. W., Lyons, B. D., & Kavanagh, M. J. (2007). The effects of training design, individual characteristics and work environment on transfer of training. *International Journal of Training and Development, 11*(4), 282–294.

Wainrib, Gilles, (2017). *Interviewed at the Deep Learning in Healthcare Summit, London.* Retrieved from https://videos.re-work.co/videos/395-interview-with-gilles-wainrib-owkin

Weissbein, D. A., Huang, J. L., Ford, J. K., & Schmidt, A. M. (2011). Influencing learning states to enhance trainee motivation and improve training transfer. *Journal of Business and Psychology, 26*(4), 423–435.

Wexley, K. N., & Latham, G. P. (1981). *Developing and training human resources in organizations.* Scott Foresman.

Whelan, T. (2018a). *70-20-10 and the concept of the OSF ratio.* Retrieved from https://trainingindustry.com/blog/strategy-alignment-and-planning/70-20-10-and-the-concept-of-the-osf-ratio/

Whelan, T. (2018b). *Research report: Deconstructing 70-2010.* Training Industry. Retrieved from https://trainingindustry.com/content/uploads/2018/07/Deconstructing_702010_Preview.pdf

# The Future of Work

As is evident from previous chapters, the 4th IR is changing the terrain of the work-place, including how both repetitive and non-repetitive tasks are being done, services are being provided, decisions are being made, and the relationship between humans and technology as work is being done. These changes have given raise to the popular question "What is the future of work?" Underlying this question are questions regarding the essential components of the relationship between humans and intelligent technologies. However, a number of factors are contributing to how the future of work will evolve. These include how remote learning necessitated by the Covid pandemic has changed how employees and employers have developed new preferences regarding how work is managed, the changing mix of generations composing the workforce and their expectations, globalization of industries, the acerating pace of innovation and change, and pressures regarding environmental sustainability.

In short, the dynamics determining the future of work are complex as these various factors not only evolve themselves, but also interact among and shape each other. Returning to the acronym at the beginning of Chap. 1, the future of work is evolving in a world of VUCA: Volatility, Uncertainty, Complexity, and Ambiguity. That said, it doesn't mean it's not possible to identify necessary skills and practices for learning, adapting/transforming, and performing through the uncertainty and ambiguity regarding the future of work. It should be noted that addressing the future of work is an issue facing both employees and organizations. For employees, and students preparing for careers, the challenges are trying to plan for much more fluid career paths that are less secure and require changing skill sets. For organizations, the challenges are creating processes for managing a workforce that is capable of performing in this world of VUCA and is also very fluid in terms of continuously seeking new employment opportunities. Perhaps ironically these challenges provide a foundation for integrating talent management/HRD practices with aspirations and needs of the workforce even as everything changes.

L. Yorks et al., *Strategic Human Resource Development in Practice*, Management for Professionals, https://doi.org/10.1007/978-3-030-95775-9_9

However, to execute this foundation, members of the workforce will need to be prepared for navigating through uncertainty. Developing this capacity is not easy but doing so needs to be a priority on the talent management agenda. As previously noted, people don't resist change, they resist loss. Anticipating and preparing for change in the workplace trigger fears of loss of security, identity, status, relationships, and lifestyle. Change in the workplace can be interconnected with other segments of the socio-economy complex, especially as the pace of change accelerates. This accelerated pace change comes with increasing levels of uncertainty in terms of work which in turn can raise fears of change among members of the workforce.

Additionally, as noted in Chaps. 7 and 8 how learning is provided to the workforce has changed with more emphasis placed on self-directed, informal learning. Of course, the implications of this will transition as generational changes take place in the workforce with younger members having grown up with new technologies and shifting career options being the new normal. However, there are important implications for the education industry having to include learning experiences that focus on developing competencies for applying strategic learning practices (practices that will continue to evolve as technologies and work/living venues continue to evolve) and a more "post conventional" mindset.

## 9.1   The Future of Work

Although the title of this chapter (and this section of the chapter) has been a popular one for several years, making a conclusive declaration about the future of work for most occupations is not possible. The uncertainty of what the workplace and workforce will be like over the course of the next 5 years and beyond is too high for specific predictions to be made. A review of existing studies and surveys of talent management executives suggests that a majority of members of the workforce (around 70–85 percent) are in occupations with uncertain prospects (Schwartz et al., 2019). This uncertainty is being driven by advances in AI. However, at least initially the changes in the workplace in terms of AI causing job elimination as not been dramatic as the initial hype suggested. A final report in November 2020 by the MIT Task Force on the Work of the Future stated, "In the two-and-a half years since the task force set to work, autonomous vehicles, robotics, and AI have advanced remarkably. But the world has not been turned on its head by automation, nor has the labor market" (Davenport & Westerman, 2021). More on this later in the chapter.

However, even given the difficulty of predicting precisely what changes will happen and when, it is possible to identify some of the challenges that lay ahead that will need to be addressed along with general guidelines for addressing them. Crowd sourcing of more than 250 C-suite and senior level executives attending *The Future of Work: The Strategic HR Joint Council Meeting* held in Chicago by The Conference Board in May 2018 (Mitchell et al., 2018). Three of the themes that emerged and are increasing reflected in how work is being organized were an emphasis on (1) teams and horizontal cross-functional work, (2) continuous learning for addressing skill deficits for developing the organization's existing talent, and (3) effectively balancing and leveraging contingent and full-time workers.

### 9.1.1 Teams and Horizontal Cross-Functional Work

One of the major themes that emerged from the Conference Board's joint council meeting of senior executives was that HR systems, and by extension HRD practices, need to support collaboration by placing value on work done in teams. Traditionally, rewards have been based on individual performance. However, increasingly work is being organized around cross-functional project teams brought together for specific projects and then disbanded with the team members moving on to other diverse projects. "As teams become a centerpiece of human capital strategy, companies need to emphasize the collaborative aspects of culture. The challenge is developing a rewards system that values work in teams" (Mitchell, Young, & Popiela, 2018, p. 13). This challenge reflects the need for aligning HRM functions such as compensation with systemic cultural change as depicted in systemic interplay of HRM, L&D, & OD framework (Fig. 9.1).

This trend toward transient teams has significant implications for the role played by managers in organizations. With the shift from structured hierarchies to collaborative work done by fluid and often self-managed teams, the role of managers will

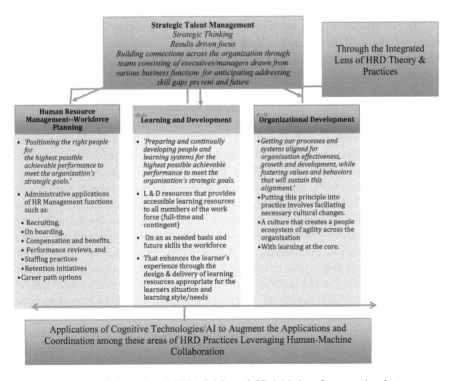

**Fig. 9.1** The systemic interplay of HRM, L&D, and OD initiatives for strategic talent management in HRD practice facilitated by technological innovation involving human–machine interaction

shift from being a monitor of work to that of being a performance coach for teams. "But its more like coaching an improvising jazz band than a football team with well-defined roles and a structured playbook." Mitchell et al. (2018, p. 14) raising the need for HRD practitioners to develop and facilitate learning and development processes that train managers how to train teams through coaching. Connecting both compensating team performance and coaching teams is the need for assessing performance not only in terms of what teams achieve, but also how the team achieved it. In the words of one participant in The Conference Board Joint Council Meeting:

We still have to assess an individual's impact and award compensation. But now are trying to get away from individual achievement and include more collaborative measures, such as, how did you contribute to other people's performance? (p. 19)

### 9.1.2   Continuous Learning for Addressing Skill Deficits for Developing the Organization's Existing Talent

As AI is changing the roles people play in organizations, it is necessary to provide members of workforce with the access and time for learning new skills. This access can involve options such as AI supported learning through individually accessed systems, reverse mentoring, and periodic webinars. As one of the presenters at The Conference Board session on the Future of Work stated "digital skills today stay fresh for about 18 months before they are outdated … individuals need to become continuous learners because there is a chance their job now won't be the same in six months" (Mitchell et al., 2018, p. 16).

As Revin Jesuthasan and John Boudreau wrote in early January 2021 "Organizations are held back by the obsolescence and stubborn inertia of a traditional work operating system that was built for the Second Industrial Revolution with *work* defined as 'jobs' and *Workers* defined as 'job-holding employees'" (Jesuthasan & Boudreau, 2021, p. 6). They argue this focus on "jobholders" obscures specific skills gaps because it takes the focus away from identifying connections between changing work and the "specific skills of those who might perform the work." (p. 6). Their proposed alternative is a process of deconstruction of jobs into discrete tasks and adopting agile processes in which work can involve collaborations across functions as work is conducted. And as digital technologies are adopted at an accelerating pace, identifying what jobs will be eliminated and what training will keep existing employees relevant is a necessary aspect of the talent management role. We note that the application of augmented AI on the skills data can accelerate the process of identifying training and development needs by providing talent management professionals in the organization with needs analysis and suggested training options for employees while also providing career options to the employees.

Jesuthasan and Boudreau make the case that a focus on what skills are becoming obsolete and what skills are increasingly necessary provides a database for organizing learning content and also bringing the attention of the workforce on both the need for and the opportunity to develop new skills. For example, "a global telecommunications company is transparent about what jobs will evolve with technology advancements and helps employees develop the skills they will need to shift to a new role" (Mitchell et al., 2021, p. 8). Consistent with this argument is a McKinsey Blog posting (Field et al., 2020)) that organizations should assess candidates for jobs based on their skills, rather than past job titles, as a way for filling critical roles with the best talent. Field et al. advocate for skills-based matching as "an approach that assesses candidates based on their holistic set (including adjacent skills across industries) rather than just industry experience or certain educational credentials. Assessing candidates based on skills, instead of their last job title, can help fill critical roles with the best talent." Their blog demonstrates how skills-matching is effective for assessing external talent candidates and for assessing, allocating, and developing internal talent as well. Companies such as IBM, Cisco, and Unilever are at the forefront of this transition to a skills-based approach (Devine, 2021). The focus on skills, not jobs also provides for transitioning to a third major theme that surfaced during The Conference Board's joint council meeting on the future of work, the need for balancing and leveraging contingent and full-time workers.

### 9.1.3 Effectively Balancing and Leveraging Contingent and Full-Time Workers

Terms like contingent workers, the gig economy, and nonpermanent talent have become widespread during the second decade of the twenty-first century, creating the view that the future of employment is workers and organizations having to construct a tangential set of employment relationships. There is no question that many workers will be part time in the future; that is already the case. In the words of one participant in the joint council meeting, "All this adds a new layer to the workforce, such as crowd-sourced workers and project-based data scientists, which can be found on online platforms such as Kaggle. These individuals never actually come into your organization, but they are part of your workforce." Another participant noted that this means that organizations will need to keep good data on the nonpermanent talent they use, not just on their full-time talent and "to expand its view on who we serve. Contingent workers need financial security just as much as full-timers do."

This evolving shift in the configuration of the workforce comes with its own challenges. "Both CEO's and other C-suite executives foresee major problems in finding enough workers with appropriate high-demand skills within the contingent, nontraditional workforce pool. They also believe the greater use of contingent workers will make it even more challenging to engage and retain not only the part-time and project workers needed to fill the mushrooming talent and skills gaps but also existing full-time employees" (Mitchell et al., 2018). Returning to the need for keeping good data on the workforce, organizations need to understand their permanent talent base and their freelance talent, building engagement with both groups. Some companies are beginning to consider what kind of benefits to offer to their contingent workforce, while also creating opportunities for understanding the future career paths that exist, or are emerging, for full-time members of the workforce. Although currently there is a growing focus on contingent workers, there is also the realization that reskilling and adapting full-time workers are important for addressing the increasing challenges of obtaining contingent workers on an as-needed basis. Another factor in play in both providing benefits and reskilling options for both contingent and full-time workers are the needs for building an engaged workforce that is available when needed and emerging societal concerns.

As previously stated above, all three themes demonstrate the need for effective coordination between the administrative applications of:

(a) HR management functions such as recruiting, on boarding, compensation and benefits, performance reviews, and staffing practices;
(b) L & D resources that provide accessible learning resources to all members of the workforce (full-time and contingent) on an as-needed basis and future skills of the workforce;
(c) A culture that creates a people ecosystem of agility across the organization.

Given the need for focusing on skills and the increasing pace of technological change making some existing skills less relevant, even obsolete, with new skills being necessary, we turn now to the skilling of the workforce for the future, which needs to be a fundamental focus for strategic HRD.

## 9.2    Skilling the Workforce for the Future

As the content throughout this book implies, learning & development functions have had to transform over the past couple of decades to stay relevant for meeting the needs of their organization and the people who are populating them. While traditionally L&D functions have been largely siloed in various parts of the organization, in the world of VUCA, AI driven change, the need for continuing reskilling and/or upskilling members of the workforce is an integral part of sustaining organization performance and realizing strategic objectives. In this context, L&D functions have to be strategically aligned with the organization's goals and change initiatives which requires breaking through the silos and having an enterprise-wide L&D function. Accomplishing this aligns L&D across the talent management functions and the business. In 2015, a research working group (RWG) convened by the Conference Board comprised of "human capital practitioners, researchers, and other experts in the field" to identify ways organizations could "break down these silos in an effort to build future capabilities" was formed (Abel & Nair, 2015, p. 4). The RWG adopted the concept of an environmental ecosystem comprised of organisms that continually interact with one another and their environment, exchanging energies enabling the emergence of system level processes as an analogy for a "People Ecosystem" in organizations that develops "structures, tools, and capabilities for anticipating disruptive changes and respond with maximum agility." They used the analogy for creating a framework for developing holistic talent systems coordinating and integrating HR practices like recruitment, compensation, and L&D in alignment with business strategies and enabling the organization to anticipate and respond to disruptive changes with maximum agility.

A people ecosystem brings together people across the organization with diverse perspectives and ideas for collaboration that creates synergies and alignment of talent management with the goals of the business. This openness is intended to engage talent across the organization and enabling it from becoming obsolete. Key components are:

- *Strategic Talent Planning* based on assessment of the business context, prioritization of issues and challenges, and developing initiatives integrating the execution of HR functions (e.g., recruitment, compensation, career planning, L&D, etc.);
- *Results Focused Execution* with good leadership, diligence, and accountability;
- *A Talent Management Strategy for Learning and Development* that is (a) aligned with the business strategy of the organization, (b) enhances the learners' experience of utilizing the learning and development resources, and (c) provides oversight by an executive leadership team across the organization comprised of members from business functions as well as L&D. These three components provide guidelines for organizing reskilling the workforce for the future.

### 9.2.1  L&D Strategy Aligned with the Organization's Strategy

Like all talent management initiatives, L&D needs to align its projects and programs with the organization's strategy, with clear links regarding the impact on the organization's performance. These links need to be based on analytics and tracked across the enterprise. L&D professionals need to assess the results of their initiatives in terms of measuring the impact on performance and/or other outcomes such as retention of necessary talent. To use an analogy regarding this point, Tej Anand, a lecturer in the Executive Master of Science Program in Technology Management at Columbia University and Clinical Professor and Academic Director of the Master of Science in Information Systems, shared with one of the authors "More technology initiatives and programs fail than succeed when not connected to outcomes; More technology initiatives and programs succeed when connected to outcomes." (comment made when collaborating as a lecturer in the HRD course at Teachers College, Columbia). The same is true in talent management in today's world of VUCA.

In terms of forward-looking initiatives, the L&D function needs to be following the organization's strategic plans for organizational changes, mapping the implications for skills gaps in different parts of the organization and be preparing the learning portfolios that will be provided for addressing these gaps. Chief Learning Officers and members of their team will need to work horizontally across the organization to stay current on the forthcoming changes anticipated by the different functions in alignment with the organization's strategy. A focus of these horizonal relationships is to determine what reskilling needs exist, or will be emerging, given the forthcoming changes, both immediate and projected for the near future. Another purpose of these horizonal processes is to provide "think tanks" that brainstorm future possibilities regarding changes in staffing needs based on trends in the broader environment.

During and following these assessments, ongoing coordination with HR administration functions such as recruitment, onboarding, and career management should take place, determining what necessary skills can be obtained through new hires, using contingent workers, or providing reassignment opportunities to the existing workforce. For each of these options, what are the likely skilling needs that might be necessary to address is a question to be answered. Also, what up-graded skills will be necessary for workforce members who will remain in existing roles given the changes in work related systems.

Throughout this process, alignment with the strategic focus of the organization must be retained. Accordingly, the process has to be guided by the strategic goals of the organization, with horizontal discussions taking place at the strategic, tactical, and operational levels of the organization being aligned. Updates need to periodically take place "vertically" and the return on investment from reskilling efforts tracked. These horizonal and vertical collaborations are vital for putting the right people with the right skills in the right position at the right time; failure to do so can derail the organization's strategic and operational plans. L&D can no longer be comprised of silos, not coordinating with other functions.

## 9.2.2    Learning Resources and Programs Need to Provide an Enhanced Learner

### 9.2.2.1 Experience
Providing an enhanced learner experience goes beyond their basic satisfaction with using a learning resource or attending a program. Rather an enhanced experience is one that highly connects with the learner in terms of usability, novelty, a sense of felt involvement, and endurance (Abel & Nair, 2015). AI technology is providing ways to deliver training that makes access flexible and can provide this sense of felt involvement that enhances the learner's experience. One example is the numerous and rapidly growing applications of virtual reality. In 2020, Johnson & Johnson, partnership with Osso VR, began distributing Oculus Quest virtual reality headsets to train surgeons who use its products (Berg, 2020). Similar applications of VR have been used in various companies to provide experiences of holding difficult conversations or preparing learners for different cultural experiences. Other applications of technology-based delivery systems for enhanced learning experiences include games, simulations, and online discussion forums.

In the past learning, interventions have been largely designed by L&D professionals more or less as a "one size fits all" design that was somewhat tailored based for the population of learners based on a need's analysis. Training programs and materials were designed following a particular framework across the organization.

Today, the design of learning resources has made meeting the learners' preferences for how learning is provided a necessity. And the expectations of learners vary as the diversity of the workforce become more diverse in terms globalization, demographics, career backgrounds, and prior experiences. Providing a learning experience that meets their needs and expectations requires understanding the mix of learners that will receive and use these resources and how that mix varies.

For example, the RWG developed a framework that differentiates five "types of learners" (Abel & Nair, 2015, p. 29) drawn from the literature and based on demographics and career states:

- The *Ageless* Learner—With lifetimes extending due to changes in lifestyle and medical care, many workers are unwilling to leave the workforce at traditional retirement ages (Cogan & Gencarelli, 2015). Their experience and commitment to the business can be valuable to the organization. While the number who are adapting to new technology in the workplace is growing, many remain unwilling to learn the new skills needed to work effectively with new technologies.
- The *Digital* Learner—Most millennials and Generation Z are digital natives who speak the digital language and naturally respond to digital technology devices (Prensky, 2001). When new adapters ("digital immigrants") to technology design learning resources and programs using digital technology, challenges with the design may emerge that disengage the digital native learners.
- The *Global* Learner—With technology enabled globalization having workers and processes "crisscrossing the world to get the job done in time and on budget" (Gargiulo, 2011) L&D practitioners need to be mindful of cultural nuances when designing learning processes.
- The *Returning* Learner—Learners who are returning to the workplace after a leave of absence for family, healthcare, pursuing an educational degree or certification, military service, or some other purpose (Warner, 2013) may need learning resources that provide new skills for using digitally enabled technology.
- The *Flexible* Learner—Contingent workers such as contractors, part-time, gig employees (United States Department of Labor, 2017) may need learning that focuses on the functional knowledge of a product and/or service.

While these categories are distinct, they are not necessary mutually exclusive. For example, returning learners may also be global and/or digital learners. Types of learners can have a bit of complexity. Rather than thinking of these as individualizing categorizations, the framework provides a window for thinking about the design considerations that need to be taken into account given the particular set of workers for whom the learning is being provided. While the analysis process can be complex, assisted and augmented AI can facilitate the process by grouping members of the workforce and highlighting primary groupings. AI can also be used for aggregating data from pilots and early distributions of learning resources based on both employee assessments of their experience, tracking their subsequent performance, and highlight issues for future revisions.

Returning to the focus on skills rather than past job descriptions in the talent management process, the learning needs of members of the workforce can vary considerably as they onboard into a new function or how changes in technology impact their roles and skill sets. This is another aspect of the reskilling process that is critical for enhancing learners' experience through providing needed resources that smooth the process of making transitions. Being able to stay current on the mix of employees and their learning needs requires that learning and development professionals collaborate horizontally across functions and with the technology function regarding design and delivery of learning resources.

### 9.2.3  Oversight by an Executive Team Comprised of Members from Various

#### 9.2.3.1 Functions Across the Organization As Well As L&D

As L&D becomes more strategically integrated into the performance assessments of the organization with the design and delivery of learning resources taking place across the organization, an oversight team needs to be established. The purpose is not to "dictate" but to make learning initiatives and resources work better across the organization. This includes establishing metrics for assessing effectiveness the learning function and curating plans for enabled continuous individual, functional, and organizational improvement in alignment with organizational priorities. Essentially this is a process of ensuring the learning and development function operates like a business that is connected to and positively impacts the performance of the organization. This oversight also coordinates the L&D function with the transformations that are taking place in the organization and enables sponsorship of transformative initiatives being driven by L&D. In short, it provides a positive space for L&D in the political economy of the organization. When the designs of learning resources are linked with organizational performance, designs are informed by inputs from groups across the organization and an executive oversight team is established with members from various functions as well as R&D, being a "business partner" is no longer a cliché; it's reality with strategic HRD, an essential component of the overall organization's strategy.

### 9.3  A Culture Enabling the Development of the Workforce of the Future

The changes described above in this chapter will need to increasingly take place concurrently in organizations given the pace of change and the need for agility as digital technology drives changes in both the external and internal political economy of the organization. This need can only be met through vertical and horizontal interactions described above. These interactions will also change the culture of the organization. Changes in performance assessments and compensation that consider contributions members of the workforce are making to help the performance of other team members described above create incentives for these and other new workforce behaviors.

As internal and external networks become more fluid and organizational structures more flattened with cross-functional teams, senior executives and managers need to "assess their culture and take steps to ensure that risk-taking, collaboration, and innovation are strong values" (Young & Nair, 2017, p. 11). These assessments can take place through periodic surveys, comments made on discussion boards, and informal conversations that take place while walking around in social gatherings. Talent management professional need to be continually putting on their "anthropologist hats" or "organizational development hats" and be paying attention to what cultural values are manifest across the organization. Learning and development have a role to play by providing learning resources developing skills related to collaboration and inquiry. These skills are becoming more important than ever before as AI changes the roles employees are given that involve working in and across teams and functions. Effective adaption of technologies also plays a role in establishing a culture of learning. See Box 1.2 in Chap. 1 providing an example of how IBM has been enabling a culture of learning through mobile and social engagement.

Given the increasing need for reskilling and upskilling developing a culture of continuous learning is an important aspect of the culture of twenty-first century organizations. This is the glue binding together the various functions engaged together for creating and implementing innovative changes through the complex socio-technical ecosystem of the organization. "Amidst the current and future business complexities, a learning culture will be the differentiator that enables employees and organizations to stay relevant" (Abel & Nair, 2015, p. 33). For a case example, see the case study Cultural Transformation at Novartis: Learning at the Core in the Case Examples section of this book following this chapter.

## 9.4    Summary and Conclusion

While it is impossible to conclusively know what will be the future work given the complexities and uncertainties involved, it is clear that changes in how work is performed will be occurring more rapidly than in the past and talent will be defined and allocated across the organization based on skills not job descriptions. Further organizations will need to strategically plan for strategically utilizing both full-time and contingent workers. Effectively reskilling and/or upskilling the workforce will be an ongoing continuing practice. Adapting the workforce to the future of work requires effectively coordinating the three main elements of Strategic HRD practice; Human Resource Management—Workforce Development, Learning & Development, and Organizational Development—Establishing a Culture with Learning at the Core. Accomplishing this involves establishing coordinating teams drawing on executives from various functions across the organization including HR in the process of designing learning interventions and providing governance. All these initiatives need to be linked to the strategic goals of the organization. As these initiatives unfold, it is necessary for the L&D professional to have business acumen as they engage in dialogues with executives and managers across the organization. Also, it is necessary for L&D, and HRD professionals in general, to be conversant regarding the application of digital systems and be able to explain how they have been created as they are implemented and impacting the workforce.

While preparing and continuing to development people and learning systems for the highest possible achievable performance to meet the organization's strategic goals, while adult and organizational learning competencies remain central for L&D professionals, the portfolio of how learning is delivered will continue to evolve. Technology-based delivery of learning will continue to advance. Like all members of the workforce L&D professionals will have to continually upskill. Further, the functions of HRM, L&D, and what has traditionally been called OD will continually become interconnected and overlapping. Again, like the rest of the organization members of the "talent management through HRD workforce" will be allocated to projects and assignments based on skills rather than job/functional titles. We invite all members of the HR function to revisit the "Core Question Guide for Situation Analysis" provided at the end of Chap. 6. The challenge is not only teaching or facilitating strategic thinking, but to have become part of one's habitus.

We conclude with a projection regarding an expanded role of HRD practice; specifically connecting talent management with societal learning; strategically taking organizational actions that address challenges facing both the organization and a segment of the larger society. For example, increasingly a college degree is required for various roles that previously did not require them. This is making upward mobility more challenging for many in families and communities with limited resources, especially given the increasingly high cost of a college education. Approximately 60% of American workers don't have a degree; 70% of rural workers don't have a degree while technology is making many of their jobs obsolete. The question is are we leaving talent on the table? Particularly at a time when companies are dealing with challenges in finding talent for jobs requiring coding and related kinds of technology skills.

For example, IBM needed to obtain more software engineers. IBM has found one solution to this need and also addressing the growing problem of upward mobility to middle class jobs by creating an apprenticeship program for workers without a college degree or even any college attendance. Apprentices in the program have worked in low paying jobs like mining coal, working on oil rigs, and in coffee shops and have transitioned to new career paths as software engineers and cyber security engineers. Upon completion of the program, the apprentices have full-time roles almost tripling their prior income. IBM hasn't built the kinds of red flags into the recruiting process that would just reject applicants without assessing potentially relevant skills and motivations. The initiative is targeted on those without degrees and has been successful in working with a diverse set of applicants from traditionally marginalized populations. In assessing the program, IBM has partnered with the American Council on Education and it has been determined that completing the apprenticeship program is equal to 45 college credits and can be transferred into a degree program if the person decides to pursue a degree. But in terms of his or her current role, it is their skill set and performance that is important and shaping their initial career path.

This is an interesting strategic initiative that not only addresses the company's needs but also reflects one response for addressing a broader social issue—how expensive attending college has become and how that has impacted upward mobility for a segment of our society. It illustrates the broader socio-economic and cultural impact for positive change that is a potential for talent management practices by connecting initiatives designed for addressing organizational needs and needs for social change. Of course, they need to be done ethically. Given the many issues being created by the rapid changes that are producing loser along with 'winners' this is an important dimension of HRD practice.

Another example of the changing territory of learning and development is the Grow with Google career certificates initiative. On October 29, 2021 a press conference was held in Middletown, CT featuring Governor Ned Lamont, Connecticut State Colleges and Universities President Terrence Cheng, and Alphabet's Chief Financial Officer Ruth Porat to announce that Google was partnering with Connecticut to provide the full suite of Google Career Certificates across the Connecticut state college and universities system. The program is now available to all community colleges and career and technical education high school across the U.S. Provided online the certificates prepare students for in-demand technology related jobs within 3–6 months. No degree or experience required. The program will prepare a diverse population of Connecticut residents with the training to fill positions in data analytics, IT support, project management, and UX design fields that are projected to grow over the coming decade. After completing the program, graduates can share their resume with an employer consortium of more than 150 companies such as Infosys, Verizon, Walmart, Wayfair, and Google. Yes, the political economic spectrum of HRD initiates is transforming in the skills focused labor market.

A conversation that needs to be continued.

## References

Abel, A. L., & Nair, S. (2015). *Future-skilling your workforce: Leveraging people strategies for developing future capabilities*. The Conference Board.

Berg, J. (2020). J&J rolling out VR headsets to train surgeons. *MedCity News*. Retrieved from https://medcitynews.com/2020/02/jj-rolling-out-vr-headsets-to-train-surgeons/

Cogan, B., & Gencarelli, T. (2015). *Baby boomers and popular culture*. ABC-CLIO, LLC.

Davenport, T. H., & Westerman, G. (2021). How HR leaders are preparing for the AI-enabled workforce. *MIT Sloan Management Review*, March 17th. Retrieved from https://sloanreview.mit.edu/article/how-hr-leaders-are-preparing-for-the-ai-enabled-workforce/

Devine, M. (2021). *Navigating to a skills-based approach to talent development*. The Conference Board. Retrieved from https://www.conference-board.org/topics/next-generation-HR/skills-based-to-talent-development

Field, E., Majumder, S., Pereira, C., Schaninger, B., (2020). *Hire more for skills, less for industry experience*. McKinsey Blog, December. Retrieved from https://www.mckinsey.com/business-functions/organization/our-insights/the-organization-blog/hire-more-for-skills-less-for-industry-experience

Gargiulo, S. (2011). *The global workforce: Challenge or asset?* CNN, Cable News Network, Turner Broadcasting System, Inc. Retrieved from https://www.cnn.com/2011/10/27/business/global-workforce/index.html

Jesuthasan, R., & Boudreau, J. (2021). Work without jobs. *MIT Sloan Management Review, 62*(3), 5–8. Fronters. Retrieved from https://sloanreview.mit.edu/article/work-without-jobs/

Mitchell, C., Young, M., & Popiela, A. (2018). *The future of work: Frontline challenges in an era of digital transformation.* The Conference Board.

Prensky, M. (2001). Digital natives, digital immigrants. *On the Horizon, 9*(5), 1–6. MCB University Press.. https://doi.org/10.1108/10748120110424816

Schwartz, J., Hatfield, S., Jones, R., & Anderson, S. (2019). *What is the future of work? Redefining work, workforces, and workplaces.* Deloitte Insights, April 1. Retrieved from https://www2.deloitte.com/us/en/insights/focus/technology-and-the-future-of-work/redefining-work-workforces-workplaces.html.

United States Department of Labor. (2017). *Contingent workers.* News release, August, Retrieved from https://www.dol.gov/newsroom/releases/osec/osec20180607

Warner, J. (2013). The opt-out generation wants back in. *The New York Times,* August, 7th. Retrieved     from     https://www.nytimes.com/2013/08/11/magazine/the-opt-out-generation-wants-back-in.html

Young, M., & Nair, S. (2017). *Driving digital transformation: Why culture & structure matter.* The Conference Board, June Research Report.

# Case Studies of Strategic HRD Practices in the Twenty-First Century

The previous chapters have provided core frameworks and processes for strategic learning and management of HRD practices in organizations. In this chapter, we provide case studies of effective HRD initiatives.

## 10.1 AstraZeneca: Using Artificial Intelligence Coaching Models to Improve Sales Performance

This global pharmaceutical organization aims to push the boundaries of science to deliver life-changing medicine. As the pace of change in health care (including pharmaceuticals) continues to accelerate—through legislation, how medical practices are organized, and how employment has changed over the years—managing through those changes is critical to the success of the organization and the individual. Within the chaos of change, AstraZeneca has turned to coaching as a strategy to help manage through it. For its US-based salesforce of 4000 people, AstraZeneca focused on elevating the coaching expertise of its 600+ field leaders whose reach can influence thousands of others through their daily interactions with customers, managers, and sales representatives.

As AstraZeneca began its coaching approach, it clearly defined what coaching means in its environment and rolled out an implementation plan. As the coaching approach gained traction, the company focused on how to coach well and measure how well it was working for coaches in the field. The most straightforward way, directly observing a conversation, is difficult to do with managers and sales representatives in the field.

### 10.1.1  Beyond Field Coaching Forms

Like many sales organizations, AstraZeneca uses a field coaching form that's designed to capture each day between the manager and sales representative, documenting what went well, what could be done better going forward, how each is feeling, what the coaching focus is, and more. As a result of this continuous documentation, thousands of field coaching forms are submitted each year. Leaders want to analyze all the forms and find ways to help their salesforce improve, but their own daily demands make it difficult.

In late 2017, AstraZeneca asked itself how it could use artificial intelligence (AI) to automatically read every field coaching form just as a human would read it by evaluating it and providing feedback. To build the model, AstraZeneca asked what it was measuring and why. For the manager and sales representative, the focus is a two-way dialogue about coaching. While researching the factors in a field coaching form that drive performance, AstraZeneca uncovered a rubric that correlates how a field coaching form is written to improved business performance. For humans, reading a form, evaluating it against a rubric, determining what's going on, and finding correlations on a consistent basis is difficult. So AstraZeneca built an AI model to do that and provide insights for all field coaching forms.

### 10.1.2  Driving Behavior Change

Since its inception 1.5 years ago, the program has provided a dashboard of what coaching looks like by geography and even by individual. For example, a manager in Oklahoma City with a team of 10 people coaches them throughout a quarter, resulting in dozens of submitted field coaching forms. The AI model can read those forms and tell that manager how focused the manager is with each person on the team. It can pinpoint how many different things the manager brings up in the coaching conversation and what the representative is doing well or needs to work on. The AI model can then make recommendations on if the form is focused, which allows the manager to make any needed adjustments for the future. The model produces a graph showing what is most talked about in the field coaching forms and how it varies across the sales team. While seeing the actual data points is less critical, the true value lies in using the data to have a coaching conversation. This allows coaching managers to dive deeper into what the salesperson is trying to achieve, what the manager's goals are with the team or representative, how what the manager sees in the dashboard aligns with what the team is trying to accomplish, how the dashboard matches up with regional/national initiatives, and more. These questions, which weren't asked before the existence of this dashboard, enable managers to reflect on their coaching conversations and tailor their approach by individual.

### 10.1.3  Objective Performance Evaluations

Another intriguing, insight came around performance evaluation. AstraZeneca found that 90 percent of performance ratings on the field coaching forms were a 3 or 4 (on a 1–5 scale, with 5 being best), indicating a highly subjective and perhaps less valuable conversation around performance. While the ranking is of less importance, it sparked a conversation around giving managers more tools and resources to have more objective performance conversations.

### 10.1.4  Taking the AI Leap

Through the pilot, AstraZeneca found an opportunity to partner with machines to offload "busywork" that is tedious or difficult for humans. The company has been using this partnership to inform its broader efforts to work with people who have different perceptions or preconceived notions about AI, framing the use of the AI model around growth and development.

AstraZeneca initially sat with the pilot group to reflect on what they are doing and not doing, with the aim of helping leaders and managers be better coaches. The program was not about measuring them, identifying if they did something wrong, or assigning them a number that they need to improve on. Rather, it was designed to be a partnership between human and machine to improve individual performance through coaching.

To ensure that human–machine connection stays present, AstraZeneca reminds participants that humans are the ones who developed the AI model, and humans can adjust it. Today, a broad governance panel periodically checks on the AI model to make sure it is on task and aligned to the present objectives while giving the company flexibility to adjust the model as needed.

### 10.1.5  Program Results and Future Plans

The AI model for the field coaching forms is an ongoing program, and AstraZeneca continues to analyze incoming data. Overall, there has been a very positive sentiment about the initiative, and it has had an impact on people. For some managers, it's been an opportunity to change their coaching approach with struggling sales representatives to enable them to accelerate their sales growth. For others, a deeper level of engagement between the manager and sales representative has led to a move away from a directive approach to one focused on problem-solving, self-awareness, and reflection.

AstraZeneca is in the process of rolling out the AI-based field coaching program across its US salesforce and anticipates a positive response and impactful behavior change. Further, the company is exploring ways to analyze trends and connect people who have been successful in dealing with certain challenges.

*This case study is based on telephone conversations, interviews, and a podcast with Kevin Murray, Associate Director, Commercial Leadership Excellence, AstraZeneca Pharmaceuticals.*

## 10.2    McMains Children's Developmental Center Identifying the Most Important Customer (MIC) and Creating Value Curves (VC) to Plot a New Strategic Direction

Current Managing Director:  Anne Hindrichs

Managing Director at time of case study:  Janet Ketcham

Location:  Baton Rouge, LA

Founded:  1954

Industry Sector:  Non-profit Rehabilitative Medical Services

Number of Employees (2020):   18 full-time therapists and administrative staff; 2 Part-time staff, 1 contract Medical Psychologist, 5 volunteer physicians

Mission:  Advance the quality of life for children and their families by providing physical, developmental, psychological, academic, and communication services.

### 10.2.1  Background and Organization History

The McMains Children's Developmental Center (MCDC) began as The United Cerebral Palsy Association of Greater Baton Rouge, Inc. in 1954. Created by a group of concerned parents and community leaders including orthopedist Dr. Frank McMains, MCDC served children with cerebral palsy by providing physical, occupational, and speech therapy services. When the MCDC was founded, there were no other facilities in the greater Baton Rouge area providing similar services for children with cerebral palsy; parents of these children had to take them to New Orleans (an hour and a half drive away) or to Alexandria, LA (a two-and-a-half-hour drive) to the state hospital and school to receive such care so having such services locally was a significant benefit for these families. Since that time, MCDC has expanded its capabilities to include educational and medical psychological services and expanded its reach to include children with other physical, speech, learning, and developmental challenges. Although the "only game in town" providing such services when founded, by the beginning of the twenty-first century, other non-profit as well as for-profit organizations had begun operations in the greater Baton Rouge area providing similar services for children with physical, developmental, and learning disabilities. In 2011, the then Managing Director of the MCDC asked Innovation Insights, a consultancy, to facilitate a strategic assessment of the organization to increase new patient referrals by assuring it maintained its reputation as the leading clinic in the Baton Rouge area providing a broad range of services for children with developmental challenges using Value Innovation (VI) methodology.

### 10.2.2  VI Methodology

VI methodology is based on the reconstructionist strategic concepts of W. Chan Kim and Renée Mauborgne, first introduced in Harvard Business Review in 1997, "Value Innovation: The Strategic Logic of High Growth" (1). This, and subsequent Kim and Mauborgne publications, were later compiled into the best-selling business book, *Blue Ocean Strategy* (2). The basic strategic premise of Blue Ocean Strategy is that the ideas and actions of the enterprise/company/organization shape the environment in which it operates, as opposed to the constructionist strategic mindset where the operating environment dictates how the enterprise/company/organization functions.

A Blue Ocean Strategy is accomplished by visualizing strategy and opportunities to increase value for its customers using a strategy canvas. Visually, in one graph, the strategy canvas pictures where an organization and its competitors are investing time, effort, personnel, and funding (along the horizontal axis) and the value provided to their customers in terms of products, service, and delivery (on the vertical axis). Identifying and implementing how the enterprise/company/organization can increase the value provided to their customers can create a Blue Ocean environment of uncontested market space, thereby making the competition irrelevant.

All well and good, but actually identifying Blue Ocean opportunities and implementing the tactics to move into uncontested market space can be daunting. In order to develop practical solutions to create Blue Ocean opportunities, a series of working groups, in which the author of this case participated, sponsored by the Industrial Research Institute (rebranded the Innovation Research Interchange in 2018) met from 1999 to 2005 and created practical tools to make Blue Ocean Strategy work (3,4,5). From these working groups, and a subsequent book by Dr. Richard Lee and Nina Goodrich, working group facilitators, providing examples in practice (6), three fundamental tools emerged:

1. Understanding the enterprise's/company's/organization's Value Chain:

    (a) Each company/entity/function/person that is involved in a buying/selling/ using *or influencing* transaction between the product or service my enterprise/company/organization provides and the ultimate end user as it relates to the focal point question

2. Identifying the Most Important Customer (MIC) in the Value Chain; ask three questions:

   (a) If there's a problem/issue with my enterprise's/company's/organization's product or service, who in the Value Chain is responsible for taking the necessary immediate action to rectify the situation

   (b) Who in the Value Chain stands to lose the most financially if there's a problem/issue with my enterprise's/company's/organization's product or service

   (c) Who in the Value Chain is the most likely to recognize the value provided by my enterprise's/company's/organization's product or service

3. Visualizing Blue Ocean Opportunities by creating Value Curves (Fig. 10.1)

### 10.2.3 Applying VI Methodology and Tools to the MCDC Strategic Assessment

The first step in a VI assessment is to meet with the senior executives requesting the assessment, in this case the Managing Director of the MCDC at the time and members of the MCDC Board's Strategic Planning Committee, to outline the scope of the project, the focal point question (how do we attract new patients by assuring the MCDC maintained its leading reputation in the greater Baton Rouge area) and define the MCDC Value Chain (Fig. 10.2)

Discussions with the Managing Director and Board Members revealed three pathways for attracting new patients: (1) Donor recommendation to parents of children with disabilities; (2) physicians referring new patients to the MCDC; and (3) word of mouth of the capability of the MCDC therapists to parents of children who

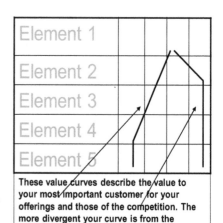

- **It's divided into two halves:**
  - On the left side of the curve are the elements of performance that define the product or service. In aggregate these define the total product or service offering
  - On the right side are the values to the Most Important Customer for each element

These value curves describe the value to your most important customer for your offerings and those of the competition. The more divergent your curve is from the competition, the more distinct your offering.

**Fig 10.1**  What is a value curve?

**Fig. 10.2** MCDC Value Chain for the focal point question

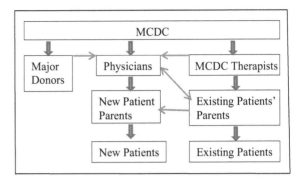

would benefit from the services provided by the clinic as well as feedback to their children's physicians. Further "peeling back the onion" indicated that the predominant Value Chain path for attracting new patients was through physician referrals. (As an aside, the Value Chain may look different depending on the focal point question being addressed. For instance, if the focal point question had been how does MCDC improve services for our patients, the Major Donors, and Physicians would not be in a direct Value Chain, but outside the direct Value Chain in what is called a Value Web where they are influencers; still important entities to be considered in the next phase of the VI process, identifying the MIC, but not in the direct Value Chain.)

Once the Value Chain is established, the next step is to identify the MIC using the three questions. In the case of the MCDC, the three questions indicate different entities in the Value Chain:

Question 1 points to three entities:

- Major Donors (if there is a serious issue with the services provided, they will take steps to rectify it by putting financial pressure on MCDC by reducing or even withholding funding).
- Parents, obviously, who will rectify the situation by removing their children.
- Physicians who will discontinue referring children to the MCDC.

Question 2 points to the parents for it is the parents who have the most to lose financially as well as in time and effort to find another clinic providing services (even if services are covered wholly or partially by insurance and/or Medicaid, there is still the time and effort to find and get accepted by another clinic).

Question 3 points primarily to physicians, who are in the best position to recognize the value (and quality) of the services offered by the MCDC and in a position to compare with services offered by other clinics.

In identifying the MIC, ideally, all three questions point to only one of the entities in the Value Chain. In the real world of Value Chains and identifying the MIC, the MCDC is more common, where there is not a clear entity that stands out as the MIC. In the case of the MCDC, three MICs (physicians, parents, and major donors) were chosen for the next step in the VI process, contextual interviewing to identify gaps in value provided for MCDC services. Since two of the three questions (Question 1 and Question 3) point to physicians as having the greatest influence on referrals to the MCDC, the majority of interviews were with physicians (some who routinely referred patients to the MCDC, and several that rarely or had never referred patients to the MCDC). The number of interviews were 7 with physicians, 3 with major donors, and 4 with parents. In addition, a group session was held with MCDC therapists and staff. For each of the interviews, including the group, the interviewer facilitated the interview along with a scribe to capture comments from the interviewee. Lead-in questions were sent in advance to the interviewee (Fig. 10.3). Based on the initial response to each lead-in question, the interviewer asked follow-up questions to further clarify the initial response. Depending on the interviewee, each interview lasted between 30 and 90 min.

Once the interviews were completed and the responses to questions transcribed, computer-assisted qualitative text analysis software along with manual review of the interviewee responses was used to identify common themes from the interviews and create the MCDC's Elements of Performance (Fig. 10.4).

Based on number of interviewee responses that corresponded to each Element of Performance, the thirteen Elements of Performance were ranked from the highest to the lowest in importance using Analytic Hierarchy Process statistical software. Based on interview responses, a "value" from 0 to 5 was assigned to each Element of Performance, with 0 being of no value provided by the MCDC for an Element of Performance to 5 being very high value provided by the MDCD for the Element of Performance.

---

**Donors**
- What keeps you awake at night re. services in Baton Rouge for children with disabilities
- What trends to you expect may impact future donations
- How do you determine funding (amount and organizations)
- What is your impression of MCDCs services & capabilities compared to other comparable organizations
- What services are not being provided by any organization that should be

**Physicians**
- What keeps you awake at night re. services in Baton Rouge for children with disabilities
- What services are you aware of provided by MCDC
- What organizations do you refer your patients and why
- What is your impression of MCDC's services & capabilities compared to other comparable organizations
- What do your referrals say about MCDC
- What services are not being provided by any organization that should be

**Parents**
- What services does your child receive at MCDC
- Why did you select MCDC
- What is your impression of the services provided at MCDC
- Would you recommend MCDC to a friend or co-worker
- What services are not provided by MCDC that your child is receiving elsewhere
- What services are provided by MCDC but your child is receiving elsewhere
- What are you most concerned about re. services at MCDC

**Staff**
- What is the process from referral, providing services, billing and collection of fees
- Where are there bottlenecks in the process
- What are MCDC's strengths and capabilities and how would you rate them
- What do you like and dislike about being on staff at MCDC
- What are you most concerned about regarding services at MCDC

**Fig. 10.3** Lead-in interviewee questions

**Fig. 10.4**  MCDC
elements of performance

- **Business Model Sustainability**
- **Therapies provided**
- **Complementary services provided**
- **Complementary services quality**
- **Wait time to 1ˢᵗ appt.**
- **Therapy Quality**
- **Location**
- **Physician Awareness**
- **Front office functionality**
- **Therapists clerical support**
- **Physical plant layout / appearance**
- **Partnerships/Alliances/Collaboration**
- **Leadership Succession / Coaching**

# Slalom® Assessment

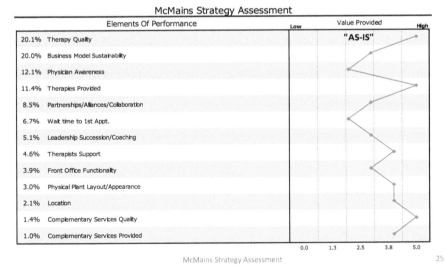

McMains Strategy Assessment

| | Elements Of Performance | Low | Value Provided | High |
|---|---|---|---|---|
| 20.1% | Therapy Quality | | "AS-IS" | |
| 20.0% | Business Model Sustainability | | | |
| 12.1% | Physician Awareness | | | |
| 11.4% | Therapies Provided | | | |
| 8.5% | Partnerships/Alliances/Collaboration | | | |
| 6.7% | Wait time to 1st Appt. | | | |
| 5.1% | Leadership Succession/Coaching | | | |
| 4.6% | Therapists Support | | | |
| 3.9% | Front Office Functionality | | | |
| 3.0% | Physical Plant Layout/Appearance | | | |
| 2.1% | Location | | | |
| 1.4% | Complementary Services Quality | | | |
| 1.0% | Complementary Services Provided | | | |

0.0   1.3   2.5   3.8   5.0

McMains Strategy Assessment                                                      25

**Fig. 10.5**  MCDC "As-Is" value curve

The next step in the VI process is to create the "As-Is" Value Curve for the MCDC using Slalom® Software (7) and shown in Fig. 10.5.

The final step in the VI Process is to meet with the organization's senior team, in this case the Executive Director at the time and the Board Members on the Strategic Planning Committee to review the findings of the assessment and to identify areas for improvement in value provided. In general, resources in most, if not all, organizations are limited so that improvement in all Elements of Performance cannot be tackled at the same time. Organizations should work on improving areas where the value provided is 3.0 or less (on a 0 to 5 scale), but also not lose focus on those areas where high value is already being achieved (in the MCDC case, Therapy Quality and Therapies Provided) so the high value can be maintained. At the workshop to review the assessment results, the recommendation was for the MCDC to work on improving value for Business Model Sustainability, Physician Awareness, Wait Time to 1st Appt., Partnerships/Alliances/Collaborations and Front Office Functionality.

- Business Model Sustainability. At the time of the VI assessment, a significant amount of funding for the MCDC came from agency grants, which by 2011 were declining as a result of the 2008–2009 recession, as opposed to fee for services from patients' health insurance plans and/or Medicaid. MCDC was not an in-network provider for several commercial insurance plans. Also contributing to Business Model Sustainability concerns was operation hours for the MCDC. The MCDC followed the school schedule for major holidays. Thus, the MCDC was closed when the schools were closed for Thanksgiving Holidays (1 week); Christmas/New Year Holidays (2 weeks); Mardi Gras (2 days) and Easter/spring break (1 week). The MCDC also closed for two weeks during the summer.
- Physician Awareness. What became apparent during the physician interviews was that many were not aware of the breadth of therapy services provided by the MCDC; many thinking it only provided physical therapy services for mainly children with cerebral palsy. Others were aware of the range of services provided by the MCDC, but when referring their patients to the MCDC learned that the MCDC was not in their patient's insurance network.
- Wait Time to 1st Appointment. Interviews with both physicians and parents revealed extensive wait times for some patients to get their first appointment or assessment.
- Partnerships/Alliances/Collaboration. Several physicians interviewed as well as the major donors suggested this might be a way to extend the capabilities of the MCDC
- Front Office Functionality. Parents, physicians, and donors all commented that the MCDC front office was often not staffed, phone calls went to voice mail and in some cases, patients and their parents were left standing at the front office for up to 15 or more minutes (or up to an hour if during lunch time) waiting to be checked in.

## 10.2.4  Steps taken to improve value provided by the MCDC

As a result of the VI Assessment, several steps have been taken to improve the value the MCDC provided for the Elements of Performance:

- To improve business model sustainability, the MCDC has increased the number of commercial insurance plans it accepts. Opening times are no longer tagged to the East Baton Rouge Parish school schedule but follow the normal federal and state holiday schedule and remain open throughout the school summer vacation months. Revenue is not as dependent on agency grants as it was with an increasing percentage of revenue coming from insurance reimbursements. Increased community fund raising activities and corporate financial sponsors and in-kind donations have also been established.
- With an increased focus on physician awareness and referrals as well as community awareness, a Communications and Marketing Manager position was established.
- Wait time to first appointment as well as improved front office efficiency has been helped by adding additional therapists in Occupational Therapy and Speech Therapy as well as staff (a Medical Receptionist and an Intake Coordinator). Following the normal federal and state holiday schedule rather than the school opening schedule has also reduced waiting times. The front office is also staffed throughout the day; there is not a time when someone is not in the front office to answer calls and check-in patients.
- Increased collaboration with major healthcare groups in the Baton Rouge area has been established to further increase referrals to the MCDC.

The improvements from the above changes are reflected in the financials of the MCDC from 2011, when the VI Assessment was carried out, to the present (2019 data):

| 2011 Revenue | 2019 Revenue |
|---|---|
| $925,000 | $1,639,000 |

The MCDC is well positioned to continue its growth and service to the greater Baton Rouge area. One of the MCDC's donors best described the MCDC in the 2019 Annual report:

"There is no other facility in our area that is solely dedicated to the physical, mental and social well-being of all children with disabilities and their families. To see the reaction of children and their families when they accomplish something once thought impossible is truly amazing"

*This case was written by H.R. Penton Ph.D., President & Founder, Innovation Insights*

## 10.3  Cisco: Career Management for What's Ahead

| | |
|---|---|
| CEO | Chuck Robbins |
| Headquarters | San Jose, CA |
| Founded | 1984 |
| Industry sector | Network hardware & software |
| Number of employees | (FY2018) 74,200 |

### 10.3.1  Two Ambitious Initiatives to Effectively Compete in the Market for Talent

The Cisco talent management team recognized that for Cisco to remain competitive for talent in its industry, as well as in the market,, they needed to anticipate the skills required for the future. And in the face of skill and talent shortages, they needed to retain their existing talent. These realizations led to two ambitious, intertwined initiatives that together are redefining how Cisco helps its employees manage their careers. They know that "prescribed, leader-directed career paths" are not what we see in our place of work today. Instead, they are paving the way for employees and managers to share ownership for dynamic, fluid career paths that evolve, step by step, over time.

### 10.3.2  Coupling Analytics and Organizational Network Analysis for Insight

The first initiative involved a comprehensive analysis of core roles and key skills, regardless of job title. With the help of Burning Glass, other external resources, and both their own and their competitors' employee populations, they identified a skill taxonomy that can be refreshed over time, consisting of 16 groupings of 54 skills, based on roles (not job descriptions). Then, they identified skill gaps by identifying their most critical anticipated skills and comparing the skills within their employee population to those of their competitors.

Cisco is now experimenting with applying adjacency modeling to identify potential job moves, or career steps, from one role to another. For example, Role X, which may have a shrinking demand, may require skills A, B, and C, while Role Z, which may have a growing demand, may require skills A, B, and D. With some further training, employees in Role X with the "skill and the will" can move into Role Z.

Cisco is taking adjacency modeling one step further by combining it with Organizational Network Analysis (ONA) to identify potential job moves based on interactions among people in different job roles. For example, ONA revealed that User Experience (UX) designers interact heavily with people in marketing and sales, who provide the UX designers with valuable insights about user needs and preferences. This can lead to identifying individuals in sales and marketing roles as potential candidates for UX design roles. By focusing on how the work gets done, new job moves and career steps emerge.

### 10.3.3  A Comprehensive Study of Careers Yields Further Important Insights

In the second initiative,, Cisco performed a cluster analysis on all of the transactional data about job role changes available over the 35 years of the company's existence. This helped them to identify patterns of career movement which formed a series of personas. They further conducted an employee survey, focus groups, and 200 in-depth, one-on-one interviews about what a career looks like. Some key findings from this research include:

- The importance of attention to and regular conversations with employees about their careers
- A strong linkage between a person's ability to play to their strengths (i.e., doing work that energizes them) and employee engagement
- The recognition that while linear career paths are no longer the norm, the perception that they are still remains
- The insight that people aren't looking for formal mentoring programs. They want help identifying others who have things in common with them and can become part of a dynamic network of informal mentors and champions over the course of an individual's career
- Given how dynamic roles and skills are, career steps are more meaningful and relevant than career paths

### 10.3.4  Translating Insights into Action

While Cisco continues both of these research initiatives, they are also implementing a series of practices that apply the insights they have gained about careers in action.

- Weekly check-ins—Cisco uses a team technology platform, called Team Space, that is designed for team leaders and team members to check in each week. Unlike traditional check-ins, which are initiated by the team leader, Cisco's check-ins are initiated by the team member. It gives them the opportunity to share their priorities, emotional experiences to the work, and where they need help with their team leader. A live conversation between the team leader and team member follows the virtual check-in via Team Space. Team Space also yields a rich data set that reveals positive correlations between the attention employees receive through weekly interaction from their team leader and employee engagement.
- Professional development for people leaders—Since leaders have the greatest influence on the distinctive local experience of a team, Cisco has dedicated a full day focused solely on leadership development. They call it Leader Day. It's an annual event where all 11,000 people leaders go offline for a day, connect with other leaders via Cisco's collaboration technology, and develop their unique and authentic approach to leading. Leader Day also sends a signal that team leadership really matters at Cisco.
- A new design for performance management—Research reveals that human beings are unreliable raters of other human beings (called the idiosyncratic Rater Effect). However, research also reveals we're really good raters of our own future intent. And so, four years ago, Cisco eliminated performance ratings. Since then, they've launched a new approach that does not involve rating or ranking another person, but rather focuses on the investments people leaders plan to make in their employees and the actions they will take to support them. All people leaders have

received consistent guidance to hold a development conversation with each employee at least once a quarter and a talent review twice a year. These conversations are in addition to the weekly check-ins. Thus far, almost half of all people leaders have submitted their investments and actions, and a correlation is emerging between a submission and higher levels of engagement.

### 10.3.5  Moving Beyond Engagement to Fulfillment

While Cisco is realizing increased engagement as a result of these initiatives, they are interested in moving beyond how they engage their employees, how they *fulfill* their employees. As one member of the Cisco team shared, "engagement as a construct is fundamentally about getting employees to be more productive." Cisco has an even bolder aspiration to create an environment where all employees can grow, learn, and be at their best.

## 10.4   Center for Entrepreneurship and Innovation Breaking from Higher Education's Traditional Learning Model: From Pipeline to Platform

### 10.4.1  Background

The speed of technological innovation and industry demands are moving faster than higher education's ability to adapt. Although there is a major move to adopt project-based learning—doing away with the usual focus on lectures and exams—the system is not fully equipped in preparing students to enter today's workforce. As the Chronicle of Higher Education states, "Universities are respected for their traditions and commitment to academic standards, but often challenged to respond to dynamic changes and modern expectations of students and employers" (2017).

### 10.4.2  A Snapshot of the Twenty-First Century Learners

The current trend in higher education reflects a need to bring postsecondary education accessible to adult learners: displaced workers, employees with degrees seeking career advancement, the unemployed or underemployed returning to school, retirees seeking post-retirement jobs, employees shifting to a new field, and other lifelong and wide-long leaners seeking to learn out of personal interests. These learners have different needs from traditional college students fresh out of high school and are seeking a degree.

### 10.4.3  Some of the Challenges of Traditional Two- and Four-Year Public Colleges

1. The pandemic resulting in urgent shift to remote learning.
2. Shrinking funding (resulting to limited professional development, freeze hiring, antiquated software programs, dated equipment, and tools).
3. Relevance of existing courses and programs.
4. Turn-around time to secure approval for new courses and modification of old ones.
5. Trained faculty to deliver and facilitate cutting-edge tech driven programs and/or courses.
6. Changing demographics of community college learners (almost half the students are over the age of 25 (Kasworm, p. 231).
7. Cost of higher education, i.e., student loan in relation to potential income.
8. The lure of technical certification and badging offered by industry leaders.

### 10.4.4  New Frontier: Breaking with Traditional Learning Model

In 2018, the Center for Entrepreneurship and Innovation (CEI) was founded by a former entrepreneur-faculty of the Business department. She was also a corporate intrapreneur leading the marketing division of a global bank prior to shifting to academia. The Center was founded as a College-wide incubator of disruptive ideas that students bring to life from concept development to market testing all the way to impact. Its mission is to make entrepreneurship education inclusive and accessible to San Francisco's lower-income and underrepresented student population.

With very limited funding, the founder rolled up her sleeves and proceeded in running this academic unit as a startup. Borrowing from the business playbook, she embraced the idea of bootstrapping and adopted an agile and disruptive new model of teaching and learning. The pandemic triggers a massive shift of business models across major firms across the world, with consumers getting more accustomed to online shopping, streaming from their devices and online learning. Even late technology adopters and not-so-tech savvy consumers realized that these seemingly "scary" and intimidating alternatives offer conveniences that they feared in the past. To remain relevant and stay in business, businesses pivoted and adjusted to this new world. With this changing landscape, higher education has to quickly adapt, which entails redesigning its business model.

It might be helpful to start with the definition of a business model, defined as a blueprint that describes how a company creates, delivers, and extracts value. One particular program that I will use is Stanford's Idea to Market to illustrate a business model architecture (Fig. 10.6).

Each of the sections outlined in the diagram entails strategic actions that would support and complement each part to achieve business growth. Using the same framework, the Higher Education Learning and Teaching model illustrates how this applies to higher education (Fig. 10.7).

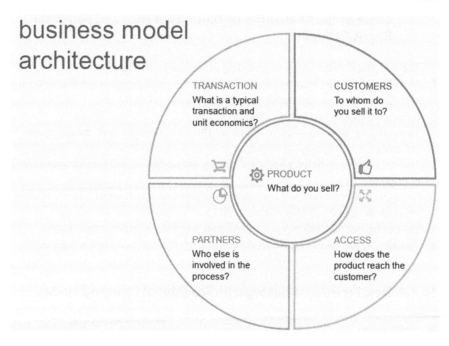

**Fig. 10.6**   Source: Idea to market program, Stanford Center for Professional Development, 2020

**Fig. 10.7**   Higher
education learning and
teaching model

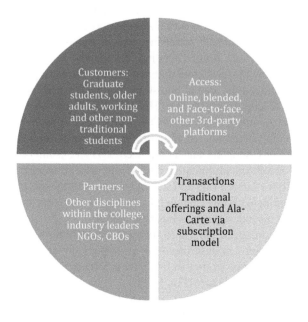

In evaluating the feasibility and viability of CEI using this architecture, I offer the following strategic courses of action. At the center of this diagram is what CEI sells, which right now are six interdisciplinary certificate tracks (all for credit units and for CSU transfer) and not-for-credit certificates for ala-carte participants. The degree programs (AS and AA) are underway.

1. Customers (end users)—Diverse set of learners who are craving for entrepreneurship education to support their nascent venture or for a degree.
2. Access (how does the product reach the customer)—CEI courses are offered F2F, hybrid, and online. Even prior to covid19, the key courses are designed for online offering.
3. Partners (who else is involved in the process)—This is where the major shift in strategy is happening. Several industry collaborations are now in place:

   (a) Entrepreneur-In-Residence program where industry thought leaders, entrepreneurs, and VC partners are tasked to provide mentorship and coaching to students.
   (b) Wider breath of partnerships such as Intuit, HP Life, and Stanford Center for Professional Development who provide training for faculty.
   (c) Intuit Financial Management and Design Thinking courses from Intuit and Michelson Institute for Intellectual Property for IP and other legal services.
   (d) Active membership with other organizations such as Kauffman Foundation, Ratcliffe Foundation, and Nasdaq Entrepreneurship Center offer support.
   (e) Transactions (typical transaction and unit economics)—CCSF offers "Free City," a partnership between CCSF and the City and County of San Francisco. To acquire students, CEI offers its Workshop and Lecture series (facilitated by industry partners) for free even for non-CCSF students. Today, it is common among new startups to offer a "Freemium" revenue model, for CEI this is their freemium offering which helped in gaining traction. To those who want more, they need to "upgrade."

### 10.4.5  A Disruptive Business Model: Moving from Pipeline to Platform

CEI secret sauce lies in its adoption of a platform model. As an overview, two commonly used models are pipeline and platform. As Fig. 10.8 illustrates, pipeline is typical of traditional businesses such as Macy's, Nokia, Zappos. It is linear and flows from producers of goods/services to end users of finished products. The production process is directly contracted by the firm, through direct manufacturing or outsourcing while distribution channels are identified to serve its target market or the end users.

Translating this model to higher education, the pipeline model would have the following elements (Fig. 10.9).

Today, we see more and more businesses migrating or adopting a platform model. Some of the most popular brands using this model are Uber and AirBnb,

**Fig. 10.8**   Source: Stanford Center for Professional Development, Idea to Market Program, 2019

**Fig. 10.9**   Higher Ed pipeline structure

**Fig. 10.10**   Source: Stanford Center for Professional Development, Idea to Market Program, 2019

which are both tech platforms. The platform business structure is more dynamic as it allows to serve dual or multi-sided customer segments, the content providers (supply) and users (demand) are highly dependent of each other. As long as each party provides value, it can achieve exponential growth through network effect. Figure 10.10 illustrates this relationship.

Using this model in academic setting, Fig. 10.11 shows how CEI operating as a hybrid learning platform generate value from wider and deeper collaborations with new types of partnerships. It has its pull effect as students benefit not only from relevant and cutting-edge contents and delivery but also the partner's brand equity. To clarify, CEI is not operating as a tech platform, for example, Amazon Web Services is a technology platform that is not based on a platform business model. What is key here is to ensure that it is a controlled platform (like Apple's). Here are some key strategic changes that CEI adopted:

1. Platform firm does not manufacture the products that they sell (e.g., Alibaba).
   CEI still develops its own products (courses, program) but was augmented from

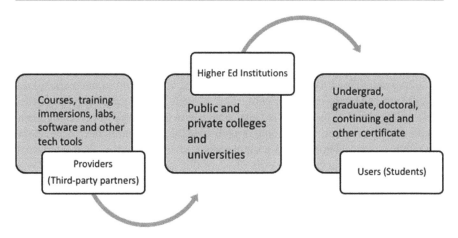

**Fig. 10.11**   Higher Ed platform structure

    importing select modules from third-party partners, i.e., Intuit's Entrepreneurial Finance.

2. Platform does not provide the services that offer on their platform (e.g., Taskrabbit). CEI faculty still teaches the courses in partnership with industry thought leaders, VCs, entrepreneurs through its Workshop and Lecture Series that is embedded in the curriculum.

    CEI connects value creators and users (educators and learners) without handing over the "key" directly to third-party partners. The onus of ensuring academic rigor and standards still rest with CEI. The courses were audited and tweaked to make it more proprietary and are in compliance with CCSF policies and State regulatory bodies. Apple's iPhone exemplifies best how to run a platform: "anybody can write an app, but it has to pass strict tests and the firm keeps 30% of all sales." (The Economist.com, 2016).

    This model is still in its Beta stage, the program is still in evolving, but CEI has its MVP (minimum viable product) that has produced some good results. In 2019, one of its students landed a spot in HP Sustainability Challenge. This year, CEI formed a team of faculty and staff to pitch for NextGen Innovation Hub for its Trades program and won the top prize!

    The founder is aware of some push back from other faculty such as the threat of losing students to these partners, and the fear that industry training programs (or badges) are undermining the value of a college degree. These are all valid concerns to revisit from time to time as the CEI's program lead takes risks just like every startup out there. CEI as an academic program can be a disruptor too but only if it can sustain its flair for innovation and change.

*    This case was prepared by Vivian Faustino, Faculty and Program Lead, City College of San Francisco, All rights reserved, Used with permission.*

## 10.5    A Financial Services Firm Mapping the Political Territory When Adopting Cloud-Based Technologies. An Illustrative Example

In 2020, public cloud technologies are mature and mainstream in the marketplace. Readily utilized by the consumer public (e.g., Google Drive/Docs, Drop Box, Office 365), public cloud technologies are now similarly in the process of becoming mainstream in large enterprises. Leading organizations across sectors have been adopting public cloud technologies as a supplement and compliment to their traditional, on-premises infrastructure. The early phase of this journey involved software-as-a-service capabilities (e.g., Salesforce, ServiceNow, Workday) where firms buying access to the software from the provider, and that provider is running their software in the cloud. The evolution of public cloud technologies has expanded, however, toward Infrastructure-as-a-Service and Platform-as-a-Service hosting models, where the actual software application remains the organizations (vs. a providers), but the physical infrastructure and virtualization, networking and storage are the providers. This is a significant shift in the operating model for information technology organizations who run and operate large infrastructure capabilities within their own data centers. While adopting public cloud technologies offers immense benefits to the firm, use of public cloud technologies requires a fundamental change in the existing technology organization's sense of identity, requiring a re-establishment of the value proposition of on-premises technology and the way in which it differentiates value from the public cloud.

One leading financial services firm grappling with these issues used the mapping of political territory to layout a deliberate approach to understanding and addressing the complex web of stakeholders involved in the transformation. By understanding their individual level of influence, key relationships, and potential for change, and by assessing the inter-dynamics among these stakeholders and groups of stakeholders, the organization has been able to abstract away the day-to-day human interpersonal dynamics to deliver on a significant transformation agenda.

### 10.5.1  Analyzing the Map

The firm's stakeholder map for public cloud adoption is extensive. Starting with the CEO and his leadership team, including the overall steward of the cloud adoption journey—the CIO—and cascading down to the line of business CIOs, the firm's CTO responsible for architecting the integration of public cloud technologies for the firm, and extending to the existing global infrastructure organization, and thousands of end user engineers and technologists, there is a large set of constituents. Not to mention the vendor ecosystem of cloud service providers, consultants and contractors will assist in the technical and financial operational changes which follow. Many of these constituents within the lines of business and their respective technology teams are eager for enterprise access and use of cloud technologies. The potential for agility by provisioning and de-provisioning nearly unlimited resources, on-demand is one of the primary drivers.

Leading public cloud providers like Amazon Web Services (AWS), Microsoft Azure, and Google Cloud Platform (GCP) offer their teams access to both foundational compute, storage, and networking capabilities on-demand, while also layering additional platform capabilities like the ability to perform artificial intelligence and machine learning (AI/ML) at scale. In comparison, on-premises infrastructure environments (e.g., dev/test/prod) takes days—if not weeks—to provision, and the firm is only in the early phases of establishing its own platform-as-a-service capabilities in key areas like AI/ML (compared to Google's already mature offerings).

Similarly, demand from within the C-suite is strong, with a clear and compelling business case for pursuing public cloud as a compliment to existing data centers, most notably the ability to shift fixed Capex expenses to variable Opex expense. As the organization has a lot more hardware, networking and data center space than their steady state business cycles require, to accommodate spikes, thereby spending much more on compute and storage week over week than required. Movement to the public cloud affords the organization to pay when it consumes, on a variable basis vs. the current fixed cost base for infrastructure.

Yet the organization's existing infrastructure organization has years, if not decades of history, sense of identity and purpose tied up in running and operating on-premises infrastructure. And while most firms do not anticipate abandoning the running and maintenance of their own data center space entirely, as there are resiliency and security benefits, among others, the mere directional pull toward public cloud is viewed as a threat by many. Re-establishing the unique value proposition of public cloud technologies relative to existing data center infrastructure and clarifying the ways in which they will collectively provide value for the future of the business is therefore a critical hurdle to overcome for the organization to remain successful.

## 10.5.2  From Mapping to Strategic Action

- Linking Agendas involves identifying opportunities for connecting the firm's strategy with traditional HRD initiatives, where are there win-win opportunities? In the case of public cloud adoption, one of the obvious opportunities that emerges is for large-scale workforce reskilling. Cloud-native architectures and development are the future for technologists and engineers. Learning how to navigate cloud-native capabilities on AWS, GCP, and Azure (among other providers), empowers them to not only make an impact immediately in their current role/organization, but set them up with the skills required for the next decade. Leaders grappling with aging workforce segments without the right skills required can use the opportunity for cloud adoption toward dedicated reskilling as these practitioners work on migrating their existing application workloads to the public cloud. The result is a benefit toward the organization's goal of running an increased portion of its application estate on the public cloud, while addressing talent shortages, demand for key skills and the reskilling of existing talent that risks being left behind in the waves of emergent technologies that will follow on top of the cloud. Now, those eager for public cloud capabilities, and those initially resistant, are more inclined toward participating in the journey due to the common agenda of a shared future.

- Utilizing Currencies involves identifying resources that are useful to others in the organization which therefore hold value in building and sustaining alliances. One example of relevance for this financial services firm adopting public cloud technologies was the currency of security. While information security professionals tend to cringe at the thought of public cloud technologies because of the additional risks associated with them, for example, relying on the third-party cloud provider for certain control mechanisms. Using risk mitigation as a currency also holds value, as cloud-native capabilities offer additional security that legacy infrastructure typically does not—for example, always running the latest software, hardware, and operating systems, thereby foregoing the often growing problems organizations like this firm faced, with end-of-life hardware and software operating within the estate.
- Following the Credibility Path involves identifying those within the organization who are well-respected and trusted. At this firm, that involved putting a long-tenured, distinguished engineer who had supported the firm through equally as transformational change in charge of architecting the future of the firm's public cloud capability. Engaging them early and making them the stewards of the change creates credibility for the vision/direction and helps sooth lingering uneasiness.
- Challenging Assumptions involves looking at the assumptions of those who are most resistant. What is it that they believe? In this case, digging into the perceptions that the firm would wind up vacating its Data Centers to operate in the public cloud. By open and honest conversation, leaders were able to clarify what's led to those assumptions, and the ways in which both forms of infrastructure and platforms will co-exist and complement each other.
- Facilitating Learning involves influencing others on change initiatives as an educative process and having learning focused conversations as part of the advocacy process. For this firm, having a dedicated team that uses their time engaging with and coaching application teams on the journey to the cloud—with both technical support and more strategic advisory insight. This process of understanding each team's current thinking, challenges. and areas of opportunity, with a centrally led set of subject matter experts coaching and advising, has moved the organization collectively toward greater appreciation for what is possible, and greater creativity in the ways in which each application team will embark on that journey to the cloud.

## 10.6   A U.S. Based Automotive Retailer AI for Talent Acquisition: Improving Pre-hire Assessments and the Interview Process

One of the largest automotive retailers in the United States has witnessed the substantial impacts AI brings to talent acquisition in just four short years. Before, average time to fill at the company was over 100 days. Some requisitions were open for more than two years, including a requisition with 600 applications that had never been reviewed. The Talent Acquisition (TA) team realized that to turn the chaos around, they must change the hiring process fundamentally, and technology would allow them to accelerate and sustain the change.

### 10.6.1  Application of AI for TA

The key challenge the TA team identified was that most hiring managers didn't have time to conduct both screening interviews and more detailed, in-person interviews. To ameliorate the situation, the team searched for digital interview platforms and eventually decided to partner with HireVue, an AI-powered platform that specializes in pre-hire assessments and video interviewing. In just a few minutes, HireVue can complete the following steps that used to take a recruiter much longer: screen résumé, analyze results of the pre-hire assessment, and automatically invite those who meet minimum qualifications for an on-demand video interview conducted by the machine (using assisted intelligence). As the platform conducts interviews with candidates directly, recruiters no longer sit in on those 30-minute conversations but can watch the recordings anytime that works best for them to assess candidacy.

To ensure a fair and structured process, all candidates applying for the same role receive the same questions. Each role has its own set of interview questions created by recruiters and hiring managers to ensure a close alignment with job requirements and business needs. For example, if the role is in sales, the platform asks candidates to describe a situation when they had to deal with a difficult customer. HireVue's AI scoring system also ranks the top candidates based on its analysis of the interview, providing insights and suggestions to help recruiters make more informed decisions (using augmented intelligence).

### 10.6.2  Business Impact

- Time to fill (TTF) decreases. Since the company has adopted HireVue, the average TTF in sales has decreased from 75 to 30 days; for auto technicians, a role that's extremely difficult to fill in the particular region, the TTF has also decreased drastically—from 100 to 59 days. This represented a substantial savings. The TA team calculated the ROI of a simple technician role and found that for every extra day a technician role is open, the company loses at least $500 profit.
- Candidate experience/net promoter score (NPS) improves. Candidate experience is completely different than it used to be. In 2018, the firm reached an average of 78.6 percent of candidate NPS—it even reached 90 percent for one month.
- Quality of hire improves. New sales executives sell four more cars a month than their peers.
- Cost per hire (CPH) decreases. Since the implementation of HireVue, CPH has dropped from $630 to $450.
- Turnover decreases. Employee retention has seen improvement, too. From 2017 to 2018, the turnover rate of the company declined from 37 percent to 29 percent (the average attrition rate in the automotive industry is 60–70 percent).

**Snapshot of artificial intelligence for talent acquisition: interviewing and pre-hire assessments**

| Stage | Automation (AI precursor) | Assisted intelligence | Augmented intelligence | Autonomous intelligence |
|---|---|---|---|---|
| Interviewing | Video software and scanned video interviews | Robot proactively calls and interviews candidates froma preset list of questions | Platform monitors interviews, and ranks candidates | |
| Assessments | Online skills assessment testing; generates reports | Realistic job previews with gamification and simulation | Validation and candidate ranking after pre-hire assessments | *Self-learning platform creates individualized assessments based on candidate's background and open role* |

*Note:* Italics = future possibility. *Source:* The Conference Board

*This case was written by Dr. Robin Erickson, Principal Researcher in Human Capital at The Conference Board*

## 10.7    A Singapore-Based Multinational Financial Services Company AI for Talent Acquisition: Enhancing Candidate Communication and Pre-hire Assessments

A Singapore-based multinational financial services corporation was planning to hire 40 percent more wealth planning managers to support its growing wealth management business. On average, recruiters at the company spent up to 20 percent of their time collecting information and communicating with applicants before interviewing short-listed candidates. With both staffing needs and work complexity increasing, the firm realized it was time to implement new technology.

### 10.7.1  Application of AI for TA

To be more effective and efficient in hiring wealth planning managers, the company's Talent Acquisition (TA) team and a Singapore-based start-up collaborated to develop the first virtual recruiter for banks in Southeast Asia. The virtual recruiter can review résumés, post prescreening questions, collect responses, and conduct psychometric profiling assessments (using assisted intelligence). With the virtual recruiter, TA professionals no longer have to spend many hours screening applicants. Leveraging an algorithm-based scoring system that assesses candidates' psychometric test results and background information such as education, work experience, and skills, the tool provides a short list of candidates for each role for talent advisers' consideration during the initial screening stage (using augmented intelligence). Through the chatbot feature, candidates also benefit from a more streamlined process, faster responses, and real-time interaction available 24/7 (using both assisted and augmented intelligence). The time saved by the virtual recruiter allows the TA team to perform higher-value work such as recruitment marketing, sourcing, engaging with candidates, and communicating with hiring managers.

To further improve the platform, the company conducted a pilot before officially launching it. Through the pilot, TA professionals developed the new skill of training the platform to assess candidates and answer candidates' queries. Once officially launched about five months later, the virtual recruiter had already interacted with over 600 candidates.

## 10.7.2  Business Impact

- Recruiter productivity increases. By automating the prescreening process, the virtual recruiter helps save approximately 40 man-hours a month. Specifically, it helps shorten the screening time from 32 min to 8 min per candidate.
- Candidate drop-off rate decreases. Due to the 24/7 accessibility feature of the AI-enabled platform, "Candidates' drop-off rate decreased to 4 percent from 15 percent," says a TA leader. Because the virtual recruiter can respond to 96 percent of candidate queries, TA professionals now have more time to focus on "selling" by sharing with the candidates the company culture, values, and strengths.
- Candidate experience improves. Over 90 percent of candidates who provided feedback about the platform shared positive comments. The average customer satisfaction score was 4.7 out 5.
- Interview-to-hire ratio increases. In the past, the company had to interview seven candidates on average before making an offer. With the new platform, hiring managers were able to find a qualified candidate by interviewing no more than three applicants.

**Candidate communication and pre-hire assessments**

| Stage | Automation (AI precursor) | Assisted intelligence | Augmented intelligence | Autonomous intelligence |
|---|---|---|---|---|
| Attract communication | Mail merge; record of communications; predefined response population | Candidate communication chatbot using natural language processing | Augmented job description and email writing | *Self-learning platform sends personalized messages it thinks specific candidates will find compelling* |

| Stage | Automation (AI precursor) | Assisted intelligence | Augmented intelligence | Autonomous intelligence |
|---|---|---|---|---|
| Recruit | Online skills assessment testing; generates reports | Realistic job previews with gamification and simulation | Validation and candidate ranking after pre-hire assessments | *Self-learning platform creates individualized assessments based on candidate's background and open role* |

*Note:* Italics = future possibility. *Source:* The Conference Board

*This case was written by Dr. Robin Erickson, Principal Researcher in Human Capital at The Conference Board*

## 10.8     A US-Based Multinational Restaurant Chain AI for Talent Acquisition: Increasing Sourcing Efficiency

A US-based multinational restaurant chain had been facing a staffing crisis for years: within a fast-paced industry with high turnover, all franchises and stores were expected to recruit hourly delivery workers constantly and quickly. However, stores were having a difficult time finding good candidates and following up with applicants in a timely manner. Screening numerous applications was time consuming; additionally, general managers were often not skilled in operating the recruiting tools, further elongating the recruitment process.

### 10.8.1  Application of AI for TA

With the goals of adopting a simple, user-friendly hiring platform and hiring quality candidates faster, the company partnered with HiredScore to develop an AI-powered platform. Due to its reputation in the industry, the restaurant was able to receive an immense number of applications for any delivery worker roles. The new tool's biggest contribution is that it quickly narrows the large number of applicants to a short list of candidates based on preset standard requirements. Based on candidate information such as education (whether they have a degree), work history ($x$ years of experience in food delivery), and previous records of operating safe vehicles ($x$ years of professional driving experience), the platform populates top insights and offers hiring managers suggestions by grading applicants from A to E (using augmented intelligence). Over time, the platform also learns what kinds of candidates are more likely to get hired in one location versus another (e.g., Houston vs. New York), and it changes the grading scales according to job locations. HiredScore monitors bias regularly to make sure numbers are aligned; general managers can also easily report issues if they find the algorithms are generating discrepancies or errors in hiring suggestions. To ensure positive candidate experience,

if an applicant's portfolio is untouched by a particular franchise for over 48 hours, the platform will forward the information to another franchise to avoid losing good candidates (using assisted intelligence). The new platform has received positive feedback from both general managers and candidates. Approximately 80 percent of the company's 6000 stores around the world have voluntarily implemented the new technology.

### 10.8.2  Business Impact

- Use of recruitment tool increases. General managers/hiring managers were more receptive to this new platform with an easier interface than a previous one they had used; as a result, voluntary use of the recruitment tool rose to 90 percent among hiring managers (from 30 percent for the previous platform).
- Time to delivery decreases. The duration between application submission and the first food delivery by a new hire decreased from 21 days to 12 days, and time to interview declined to approximately 3 days from 7 days.
- Restaurant sales increase. Before adopting the new platform, the restaurant had been suffering from a shortage of delivery workers, which kept some stores from meeting their sales targets. After implementing the HiredScore recruitment tool, the restaurant chain generated higher sales with the help of fully staffed delivery teams.

**Artificial intelligence for talent acquisition: sourcing**

| Stage | Automation (AI precursor) | Assisted intelligence | Augmented intelligence | Autonomous intelligence |
|---|---|---|---|---|
| Sourcing | Basic online search for exact roles | Algorithms optimize online sourcing through automated supervised search | Candidate scoring/ ranking based on predictive success | *Self-learning platform reaches out to best candidates directly* |

*This case was written by Dr. Robin Erickson, Principal Researcher in Human Capital at The Conference Board*

### 10.9    Cultural Transformation at Novartis Next-Generation HR: Learning at the Core

Business transformation often has a simple story at its kernel that vividly illustrates why fundamental change is necessary. And the most compelling stories involve the arrival of a new CEO who is more than willing to question the status quo and challenge the business. Such is the case for Novartis' cultural journey that began in 2018. "We had great people and a great drug pipeline, but we concluded that the piece that was holding us back was our culture—that was the sticking point," says

Simon Brown, Chief Learning Officer at Novartis. "We knew that if we could transform our culture, we could unlock all that potential value and exceed the expectations of our customers and investors."

## 10.9.1  The New Culture: Feel Inspired, Curious, and Unbossed

An analysis of the Novartis culture suggested that while it had served its purpose in a highly regulated industry, it would not deliver the performance the company aspired towards. The culture needed to become less expert-based and risk-adverse and more willing to question and experiment. "We had very bright people, and this manifested itself as a kind of perfectionism and a need to know all the answers," explains Simon. The company wanted to encourage people to experiment more, feel free to constantly question the status quo and seek opportunities for improvement and innovation. This also meant a psychologically safe environment to try and potentially fail—a hard adjustment for a performance-based culture.

Driven by the heads of talent management and organization development and supported by the executive committee, Novartis identified how the culture needed to shift. The company landed on three core aspirations or values for exceptional business performance: employees should feel inspired, curious, and "unbossed" (traits influenced by Dan Pink's motivational theory).

Novartis' leadership team defined culture transformation as the number one strategic priority for 2018 and a critical enabler for other priorities, such as breakthrough innovation, operational execution, data/digital leadership, and trust & reputation.

With culture at the heart of business transformation, the people strategy provided the roadmap for nurturing the three core values. This was signed off by the executive committee at the end of 2018, along with the decision to rename the HR function as People and Organization (P&O). This name change acknowledged the function's two core stakeholders—the organization and also individual associates. "Seeing our people as our critical stakeholders provided a different lens," says Brown. "It brought us to the importance of providing a great employee experience."

The people strategy focuses on crafting "moments that matter" that help nurture the new culture and aid talent attraction and engagement. The team explored these influential experiences by holding internal focus groups, talking to external recruiters, and tapping into internal data. P&O selected three moments that resonated most closely with the value of inspired, curious, and unbossed. These were "my growth," "my leadership," and "my impact." These mapped onto the three cultural values.

- *My impact* maps to being inspired, providing people with the support and opportunity they needed to make an impact in their daily work, and ultimately through the wider corporate purpose of Novartis.
- *My growth* is triggered by being curious and having opportunities to learn and develop.
- *My leadership* maps onto unbossed through having leaders that bring out the best in their people.

## 10.9.2  Learning is a Strategic Imperative

Novartis has always had a strong commitment to learning, but the new people strategy "super-charged" these efforts by elevating learning into a vital driver of cultural change. "We decided to make the business case to go big on learning" says Brown, who had taken on the CLO role at the start of 2019. He and his team convinced the executive team that the company should substantially scale up its investment in learning.

The case for making a big investment in learning was compelling. "All our data points told us, and continue to tell us, that the opportunity to learn is among the top reasons why people join and stay with Novartis. If we want the best talent, we have to offer the best learning," says Brown. A second compelling reason was that to transform and achieve its aspirations, the company needed to invest in developing a range of critical skills for the future, including leadership, operational excellence, data and analytics, digital skills, and agility.

The executive team agreed to invest one hundred million US dollars over the next five years to provide associates with the best possible learning experiences and opportunities. The team also agreed to actively support the aspiration to encourage people to spend five percent of their time, or 100 hours per year, on their own learning and development (this is an aspirational goal and not mandatory to encourage intrinsic motivation instead of compliance). "In 2018, the average was 22.6 hours of learning per person per annum, so the goal of 100 hours was an enormous aspiration," says Brown. "It was a strong signal that the company valued learning and wanted people to change their behavior and commit to building their skills." The new learning strategy entailed creating a single learning organization with one consolidated digital learning platform. The endorsement of the executive committee and the clear link between learning and Novartis' cultural journey helped create momentum. Learning is linked to cultural values and key future capabilities for Novartis, especially digital-based skills and data analytics.

Novartis' top 300 leaders, including the executive committee, acted as role models for the commitment to learning by embarking on a year-long leadership development program to increase self-awareness and build their "unboss" capabilities. This in-house program includes experiential face-to-face sessions, webinars, social learning, peer-to-peer mentoring, and personalized coaching.

## 10.9.3  Global, Divisional, and Regional Leadership

There is strong leadership and accountability for learning. The role of CLO, introduced in 2019, is a member of the P&O Leadership Team. There is a central team with a presence in every region, called the Novartis Learning Institute (NoLI). The team's remit is to support enterprise-wide capabilities and includes heads of enterprise capability, leadership development, strategy and innovation, operational excellence, and digital capability. The central team works closely with the divisional heads of learning, with each of these responsible for ensuring everyone in their division has access to tailored learning opportunities. Eleven regional NoLI heads comprise the third part of the learning organization, and their role is to facilitate local uptake and customize for local needs and preferences. Together, these three teams work to create a "learning ecosystem," partnering with talent management and other centers of expertise. The link to employee experience is being strengthened through the appointment of a work and learning experience expert to the Novartis Learning Institute, and there are close partnerships with the Novartis employee experience team in the wider P&O organization.

The leadership team has also worked to increase the agility of the learning strategy, recognizing that the company may need to upscale some learning activities when there is a disruptive shift in the external competitive environment. There has been considerable effort to consolidate learning resources and to move everything to a single digital learning platform.

COVID-19 proved to be one such disruptive shift. Novartis was able to provide targeted training instantly to help support the transition of over 60,000 associates to virtual homeworking. The company saw a huge uptake of courses on how to lead virtual meetings, work remotely, and build resilience. Recognizing the toll of the crisis, the company launched learning resources for associate families and friends to help those who needed to upskill or reskill. Over 12,000 people took advantage of this resource, which included externally certified courses.

### 10.9.4  Measuring Progress

Novartis has improved its data analytics capability, especially in data visualization, and is using a variety of data and tools to identify different indicators showing the degree to which curiosity and learning are becoming embedded in the culture. The learning organization has worked with the analytics team to develop a dashboard that enables anonymized and aggregated learning data to be cut by division, job grade, country, and even by the level of individual courses.

Signs of progress are encouraging:

- Hours of learning per person per year increased from an average of 22.6 h in 2018 to an average of 35.8 h in 2019 and are set to increase further in 2020.
- Voluntary learning compared to mandatory job-related learning showed a solid increase.
- More learning time is spent on topics that are strategically important to Novartis, and there are measurable skills improvement in key capabilities.
- The annual engagement survey has explicit questions asking about learning experiences while quarterly pulse surveys help gauge attitudes to learning. Engagement scores have risen from 68 (two points below the industry benchmark) to 72 at the beginning of 2020. Despite the pandemic, the last survey increased to an engagement score of 75.
- Talent attraction data based on over a million applications reveals that the number one reason why people joined Novartis over the last year was the learning and development opportunities.

- Internal data shows that the more learning people do, the less likely they are to leave the company.

Changing behavior is one of the most difficult things to achieve—especially for a company that has been successful for over two centuries. While the P&O function has put in a learning ecosystem, organizational support, and strong leadership, and accountability to embed curiosity as a culture value, they are taking a long-term perspective. Novartis acknowledges that they are on a journey, and that they won't get it right straight away and that it takes practice. Things will go wrong, and they need to keep at it, but if they do, then eventually the culture will monumentally shift, one person, one behavior at a time.

*This case was written by Dr. Marion Devine, Senior Human Capital Researcher, Europe, The Conference Board*

## 10.10   Agile HR at Japan Tobacco International (JTI): Next-Generation HR

HR transformation at JTI is part of a larger business transformation initiated in 2018 by the third-largest tobacco company. To keep ahead of changing customer requirements, spur product innovation, and build a sustainable business, JTI prioritized greater strategic and operating agility. Much of the transformation is about rethinking the roles of the global headquarters and regional/market divisions, scaling up global business services, and developing a new set of capabilities and culture. The company's hybrid operating model has been changed to achieve more crisp accountabilities. The global center is entirely responsible for strategy formulation, while the five regional divisions focus on implementing global strategy.

Creating a central transformation team, JTI identified five levers of transformation:
1. Clarity of roles between the center and the markets,
2. Optimizing organizational design,
3. Reducing spans of control,
4. Outsourcing and consolidating some activities into global business services, and
5. Introducing Agile working.

Seven corporate functions were selected in 2019 to pilot Agile, including HR.

### 10.10.1   HR Transformation

HR strategy is driven by the priorities of JTI: supporting the company's growth ambition by bringing new skills into the business; changing the culture and supporting the shift towards agility; ensuring leadership bench-strength; and aiding talent mobility across the global business. If HR is to deliver these priorities and work within a hybrid and increasingly agile global organization, it too must change the way it works. The function, which is now called People and Culture (P&C), introduced a new operating model in 2019. Transactional work has been outsourced to global business services. The HR team of 100 people at the corporate headquarters in Geneva, many of whom worked in functional centers of excellence, has been optimized. The HR organization now comprises:

- Three "strategic pillars," responsible for devising policies and strategies for talent, global rewards, and diversity. These pillars replace centers of excellence but have much smaller teams of experts to implement strategy.
- An Agile pool, responsible for service delivery. The pool brings together approximately 30 individuals from across a range of HR specialties. These individuals may work as internal consultants or within Agile teams on a range of HR projects within P&C.
- A small team of senior strategic HR business partners responsible for strategic accounts at Corporate Functions and Regional levels.

Each of the transforming corporate functions has adopted similar Agile pools. A senior manager acts as Agile lead, responsible for service delivery, and is also a member of the function leadership team.

Sergei Polianski is the Agile lead for P&C. He explains the benefits of the newly introduced structure: "It enables us to pool expertise from across the function, create empowered teams, and focus on the strategic work that really matters to the business. It's a way to reduce bureaucracy and break down silos. We can take a step back, find economies of scale, and shift resources to more important projects. The cultural impact is more speed, customer focus, and entrepreneurship."

## AGILE OPERATIONS ZOOM-IN

New JTI Agile people and culture structure. Source: JTI

### 10.10.2   Strategic Prioritization

This nimbler way of working relies on a process JTI calls strategic prioritization. The prime role of the Agile lead is to act as a neutral middleman by facilitating discussion between the three strategic pillars (global rewards, diversity, and talent),

HR business partners, and the rest of P&C leadership team. The aim is to find the most effective alignment between service requests and business priorities. Because the majority of HR resources are located in the Agile pool, other parts of the HR organization can no longer embark on their own initiatives but must bring their ideas and make their case to the Agile lead and the rest of the leadership team. This is a different way of working and may not always please everyone, all of the time. However, the discussion means that decisions about how to allocate resources are transparent. Another strong benefit is that the discussions help surface project dependencies, unexpected consequences, or knock-on effects.

Transparency is achieved by applying a clear set of criteria for strategic prioritization. One set of criteria helps evaluate the business value of the proposed project. How does it support the corporate and/or corporate function strategy? What business value does it help create? What is the urgency, and what are the consequences of not acting? The second set of criteria focuses on practical matters such as cost of implementation, visibility, complexity, risk, and compliance issues, among others. "In theory, it's a thorough and straightforward process. In practice, it's quite complex, and people have different priorities. While a degree of maneuvering and politics is inevitable, the end result is a positive and focused discussion," says Sergei.

As Agile's lead, Sergei decides the composition of the Agile team and decides on the most appropriate way to work, including which Agile or related methodology (Scrum, Kanban, etc.) is best. The Agile lead is also responsible for managing the team, and while the concept of less hierarchy is attractive, managing a team of 30 can be time consuming. Once a quarter, the Agile lead, along with the HR leadership team, reviews all the projects and initiatives underway to gauge progress and revisit their alignment with strategic priorities. "This is also an important means of creating a more fluid structure where we can quickly change course," Sergei explains.

### 10.10.3   Service Delivery Via the Agile Pool

The Agile teams work on a variety of projects such as implementing a new employee portal, working on a new listening strategy, evaluating performance management, and rolling out international mobility processes. The team is also responsible for day-to-day employee support for JTI global headquarters and verticalized functional, playing the role of a people partner for approximately 4000 employees. JTI is working to embed a range of Agile working methods (Scrums, stand-ups, sprints, sprint reviews, retrospectives, etc.) as well as Kanban (a visual workflow tool from lean manufacturing) for day-to-day tasks. The Agile lead appoints product owners, Scrum masters, and Scrum teams and facilitates regular sprint reviews, which then feed into sprint planning for the next work iteration.

The use of Agile teams is helping JTI to introduce cross-functional working. For example, P&C and finance have formed a joint Agile team which is working at different locations and factories to understand needs, brainstorms ideas, and ultimately design an improved headcount and cost planning process. The agile pool currently comprises four core Scrum teams which typically work on two or three different projects at any one time to help optimize their utilization. These are "stable" teams, meaning they stay together for one business quarter to help promote teamwork. They undergo a "health check" in the quarterly review to see whether changes should be made or the team should stay intact for the next quarterly cycle. In addition, the team has a pool of 12 people partners who provide support to employees by leveraging Kanban methodology.

### 10.10.4   Incubating Talent

The new HR operating model represents a significant change for HR staff. "Now that people work on a range of projects, they no longer have an anchor in one HR function, such as rewards or talent management," explains Sergei. Though they might miss that stability, they have more opportunity to work in different projects, gain new experience and skills, and also move into different roles such as a Scrum master or a business partner within their job pool.

"It's still early days" says Sergei, "but we want the Agile pool to act as an incubator for talent, boosting people's knowledge and experience before they move on." For that reason, the company looks to select people into the Agile pool with a range of skills, not just in HR but from other disciplines (such as digital, analytics, and communications) who are open to being geographically mobile and are motivated to learn and grow. It is envisaged that people will work in the Agile pool for a couple of years before moving on to other parts of JTI or the P&C function, for example, as HR leads in different parts of the business or different markets.

The P&C Agile function is looking for people with "M-shaped" profiles, where they have multiple deep competencies (for example, D&I, talent management, and total rewards) as well as broad competencies. These broad competencies include business partnering, project management, and change management. People should also be versatile in different working methods, so they can work equally well in Agile teams or internal consultancy teams. As well as providing extensive skills training, the Agile pool also has a dedicated skills development team (which includes an internal agile coach) which is tasked with supporting Agile working within the P&C function.

### 10.10.5   Key Learning

The experience of agile transformation within corporate functions like HR has shown that leadership from the top is a vital enabler, but Sergei advises that a degree of resistance from the next level is to be expected. There is also some inevitable tension between the Agile parts of the business and those that run on traditional lines, but this can be managed through open communication and by demonstrating the business benefits of Agile working, not least greater customer centricity. One big advantage has come from the Agile leads across the seven corporate functions

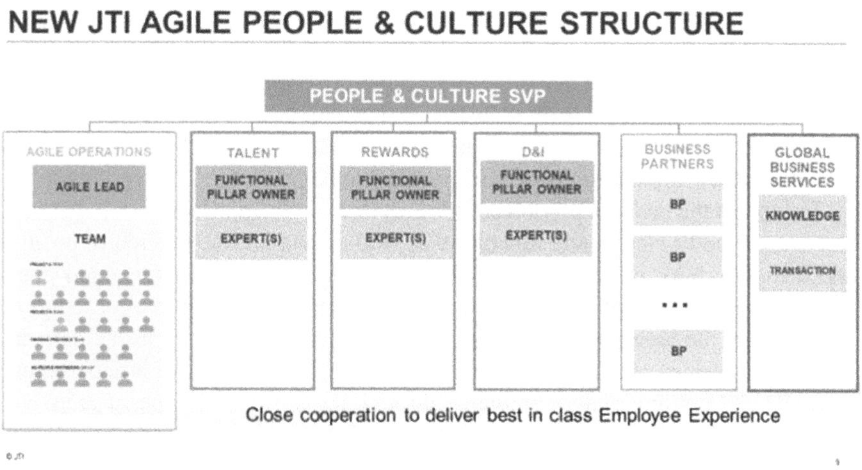

# NEW JTI AGILE PEOPLE & CULTURE STRUCTURE

**Fig. 10.12**   Agile Operations Zoom-in. Source: JTI

forming a strong personal network. "We have bi-weekly calls where we discuss common issues, share experience and learning, or focus on topics like managing careers or developing skills. This network has also enabled us to act collectively as 'Agile ambassadors' to promote agility across the whole business."

The next phase of JTI's transformation will be to scale up Agile working through other parts of the organization, both in corporate functions and in the markets. In the meantime, the seven corporate functions will aim to build their maturity in Agile working during 2021 and use their experience and insights to "stretch" agility further. For the P&C function, this foray into Agile has been an invaluable opportunity to gain first-hand knowledge of the implications of Agile in terms of culture, leadership, and performance management (Fig. 10.12).

*This case was written by Dr. Marion Devine, Senior Human Capital Researcher, Europe, The Conference Board.*

## 10.11   SAP Using Learning and Digital Strategies to Enhance Company Brand

HRD functions, such as learning and development, are becoming more integrated and are contributing to the execution of the organization's strategy. Concurrent with this trend is the shift from traditional classroom to digitally delivered learning for members of the workforce to access in the flow of work. In addition to reskilling and upskilling, digitally delivered learning is being used to transition employee mindsets and behaviors, and by extension the organization's culture into alignment with the strategic direction of the organization.

SAP is an example of an organization that is using learning strategies, supported by technology, to enhance their organization brand and support business goals. Founded in 1972, SAP is a market leader in enterprise application software, helping companies of all sizes and in all industries run at their best. Over seventy percent of the world's transaction revenue touches an SAP system and the SAP brand is consistently ranked among the world's most valuable brands.

To support the need for employees to recognize, think, and act in ways that reinforces the brand's stature and reputation as well as support the creation of positive and distinctly SAP interactions with its customers, SAP has implemented brand learning approaches that are designed to inform, enable, and inspire ALL employees based on the premise that in today's world of heighted interconnectedness any employee's actions can impact the way SAP is perceived. In short, it is a marketing, learning, and cultural change initiative through the *democratization* of employee learning which includes leaders across all lines of the business, marketing, and communications employees (including both designers and content providers), as well as employees in general beyond marketing and communications.

### 10.11.1  Democratization of Learning and Development

As digital technologies become increasingly sophisticated and are widely available through the internet, the term *democratization* has become increasingly used to describe the impact on how information and expertise are documented and shared. People are able to independently search for and acquire information from the web and also post their own content. As this leveraging of digital technology has become part of the way people individually access and share knowledge in their personal lives, organizations are transforming how learning and development are being managed and delivered. While the extent to which this is happening varies across organizations, organizations are adopting democratization as one path for building their capacity for reskilling and changing culture driven by the intensifying pace of technological transformation. The shift from the traditional classroom to digitally delivered content enabling members of the workforce to access it when needed while carrying out their job is what Josh Bersin calls *learning in the flow of work* (Bersin, 2018, 2019). To democratize learning, Learning & Development and other professionals are less providers of content than curators of content, monitoring it for accuracy. Providing learning content is less top down driven and more bottom up and horizontal across the organization. In order to provide for organizational agility in ways that build the Brand, SAP's strategic application of digital learning & development consists of focused applications.

For example, at SAP, beyond being able to access information on an as needed basis, employees are encouraged to share practical learning from their own brand-building experiences through 60 second videos. These videos are called "Brand Tips in a Minute." Employees write, narrate, and film their "Brand Tip" on smart phones using writing and producing guidelines provided to ensure clarity, benefit, and engagement with audiences. There's a proven 5 step framework for writing a minute script, for example, with most "Brand Tips" driving viewers wanting more details to SAP's internal brand website.

Helping colleagues save time and reduce headaches have consistently made this weekly series valuable. As one SAP colleague describes: "They are so helpful and every week I can learn something new." The platform where they're posted also allows colleagues to write to the narrator. "Good job!" or "very helpful. Thank you!" are often commented and foster collegiality. Interestingly, with more people working from home, even children have appeared in these videos. These get exceptionally high likes and comments. Many can relate to the blended world of work and family at home. This human connection achieved through colleague narrators, not professional actors, has proved one of the series most popular and engaging attributes as this comment indicates: "...I love these Brand Tips in a Minute. Keep them coming!" The format has also been recognized internally at SAP as a best practice, adopted by other groups within the company, and featured at many industry conferences, like the Conference Board, as a learning best practice.

## 10.11.2   Strengthen Company Brand with a Culture of Learning

As organizations evolve in changing business environments, the brand of a company may get lost or diluted in the eyes of the customer. The brand of a company may be one of its most important assets; one that would outlast a specific product or service. If the brand is negatively damaged in a significant way, that can potentially impact an entire organization. Thus, a brand needs to be strong, clear, and positively viewed, especially in fast changing business environments. Building a culture of learning about brand awareness and importance promotes and strengthens an organization brand among employees and by extension to customers.

SAP's Brand Education desired outcome is that employees can create SAP experiences that reinforce desired perceptions with customers, partners, and employees. To enable employees to create these branded experiences, the SAP brand team uses a live virtual forum called "Training Tuesdays." Different from other one hour training sessions with a subject matter expert presenting, a dialogue is fostered with the audience via a moderator who can stop the speaker at any time during the session with questions or comments as they appear in the chat room of the virtual platform. Not only does this help change the dynamic from a lecture to a conversation but it provides instant gratification with answers as questions arise.

Additionally, "Training Tuesday" content is piloted with critiquers prior to the actual sessions to ensure clarity, usefulness, and engagement for learners. This additional step can be troublesome for busy subject matter experts but it consistently results in content improvement and positive audience outcomes as this quote indicates "Training Tuesday' is such a great resource. So thank you for finding great content for all the SAP teams." For colleagues who cannot attend the three live sessions provided to accommodate SAP's global employee audience, recordings of the sessions are provided in follow-up mailings and are posted on their brand website along with other on-demand learning modules like "Why Brand Matters" and "SAP Brand Basics." These on-demand modules vary in length from 5 minute to 15, but no longer.

### 10.11.3 Leveraging Technology for Learning in the Flow of Work

Recognizing that employees don't have time or patience for learning that is irrelevant and dull in today's time pressured environment, the focus is on providing learning that can be applied to jobs through delivery mechanisms that are quick, engaging, and practical. This enables learners to access 'real-time' content in the flow of work, to support immediate needs. Technologies such as mobile phones, tablets, laptops allow even greater flexibility to how learners can access information. In the flow of work, a short learning tutorial might be all that is needed to support learners in completing a task and thus able to move on to the next task. Additionally, technology allows for creative and different ways to deliver and engage learners, such as short micro-learning sessions, videos, and gamification. "The goal is to make it easy for employees to learn and apply learning to their jobs with quick, practical, and engaging formats and content," cited VP, Corporate Identity, Joe Pantigoso who developed the formats cited here.

For example, as previously cited, the sixty second "Brand Tip" 60 second videos provide a good return on time invested: as some colleague attest to:

> "I don't always have time to read all my e-mails, click on all the links, view hour long sessions, but I always have a minute…."

> "…people get tired of reading long guidelines…perfect way to share knowledge." "…easy to digest and recall."

> "…what an amazingly small commitment I've made for a large gain!"

In addition to "Brand Tip" videos, SAP developed an Instagram-like banner for quick brand news, called "Brand Flash." This format received by employee subscribers in their e-mail provides them with in the flow of work quick guidance. Describe as "brand guidance at-a-glance," these "Brand Flashes" contain a simple headline, sub-headline, and image with a link to more. Of all the learning assets cited here, these have the highest click through on a per unit basis.

Recently, the team also developed a series of half a dozen skill-building games to engage colleagues in a different way. Racing against the clock, employees have to identity SAP experiences versus competitors—an SAP experience side by side with 3 others. This not only hones employee's ability to recognize how SAP experiences should look like but reminds them of the importance of differentiation in the marketplace, in effect seeing the marketplace as customers do. Not only were the games enjoyed—"It was so much fun"—but it tapped into colleagues intrinsic motivation to improve their performance: "Not so easy. I thought I would perform much better, so I did it several times."

## 10.11.4    Conclusion

The SAP brand team's relentless focuses on creating learning that is *useful* with practical advice on how to help employees build the brand and do their job faster with less headache, *simple* with content that is clear and quick to understand, access, and apply learning, and *engaging* with a high degree of humanity leveraging colleagues to help colleagues have made their program admired by colleagues as well as helped propel SAP into the top ranks of the world's most valuable brands.

*This case was written by Joe Pantigoso, Senior Director, Global Brand at SAP*